JN322582

The Architecture of Glenn Murcutt

グレン・マーカットの建築

The Architecture of
GLENN

The Architecture of Glenn Murcutt

First published in Japan on June 15, 2008
Fourth published on July 20, 2021

TOTO Publishing (TOTO LTD.)
TOTO Nogizaka Bldg., 2F,
1-24-3 Minami-Aoyama, Minato-ku,
Tokyo 107-0062, Japan
[Sales]Telephone: +81-3-3402-7138
　　　　Facsimile: +81-3-3402-7187
[Editorial]Telephone: +81-3-3497-1010
URL: https://jp.toto.com/publishing

MURCUTT

Produced with cooperation of Glenn Murcutt
Authors: Maryam Gusheh, Tom Heneghan, Catherine Lassen, Shoko Seyama
Photos: Anthony Browell
Publisher: Takeshi Ito
Book Designer: Tetsuya Ohta
Printing Director: Noboru Takayanagi
Printer: Tokyo Inshokan Printing Co., LTD

Except as permitted under copyright law, this book may not be reproduced, in whole or in part, in any form or by any means, including photocopying, scanning, digitizing, or otherwise, without prior permission. Scanning or digitizing this book through a third party, even for personal or home use, is also strictly prohibited.
The list price is indicated on the cover.

ISBN978-4-88706-293-1

すべて建築として建っているものは、デザインされたのではなく
見出されたのです。この発見の過程は創造的なものです。
図面を描くべく手が動き始め、意識よりも先に手が解答をつかみ始めます。
大切なことは建物を楽器のようにつくるということです。
光に呼応し、空気の動き、景色に呼応し、シェルターとして機能するように。
そのように作られた建物は、作曲家の音色を奏でる楽器として働き始めますが、
その作曲家は私ではありません。
それは、すでにそこに在るもの──それは土地の音であり、光です。
私はただ建築をつくることで、それを受け取っているのです。──── グレン・マーカット

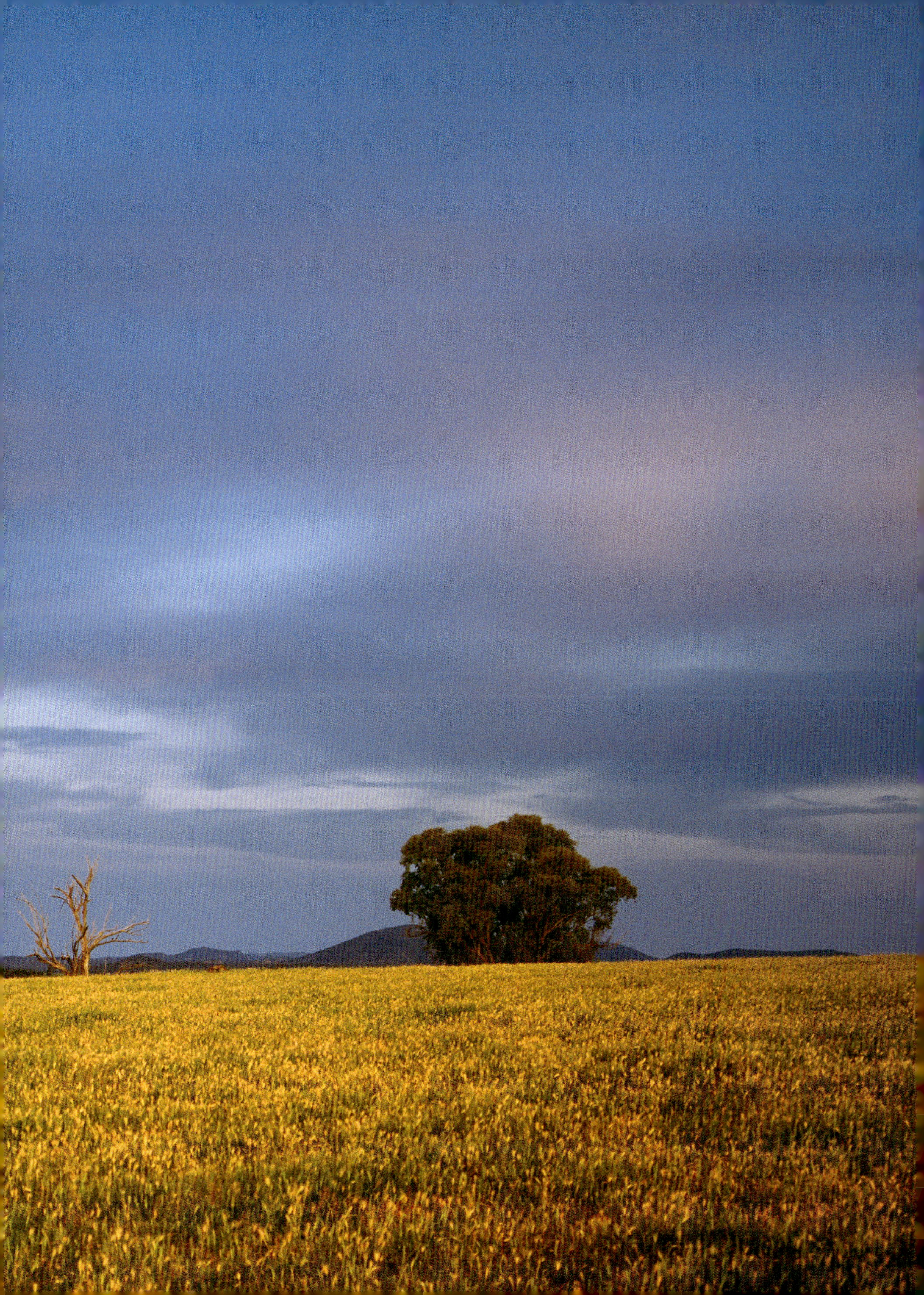

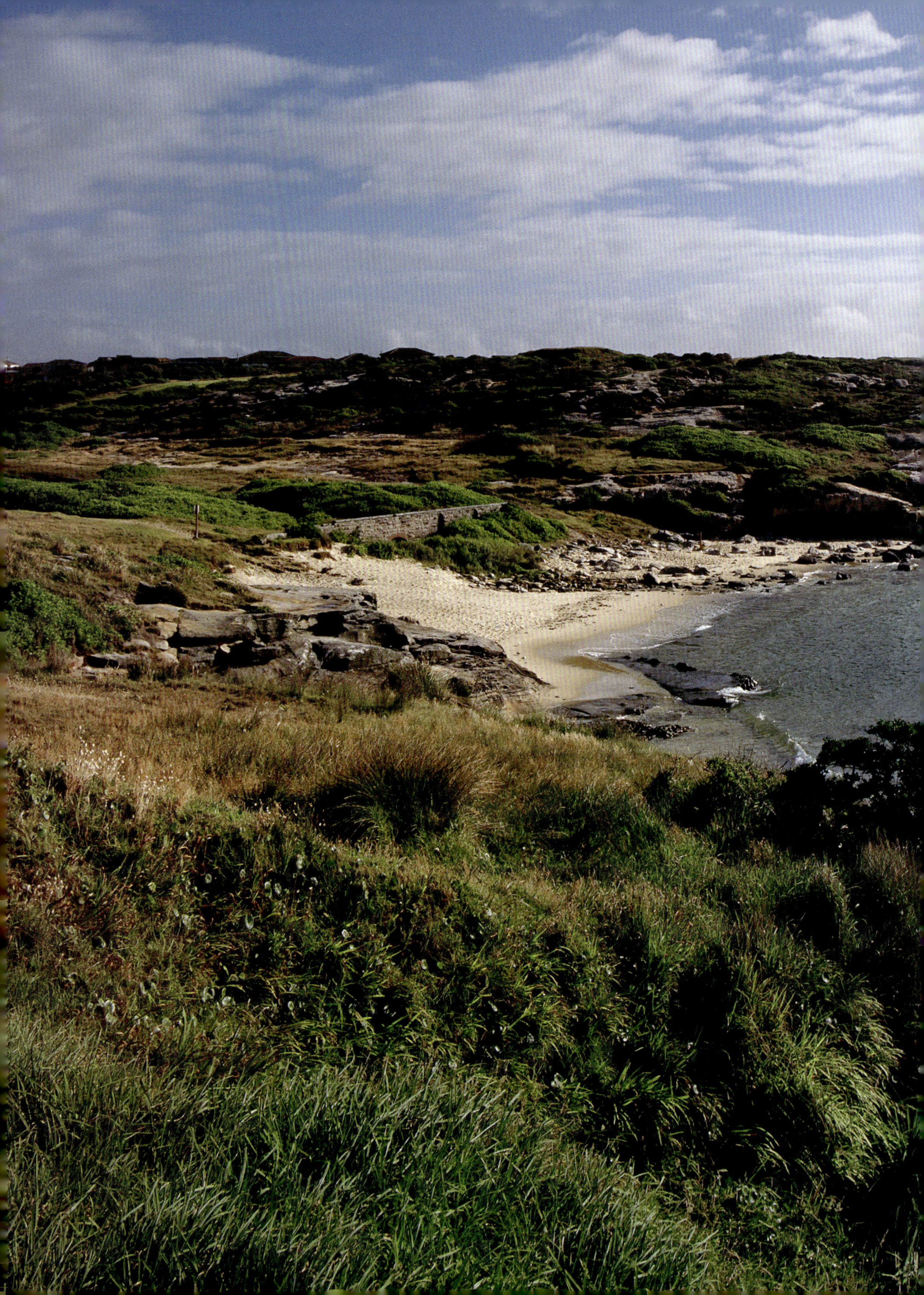

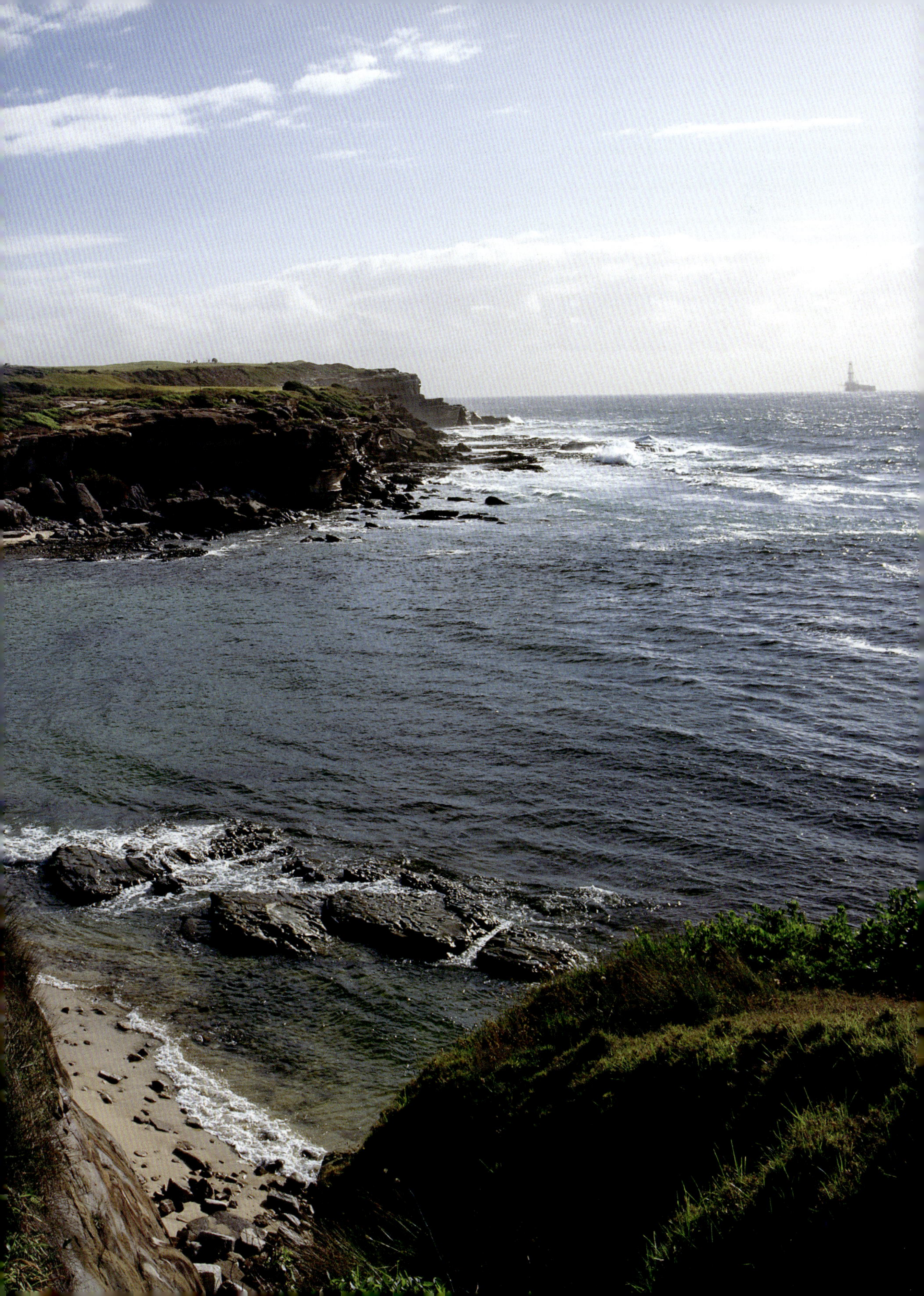

Works of architecture are discovered, not designed.
The creative process is a path of discovery. The hand makes drawings and
arrives at solutions before the mind has even comprehended them.
It is very important to me to make buildings that work like instruments.
They respond to light, to the movements of the air, to prospect, to the needs of comfort.
Like musical instruments, they produce the sounds and the tones of the composer.
But, I'm not the composer. Nature is the composer.
The light and sounds of the land are already there. I just make instruments
that allow people to perceive these natural qualities. ──── Glenn Murcutt

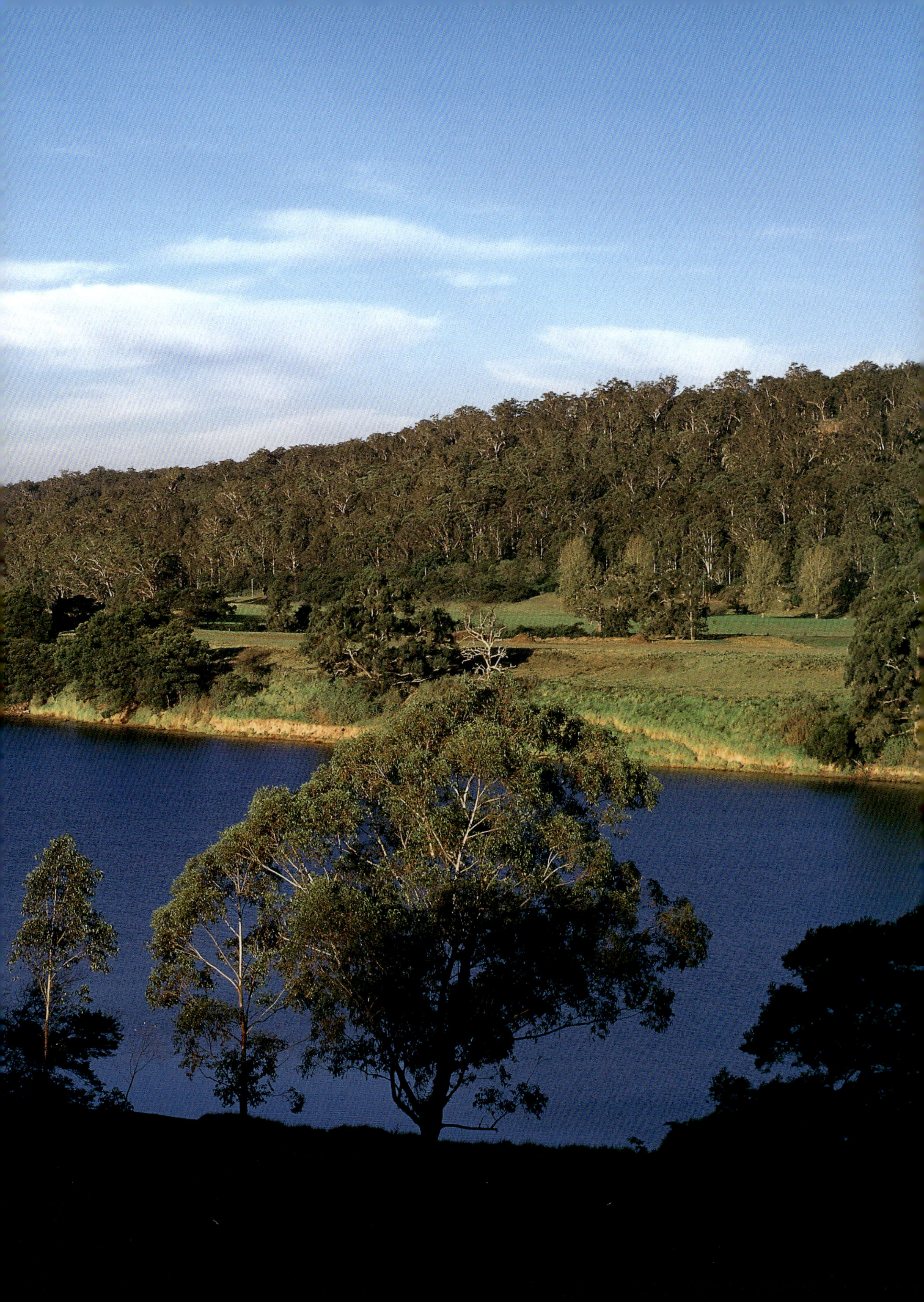

グレン・マーカットの建築
The Architecture of Glenn Murcutt

目次
Contents

012
序文：建築を教えるときに大切なこと
Preface: On the Teaching of Architecture
グレン・マーカット
Glenn Murcutt

026
推薦状
Testimonials

038
ダグラス・マーカット邸
Douglas Murcutt House
Belrose, Sydney, New South Wales

046
マリー・ショート／グレン・マーカット邸
Marie Short / Glenn Murcutt House
Kempsey, New South Wales

062
フレデリックス／ホワイト邸
Fredericks / White House
Jamberoo, New South Wales

082
マグニー邸
Magney House
Bingie Point, New South Wales

110
マグニー邸
Magney House
Paddington, Sydney, New South Wales

126
シンプソン＝リー邸
Simpson-Lee House
Mount Wilson, New South Wales

148
マリカ＝アルダートン邸
Marika-Alderton House
Eastern Arnhem Land, Northern Territory

164
マーカット・ゲストスタジオ
Murcutt Guest Studio
Kempsey, New South Wales

174
フレッチャー＝ペイジ邸
Fletcher-Page House
Kangaroo Valley, New South Wales

200
アーサー＆イヴォンヌ・ボイド・アートセンター
Arthur and Yvonne Boyd Art Centre
Riversdale, West Cambewarra, New South Wales

230
サザンハイランドの住宅
House in the Southern Highlands
Kangaloon, New South Wales

252
マーカット＝ルーウィン邸＆スタジオ
Murcutt-Lewin House and Studio
Mosman, Sydney, New South Wales

274
ウォルシュ邸
Walsh House
Kangaroo Valley, New South Wales

308
エッセイ：対話と発見
Essay: Dialogue and Discovery
トム・ヘネガン
Tom Heneghan

320
略歴
Profiles

序文　Preface

建築を教えるときに大切なこと
On the Teaching of Architecture

2007年11月シドニー大学において、グレン・マーカットへのインタビューが行われた。「もし私があなたに建築を教えるとしたら」（ル・コルビュジエのエッセイと同題）の質問により、核となる考え方や、仕事の仕方が浮き彫りにされた。

In November 2007 Glenn Murcutt was interviewed at the University of Sydney.
He was asked to respond to the theme: 'If I had to teach you Architecture…'

建築を教えるときに大切なこと

　　グレン・マーカット

私たちはそれぞれ違う能力をもっています。イメージするのがとても得意な人たちがいます。ある人はそうでないし、ある人は素晴らしい図面を描けて、図面から空間をイメージできる。多くの違った思考方法があり、それが教える時に面白い点だと私が興味をもつところなのです。

●

子供の頃、私は父よりランドスケープについて学びました。ランドスケープを学ぶということは、植物の名前を覚えることではないのです。それは、土地の構造と秩序を理解することです。父は、私を丘の

On the Teaching of Architecture

　　Glenn Murcutt

We each have different abilities within us. Some people are able to visualise things really well. Other people can't visualise, other people can draw beautifully, and can visualise through drawing. There are many different ways of thinking—and therein lies a lot of the interest I have in teaching.

As a child, my father taught me about landscape. Learning about landscape doesn't mean learning the names of plants. It's about understanding the structure and order of the land. My father would

上に連れていき、特定の植物がなぜそこに生えているかを教えます。そして、同じ植物が生える場所の違いにより、いかに違ったものになるかを見せるのです。例えば、丘陵の裾に生えるアンゴフェラ・コスタータ（シドニー・レッド・ガム：ユーカリの一種）は、丘の頂上に生えているものとはまったく違う木であると言えます。1万年以上もの長い間、地下水が浅く、強い風の吹く丘の上から、地面の栄養素が雨により流れ出されます。丘の裾野は、地下水が高く、土は深く、栄養素も含まれ、風は強く吹かない。丘の上の樹木が風圧で曲がったりひどく倒れているのと比べてまっすぐ育ちます。ですから私は、生徒にいかに1つ1つの土地が違い、それが植物へ及ぼす影響がまったく違うものであるかを教えるでしょう。

●

私は、水についても教えるでしょう。水はその日を綴る日記です。水は光の明度を高めます。水は風の動きに意味を与えます。水の中の葉が渦を巻いているなどの動きをしている時、風がどう動いているかわかるでしょう。また水の色で深さもわかります。海では、水面が穏やかか波立っているかで海流がわ

take me up a hillside and point out to me why certain plants grew where they did, and how different the same plants were depending on where they grew on the hillside. For example, an angophera costata (Sydney Red Gum, eucalyptus tree) growing low on a hillside is an entirely different tree to the same plant at the top of the hill. Over tens of thousands of years, rain has leeched the nutrients out of the top of the hill, where there is also a low water-table and strong wind. At the bottom of the hill the water table is higher, the soil is deeper, there are more nutrients in the soil, and the wind pressures are less. The trees grow more vertically than those at the top of the hill where you can see them blown down or lying back, pushed by the wind. So, I'd teach students how each place is very different and has an entirely different effect on our fauna.

I'd teach about water. Water is a diary of the day. Water can intensify the light of the day. Water gives every wind-pattern a meaning. When you see a leaf in the water moving around in patterns and eddies, you see how the wind is moving. You can see where the water is deep by the colour of the water. You can see the currents by the movement of the surface, whether it's a rough surface or a

かります。ヨットを操れば、水を読み理解するようになる。また、泳げば、水を読み理解するようになる。これらは肉体的であると同時に、知性を要求するものなのです。まず実験的に物事に没頭し、知性がそれを理解し系統立てる。自然現象を理解することは建築家にとって重要なことです。水を読み、土地を読み、水際の地形を読むことができれば、建物を建てる場所の気候要素を理解することができるでしょう。

●

人は環境に気づくには普段いる場所を去らなければならないのです。ですから私は生徒を日常の環境から連れ出します。ヨットに乗ったことがない生徒がいたら、連れていき、風や水がどう作用するのかという彼らにとって新しい現象を理解させるでしょう。また原生林（ブッシュ）に連れていき、植物の構造と秩序について話し合うでしょう。オーストラリアの自然は、規律立った条理をもっています。一見すると雑然としていますが、実際は、アルカリ／酸性レベル、地下水との関連性、海との近さなどにより成り立っているのです。私は、例えば午後の4時から日没まで生徒をどこかに座らせて、場所の匂いを特

smooth surface. When you sail, you start to understand and read water. When you swim, you start to understand and read water. This has a meaning for us physically and intellectually.
We immerse ourselves in the experiential, and with our intellect we make sense of the experience. To understand natural phenomena is extremely important for an architect. If you can read water, read land, and read the topography at the water's edge, you can understand the climatic factors of the place in which you are working.

To perceive ones own environment one needs to leave it, so I'd take the students away from their usual environment. I'd take people sailing who have never sailed, so that they can understand new phenomena—what wind does, and what water does. I'd take them into bush-land and discuss the structure of plants, and the order of plants. In our native landscape there's a very strict order.
It looks incredibly informal, but it's a very strict order, related to the acidity level, or the alkalinity level, related to the level of the water-table, related to the altitude, to proximity to the sea. I'd get the students to sit somewhere from around four o'clock in the afternoon, and I'd get them to identify

定させたり、日中から日没にかけて、また早朝から日の出にかけて、虫がどう変わるか、その声がどう変化するかを観察させるでしょう。鳥が寝ている夜間の虫の声は、朝とはどう違うか。春、夏、秋、冬でどう違うか。私たちは、普段これらのことから隔絶されているがゆえに、それがわからないのです。

●

私は生徒をいろいろな場所に連れていき、なぜこの部屋は少しばかり寒すぎるのか、もしくは少し蒸し暑いのか、なぜ窓を開けて空気を入れたくなるのかを彼ら自身で考えさせるようにするでしょう。海岸、内陸、砂漠地帯を問わず、湿度や通風はどちらも重要な要素であり、また建築を決定する因果関係をもつものなのです。われわれは、たやすく暮らしていけない環境において、人間の原則的な要求に答えるよう設計しなければいけない。私たちは、気温が14度より低くても快適でないと感じるし、28度より高くても不快に思う。オーストラリアのように、気温と気候がひどく変化に富んでいる国で、生活環境をそれに沿うように調節しなければいけない。結果として何が欲しいかわかっている時は、どうやってそれを達成するか見つけることができます。冬の間は日が射し込んで欲しいが、夏の間はいらない。ま

the smells, and identify the change in the insects' chorus, from the daytime hours to sunset, and from before day break to early morning. What is the chorus like at night-time with birds shutting down, and then awakening in the morning. What is the difference between spring, summer, autumn, and winter? We don't know these things because we are usually too removed from them.

I'd take the students into various sorts of spaces and leave them to understand why a room feels a bit too cold, or a bit too humid—and why they'd like to open a window to get a bit of air in. Humidity, wind factor, whether the location is coastal, inland, hot arid, etc, are all very important factors, with very significant consequences for architecture. In Australia, we need to design to meet human needs within an environment that we can't withstand so easily. We don't like the temperature going much below 14 deg C, and we don't like it going much above 28 deg C. We have to modify our environments in order to cope with the extremely varying temperatures and climates of a country such as Australia. When you know what you want, you can find a way of achieving it. When I want the sunlight to come in during wintertime, but not in the summertime, or if I want to

たは、北西の風を捉えて建物を通風させたい。そこには何通りものやり方があります。そして、気候のタイプに合った、美しい解答があるのです。

●

例えばマリー・ショート邸において、2つのベランダは周辺の水に関係しています。片方は川の蛇行する部分があり、もう一方は湖というように。南半球では北に太陽が昇り、ケンプシーでは南東30度より美しい夏の日の出があります。日中の高度は78度に達し、日没は南西30度に沈む。ゆえに、寝室棟をずらすことにより、夏の午後には北側のベランダが南西の暑い太陽が当たらない日陰となり、日中は直射日光がまったく室内に入りません。冬の間は、太陽は北東30度から昇り、正午の高度はわずか31度33分、そして北西30度に沈みます。ですから1日中部屋は太陽の光で満ちているのです。ヨットを進ませるには風に向かって45度に舵を取ると、一番速い速度を得ることができます。この住宅も北東の涼しい風を呼び込むために風に向かって45度振っている。そのため、北東の涼しい風が一番よく吹き抜けるのです。また、私は室内を空に向かって開くように北の太陽に面する天窓を設置しました。

catch the north-east breeze and pass it through the building, there are many ways of achieving it—ways that respond in a beautiful way to the climatic variations.

For example, at the Marie Short House the two verandas relate to water—a bend in the river on one side and a lake on the other. In the southern hemisphere the sun shines from the north, and at Kempsey there's a beautiful sunrise in summertime, rising from 30 deg south of east, coming up to 78 degrees in height at mid-day in summer, then dropping down to 30 degrees south of west. So, by sliding out the bedroom wing, the northern veranda is shaded from the south-west sun on summer afternoons, and no sun, at all, comes into the house during the daytime. In wintertime the sun rises 30 deg north of east, climbs to only 31 deg 33 minutes at mid-day, and drops back to 30 degrees north of west, so all day you've got the sun pouring into the house. When sailing, you get the greatest speed when the yacht is at 45 degrees to the wind, so I set the building at 45 degrees to the angle of the cool north-east summer breezes, and this gives the beautiful cooling north-east breezes the greatest speed through the house. I opened up the interior to the sky, through roof-

ここで、大切なことは日光を夏の間室内に入れないことだ、ガラス面を通して入射する熱を制御すればよいのだということに気づきました。ですから、天窓を冬の太陽高度に設定した角度のルーバーを春分・秋分の太陽高度55度でオーバーラップするように固定した屋外ブラインドで覆っています。直射日光の入る量によって1年のうちのどの季節かがわかるのです。正午に固定ルーバーの陰がないほど冬至に近く、陰が濃いほど夏至に近い。太陽のカレンダーと言えるでしょう。

●

私は生徒にオーストラリアの樹木の特性を教えるでしょう。木の茎は柔軟に動きます。気温の高いオーストラリアの多くの地域において、木の葉はその端を太陽に向け、太陽の動きに合わせて動くことで水分の蒸発を防いでいます。これが、太陽の光を通過させる、斑な木陰ができる理由です。私たちは、このとても美しく明るい陰と呼応する建築をつくらなければなりません。

●

このように陰について教えるとともに、光についても教えます。オーストラリアの光は、視覚的に1つ1

windows which face the northern sun, but I realised that the important thing is to control the heat entering the house through the glass. So, I covered the roof-windows with external louvers that are fixed at the mid-winter sun angle and overlapped at the equinox angle of 55 degrees. The sunlight that comes through tells you what time in the year it is. The thinner the shadow of the louvers at mid-day, the closer you are to mid-winter. As the shadow gets thicker and thicker you get closer to the summer equinox. It's a diary.

―

I'd teach students about the character of the trees in Australia. They have leafs with stems that are flexible. In many parts of Australia where the temperatures are very high the edge of the leaf turns to the sunrise and tracks the sun all day, to reduce transpiration. This lets through filtered sunlight which gives a dappled shade—a luminous shade that is absolutely beautiful shade, which we need to respond to in our built forms.

―

As well as teaching students about shade, I'd teach them about light. The character of our light in

つの物事を際立たせるように働きます。北半球では、光の明度がより低く、光は物事をまとめる働きをします。まったく反対の作用です。私たちは、光の明るさを調節できる建物を設計しなければいけません。この理由により、ブラインドや日除けの装置は私の設計において基本的に必要なものとなっています。そして日光は遮断しても通風は遮らないものとしているのです。これらの建物は調節可能なのです。ちょうどヨットを繰る時のように。水の流れに応える必要があり、水底の流れにも応える必要があり、地形が風の流れを左右することから地形にも応答する必要がある。ヨットであれば帆をたたんで風を逃したり、または帆を張って風を受ける。スピンエーカーを上げたり、下ろしたりする。シートロープを引張ったり緩めたりする。絶えずヨットを調整するわけです。私たちは衣服で同じような調整をしています。外出する時はコートを着て、暖かい室内ではコートを脱ぐ。人々は適切な着衣をします。私たちはヨットを走らせるように、また服を着るようにデザインするべきです。私は建築もそれが必要だと思っています。私の設計する建物に何層かの被服があります。フレッチャー＝ペイジ邸やウォルシュ邸においては、ルーバーが外側に設置され、鎧戸、網戸付きのガラス戸という構成になっています。この3つ

Australia separates elements, visually. In the northern hemisphere the light-level is lower, and it serves to connect objects. It's entirely opposite—one light-level is serving to separate, one is serving to connect. We have to design buildings that modify the brightness of our light levels, hence the blinds and light-shades that are fundamental in my designs, so I can shut the buildings down but not prevent ventilation. The buildings are modifiable. Like when you are sailing a yacht. You must respond to the water pattern, you must respond to the sub-water movements, you must respond to the topography because the topography defines where the wind is coming from. You are 'spilling' wind, or you are 'pulling' wind. You are putting up spinnakers and taking spinnakers down. You're pulling the sheet-rope tightly and you're letting it off. The whole time you are modifying the yacht. We do the same thing with our clothes. You have a coat to go outside, but inside it's warm and we don't need coats. People dress appropriately. We should be designing buildings like we sail yachts, and like we dress. I think architecture needs to do that. My buildings have multiple layers. At Fletcher-Page House and Walsh House there are louvers on the outside, and slatted screens, and glass windows with insect screens. These tri-partite elements give you flexibility. If the weather is

の部分からなる要素は、住宅にその時々にあった柔軟性をもたらします。暑くてすべての窓を開けて換気させたい時には、すべての要素が開かれる。防犯には鎧戸を閉めればよい。虫がいるならば網戸を閉めればよい。寒い夜にはガラス戸を出し、網戸をしまう。または日中部屋に暖をとりたい時は、鎧戸と網戸を引き込み、ガラス戸を出す。このように建物を変化させるのです。建物の中に住むだけでなく、建物と暮らすのです。他には、オーストラリアの最北にあるマリカ＝アルダートン邸が挙げられます。雨期のある熱帯気候にあり、熱帯の過酷な暑さと湿気を和らげるため、1年中通気を行うことが必要とされました。そこで、ガラス窓を省略し、鎧戸を、引き戸か突き上げ戸として使用し、日光に反応して動く植物の葉のように開いたり閉じたりできるようにしました。

●

また、自然の中の構造を理解する必要もあります。動物の体の構造を見てごらんなさい。すべての生物の構造を観察してください。どうやって貝ができているか？　貝の強度はどこからくるのか？　脊椎動物の、また無脊椎動物の構造は？　私は、構造の数学的、機械学的なことでなく、その原則を教える

hot and you want full ventilation you have everything open. For security you can just have the slats across. If there are insects you can just have the insect screens. If it's a cold night, you slide the glass in, and the insect screen in. Or, during the day, if you want to get warm, you slide the slats and the insect screen back, and let the glass take in the heat of the sun. So, the whole time you're modifying the building. You're living with the building; you're not just living in it. Another example is Marika-Alderton House, in the far north of Australia. It's in a monsoonal tropical climate, with extreme heat and humidity, and requires through-ventilation all year. So there is no glazing, and the walls are composed of sliding or top-hung plywood shutters which are solid or slatted, and which are opened or closed in response to the environment, like the leaves of a plant.

―

You need to understand structure in nature. Look at the structure of animals. Look at the structure of all living things. See how shells are made. Look at the strength of shells, look at the strength of vertebrates and invertebrates. I'd teach the principles of structure—not mechanics or the mathematics of structure—I don't think that is significant. I'd use lots of physical examples of

でしょう。私はたくさんの構造的な仕掛けの、具体的な例を挙げるでしょう。木の梯子を考えてみましょう。なぜ直径3mmのワイヤーが各段の裏の溝に入っているのか？ それは、木材は圧縮には強いが引張りにはからきし弱いからです。鉄線は圧縮には弱いが引張りには強い。梯子に足がかけられた時、木の段の下側は湾曲し、ワイヤーが働く。ですから木材は折れないし、木の段の上部は圧縮に働くのです。鉄のコアを木材で挟んだコンポジットビームを見てごらんなさい。断面上部は圧縮に対してよく働き、木が鉄板をしっかりと挟んでいるため、そのかたちが歪まず、そのため断面下部は引張りに強いのです。これは、筋肉と腱、骨が一体として働き、全体として各々の機能が独立して働くよりもより強く働くようになっているのと同じです。

●

どうして竹は立っているのか？ 節の長さと竹の背と径との関係は？ 竹は柱や補強材としてわれわれに何を教えてくれるか？ 素材としてはどう使われるか？ どれだけ素材の可能性を試せるか？ 真の性質は何だろうか？ カーンの言葉を引用すれば、「素材が何になりたがっているか？」。素材の性

structural mechanics. Look at a timber ladder—why is there a 3 millimeters thick wire, in a recess, on the back of each timber step? It's because timber is great in compression and terrible in tension. Steel cord is terrible in compression and great in tension. When you step on a ladder the bottom of the wooden step goes into tension and the steel wire starts to work so the timber doesn't snap, and the top of the step goes into compression. Look at a composite beam—with a steel core between two timber cheeks. It works fantastically well in compression at the top, and the wood holds the steel blade very stiff so that it can't warp, so it works fantastically well in tension at the bottom. It's like muscles and sinews and bones, working together, making the total much stronger than the parts.

Why does bamboo stand up? What is the ratio between the spacing of the diaphragms to the height of the bamboo to the diameter of the bamboo? What does it teach us about a column, what does it teach us about reinforcing? And, how can that material be used? How far can you push materials—what is the true nature of materials? What does a material—in Kahn's words—"want to be?" When we understand the nature of materials we understand what they want to be, and we can use them

質を理解した時、素材が何になりたがっているかを理解でき、適切に使うことができるのです。

●

クモの巣はどうなっているか？　クモは、まず一筋の糸を出し、それが風によってどこかにくっつくようにします。そこから地面に垂直に1本垂らし、斜めの糸で最初の2本をつなぎ、放射線状の巣を編んでいくのです。これは吊り構造です。吊り構造を習うということは橋を習うことです。これらはまったく基礎的な原理なのです。

●

私は、われわれの環境をどう保持するかにおいての建築の役割を教えるでしょう。どのように建てれば素材を後に再利用できるか、生徒に教えます。マリー・ショート邸では、施主が小屋にもっていた部材を使って建てました。長い年月をかけて彼女はさまざまな美しいハードウッドを集めており、それらは当時でも入手困難なものばかりでした。オレゴンパイン別名はダグラスファー（米松）ですが、これは半割にして梁に、タローウッド（ユーカリの一種）は柱に使いました。ブラッシュボックスは床に、コーチ

---

appropriately.

―

How does a spider's web work? The spider on a tree lets out its first web into the landscape and lets the wind blow it until the web catches somewhere. That becomes the first link. From that, it drops a line to the ground, and then drops diagonals, and starts knitting in a radial form. It's all about catenaries. And, when we learn about catenaries we learn about bridges. These are really basic principles.

―

I'd teach about architecture's role in the conservation of our world. I'd teach students how to put buildings together so that the parts can be re-used. The original Marie Short House was built with materials that the client had stored in a shed. Over many years, she had collected beautiful pieces of different types of hard wood, which it was hard to get, even in 1972 when we built the house. I used oregon pine for the beams, tallowwood for the columns, brushbox for the floors and I lined the walls with coachwood. Marie had told me that she might, sometime in the future, want to move

ウッドは壁の仕上げとしました。マリーは私に、将来2km先の場所へ家を動かすかもしれないと言ったので、解体と再度の組み立てができるようにボルト留めで組み立てたのです。その時は、将来自分の持ち家として購入し、改築するとは思っていませんでした。1980年の改築では、既存のベランダを新しいところへ移し、妻立面を移動し、寝室のドアだったものはリビングのドアとなり、すべての小屋梁は再利用されました。すべての既存素材が使われ捨てられたものはありません。マリカ＝アルダートン邸では、予算が少なく、村に技術をもった大工がいませんでした。そこでシドニーで完全に部材をつくりました。2つのコンテナに収められた部材はダーウィンまで陸路で運び、そこから船で現場まで運ばれて現地で組み立てられました。1日で組み立てられたので、解体する時も1日ででき、動かすことができるでしょう。ボルト留めなので部材は再利用できます。ボイド・アートセンターの軸組はオーストラリアの再利用のハードウッドです。そしてボルト留めとすることで将来の変更や、他の建物に使用できるようにしているのです。レンガ舗装までも再利用を考えて砂の上に設置しています。この、建物の要素を将来分解して再利用できるという考え方が、建物の美観を形づくっているのです。私は、これらの再

the house to a site 2 kilometers away, so I designed the house so she could unbolt the whole thing and reassemble the components in the new place. When I designed the house I never thought that I would eventually buy it, and alter it, in 1980. In the new version the verandas are used in new positions. The gable walls are used in new positions. The door to the bedroom is now the door to the living room. All the rafters were re-used. Everything was re-used. Not a single thing was lost, because I put it together, originally, in such a way that it could be taken apart. The Marika-Alderton House had only a modest budget and there were no skilled building workers available locally. So, I had the building entirely pre-fabricated in Sydney. The materials were sent to Darwin by road in two containers, taken by barge to the site and bolted together. It all was built in one day, and it can all be dismantled in one day, and moved. It's all screwed or bolted together, so it can all be re-used. At the Arthur and Yvonne Boyd Art Centre the framing is from recycled Australian hardwoods, bolted together to enable future relocation, or re-use in a different building. Even the brick paving is laid on sand so that it can be easily taken up and re-used. This way of thinking about architecture—of putting a building together so that in the future it may be taken apart—has

利用という理念に沿って、生徒に建築の工法を教えるでしょう。とても興味深い教科だと思います。

●

私は生徒にどう図面を描くか教えます。私がお話したことすべてをどのように図面にするか。1枚の図面がどれだけ空間を描写できるか。これは、人間の素晴らしい才能です。誰かが座して空間を思い描き、2次元の図面にし、違う誰かがそれを読んで建てることができる。素晴らしい行為です。建築家が考え抜いたことを、描いて大工に渡し、大工はそれを読んで、できると答える。あなたの図面から大工が空間を想像してどうやって建てればよいかわかるのです。何という人間の技でしょう！　図面を描くことは本当に大切なことです。図面を引く行為は、紙に線を引くことでなく、あなたの定義する空間をつくることなのです。多くの生徒は平面と断面を描くことから始め、それが建物をつくることだと思っています。それはある種の建物とはなっても、必ずしも建築になってはいないでしょう。

●

建築は理論ではない。現実なのです。建築は学ぶことではありません。それは知識なのです。

インタビュー構成：トム・ヘネガン

a distinct aesthetic result. So, I'd teach students about methods of assembly. It's a very interesting subject.

———

I'd teach drawing, how to document all the things I've talked about. I'd explain how a drawing can deliver a spatial understanding. It's a remarkable human ability to sit down and visualise something, and draw it in two dimensions for somebody else to look at, understand and construct. I think it's a remarkable process. You imagine something, think it through, draw it and give it to a builder, and he looks at it and says—yes, I can do that. From your drawing he can visualise it, and know how to do it. What an achievement! Drawing is absolutely important. You have to understand that every move you make is not a line on a piece of paper, but is a space you are defining. Most students think you start drawing plans and sections and that makes a building. It can eventually do that—it can make a building, but it doesn't necessarily make architecture.

———

Architecture is different from theory—it's real. It's not about learning, it's about knowing.

Interview conducted by Tom Heneghan

推薦状

2003年、グレン・マーカットへシドニー大学より
名誉建築博士号が授与された。
著名な学者や建築家によって世界各地から
寄せられた推薦文のいくつかをここに紹介する。

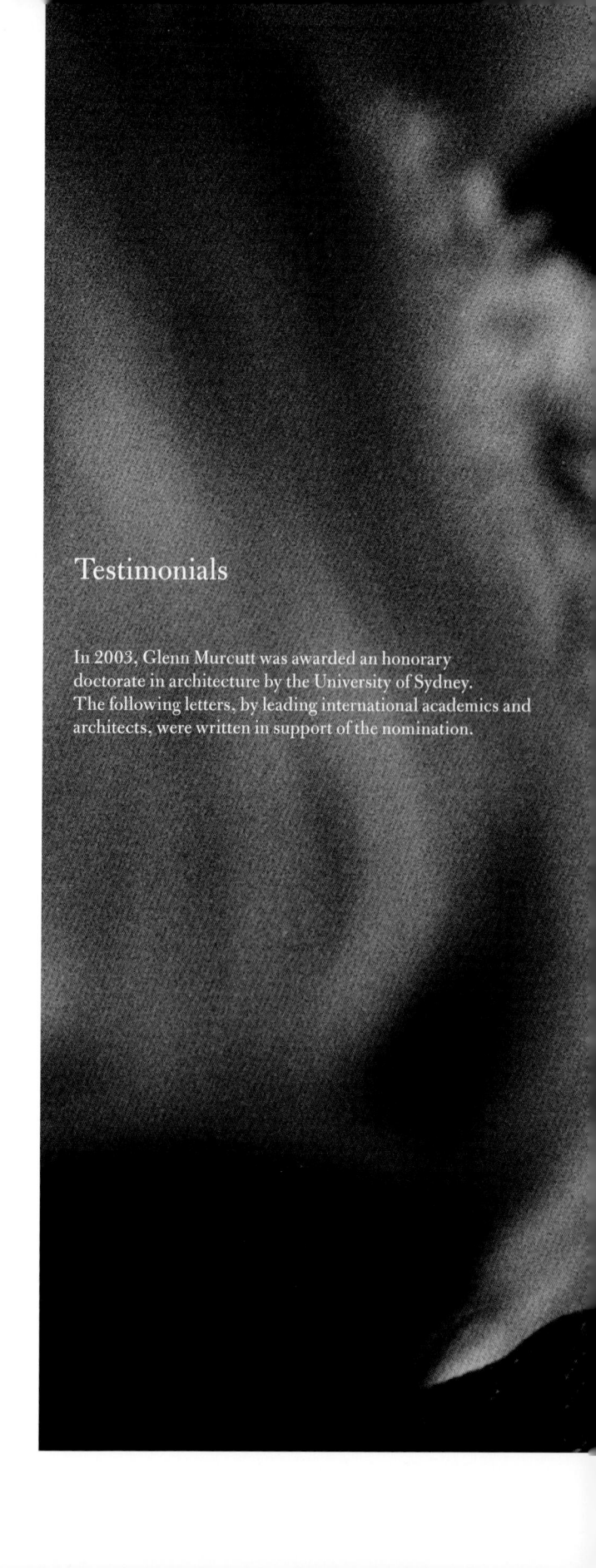

Testimonials

In 2003, Glenn Murcutt was awarded an honorary
doctorate in architecture by the University of Sydney.
The following letters, by leading international academics and
architects, were written in support of the nomination.

Glenn Murcutt

マーカットの建築文化への貢献を考える時、自然の中で、雨水が合流する時のランドスケープの樹木状の構造を考えるのもいいかもしれない。土地の上を水がどう流れるか。源泉からのたくさんの細い水脈、合流した水脈が小川をつくる。小川は河流となり、河口へ流れ込み、海へ到達する。

マーカットの仕事と教育活動は (それは切り離しては考えられないだろう?) ひとつの始まりから、長い年月をかけて大きな流れとなり、今ではあらゆる建築の系統が参照し目指すところとなっている。彼の影響は国内外を問わず大きい。畏怖の念をおこさせる彼の仕事は、自然環境の維持を信条とする多くのアイデアが束ねられたものと言える。土地——どう形づくり、その中に物事をどう沿わせるか。気候——自然の力にどう応答し、どうやってその現象を楽しむか。構造——どう枠組みして生けるものをかくまうか。そして最後に、その建築が社会道徳に忠実 (もしくは疑問を投げかける) か。これらすべてが、単純なシェルターではない、人々を養い感受性を刺激する場所をつくる偉大なマーカットの技によって織り上げられてきた。

これらの能力についてマーカットは、彼の仕事の中で完璧に提示してきた。彼の技は長い年月の中で発展し、光栄なことに、私は、シドニー大学で若い頃は一緒に教鞭をとり、友人として付き合い、それぞれの仕事を見せあう何十年もの付き合いの中で目の当たりにしてきた。

これらにより、私は、シドニー大学建築学科が博士号を贈られる際に、彼がいかに適切であるか、彼がどうそれを使い、尊敬し、任務を纏うかについて言及できる位置にいると言える。彼について話す機会を与えられたことに感謝する。

リチャード・レプラスタリエ

リチャード・レプラスタリエ
建築家。シドニー大学を卒業後、京都大学増田友也教授のもとで学ぶ。丹下健三事務所勤務のち、1964-66 年の間ヨーン・ウッツォンに師事。1999 年、王立オーストラリア建築家協会 (以下 RAIA) よりゴールドメダル受賞。2004 年には、フィンランド「スピリッツ・オブ・ネーチャー、木造建築賞」受賞。

In coming to understand Murcutt's contribution to architectural culture it may help to look at the dendritic nature of landscape's tree-like branching catchment pattern. The way water flows over land. Its many fine veins form the rill, the coalescent rills form the stream. The streams form the river, the rivers swelling into the estuary, and so on inevitably to the sea.

Murcutt's work and teaching (how can they be separated?) started like this. From simple beginnings it has become, over the years, one of the main stems to which so many branches of architecture now refer. His impact is far reaching both inside and outside our country. His formidable body of work is an interlocking trunk of the many strands that underpin the ethos of sustainable place. The land—how it is formed and how things fit to and within it. The climate—how it responds to the forces of nature and how it celebrates the phenomenal. The structure—how it frames and harbours life within. And finally how that life is true to (or challenges) the ethics of its society. All woven together with great skill to make a place that not only shelters life, but also sustains, nourishes and inspires it.

These are the skills Murcutt so consummately displays in his art. It is a skill which I have been privileged to see develop over the years, spending time teaching together in the early days at Sydney University and through our decades of friendship and individual practice.

So perhaps I am in a better position than most to say how appropriate it would be for the university to confer upon him this honorary doctorate in architecture and how well he will wear, and honour, the mantle of this particular office. Thank you for the opportunity to speak for him.

Yours sincerely

Richard Leplasterier

Richard Leplastrier
Architect. Graduated from the University of Sydney and studied at Kyoto University under Professor Tomoya Masuda. Worked in the office of Kenzo Tange in Tokyo, and in the Sydney office of Jørn Utzon from 1964 to 1966. In 1999 he was awarded the Royal Australian Institute of Architects Gold Medal, and in 2004 was awarded Finland's 'Spirit of Nature, Wood Architecture' Award.

この手紙は、シドニー大学がグレン・マーカットへ名誉学位を授与することについての私の惜しみない賛成を添えるものである。

この国において、グレンをおいてこの名誉に値する建築家を思い当たらない。私は彼と長年の親交があり、尊敬してきた。彼の最初の住宅の写真を、楽しんで見たことを思い出す。それは、他のオーストラリア全般の建築と比べた時、独創性のある優秀さをもっていた。

すべてはそこから変わっていない。マーカットの仕事は国内外を問わず無数の出版物を通して紹介され、万人を喜ばし、魅了し続けている。

ハリー・サイドラー&アソシエイツ
ハリー・サイドラー

ハリー・サイドラー
建築家。1923 年ウィーン生まれ。1944 年カナダ、マニトバ大学卒業。1945-46 年、ハーバード大学にてウォルター・グロピウス、マルセル・ブロイヤーに学んだ後、マルセル・ブロイヤー、アルヴァ・アアルト、オスカー・ニーマイヤーに師事。1949 年、シドニーに事務所設立。1976 年 RAIA ゴールドメダル、1996 年 RIBA ゴールドメダル受賞。2006 年逝去。
※手紙の使用に関して彼の妻であるペネロピ・サイドラーに了承いただいた。

This is to lend my wholehearted support to the proposal to nominate Glenn Murcutt for an honorary degree at the University of Sydney.

I can think of no other architect in this country who would be more deserving of this honour than Glenn. I have known and respected him for many years. I recall seeing photos of his very first house which I viewed with great pleasure. It was a work of unique excellence when compared to Australian architecture generally.

Nothing has changed since then. Murcutt's work continues to delight and enthrall everyone both here and overseas, where innumerable architectural publications portray his work.

Best regards,
HARRY SEIDLER & ASSOCIATES

Harry Seidler

Harry Seidler
Architect. Born in Vienna, 1923. Graduated from the University of Manitoba, Canada, 1944. Studied under Walter Gropius and Marcel Breuer at Harvard University, 1945-46, and subsequently worked with Marcel Breuer, Alvar Aalto and Oscar Niemeyer. Began private practice, Sydney, Australia, 1949. Recipient of the Royal Australian Institute of Architects Gold Medal in 1976 and the Royal Institute of British Architects Gold Medal in 1996. Died 2006.
(Permission to reproduce this letter was given by Penelope Seidler.)

グレン・マーカットの、貴大学の名誉博士称号について私は喜んで推薦する。イエール大学において、グレン・マーカットは2度、素晴らしい名誉招聘教授を務めた。どちらにおいても、彼は影響力のある教育者であり、素晴らしい建築の方法論——環境への適切性に直接的に応えるかたちの構成に重きを置く——を生徒に紹介した。彼は芸術性をあわせもつ知識者である。世界の偉大な建築家の中で、彼は誰にも劣らない。

イエール大学建築学部長
J・M・ホッピン建築教授
ロバート・A・M・スターン

ロバート・A・M・スターン
建築家。1939年ニューヨーク生まれ。1960年コロンビア大学卒業後、1965年イエール大学建築科大学院修了。ニューヨークに事務所を設立。1998年よりイエール大学建築学部長。

I am very pleased to support the nomination of Glenn Murcutt for an honorary degree at your University. Glenn Murcutt has twice occupied a distinguished visiting chair at this School. Each time he has proved an inspiring teacher, introducing students to an architectural methodology that is all too rare—one that values formal composition in direct proportion to its environmental appropriateness. His is the great gift of intelligence combined with artistry. In terms of the world's great architects, he is second to none.

Sincerely,

Robert A.M. Stern
Dean
J.M.Hoppin Professor of Architecture
Yale University

Robert A.M. Stern
Architect. Born in New York, 1939. Graduated from Columbia University in 1960 and received a Master of Architecture degree from Yale University in 1965. Private practice in New York. Dean of Yale School of Architecture since 1998.

グレン・マーカットは過去数十年にわたり、世界の建築の中で欠くことのできない存在であり続けている。彼の建築デザインにおける強く個人的な方法、素材の使い方、そして建築の発展と建築教育に対する貢献は計りしれない。

グレン・マーカットは、1992年、フィンランド建築博物館、フィンランド建築協会そして教育省より、アルヴァ・アアルト・メダルを授与された。

ここにわれわれは、グレン・マーカットに対する、名誉科学博士号の賞与を強く推薦する。

アルヴァ・アアルト財団　財団長
マーク・ラーティ

アルヴァ・アアルト協会　協会長
エーサ・ラークソーネン

Glenn Murcutt's meaning for the world architecture scene has been essential during the past decades. His strong and personal approach in architectural design, environmental design, use of materials and his contributions to the general advancement of architecture and architectural education are outstanding.

Glenn Murcutt was granted the Alvar Aalto Medal in 1992 by the Finnish Museum of Architecture, the Finnish Association of Architects and the Ministry of Education.

We strongly support the nomination of the architect Glenn Murcutt for the honorary degree of Doctor of Science (Architecture).

Markku Lahti
Director
Alvar Aalto Foundation

Esa Laaksonen
Director
Alvar Aalto Academy

グレン・マーカットの建築は、過去30年以上、とても重要であり続けている。彼の一面は、その簡素さと明快さをもつ建築の技である。その建築のもう一面は、環境であり、敷地への建ち方、存在感である。しかしながら、彼が貢献してきた最も重要な分野は、私が職業倫理と呼ぶところにおいてであり、それは、正直さと頑固さをもった、仕事のクオリティをつくる日々の仕事である。

グレンは、場所に対する繊細さと、建築への革新的で斬新な方法において名高い。多くの理由が挙げられるが、彼が私のよい友人であることをさておいても、彼を名誉科学博士へと強く推薦する。

レンゾ・ピアノ

レンゾ・ピアノ
建築家。1937年イタリア、ジェノバ生まれ。1970年よりリチャード・ロジャースと、1977年よりピーター・ライスとパートナーシップを組む。1989年RIBAゴールドメダル、1995年高松宮殿下記念世界文化賞、1998年プリツカー賞受賞。

I think that Glenn Murcutt's architecture has been immensely important over the last 30 years.
On one side it is about the art of building with simplicity and clarity.
On the other hand it is about context and presence in a site.
But the field in which his contribution has been even more important is what I call the ethic of profession: the honest and the obstinant daily work about quality.

Glenn is renowned for his sensitivity to place and his inventive, fresh approach to architecture: these are just a few reasons why, apart from being a very good friend of mine, I strongly support his nomination for the honorary title of Doctor in Science.

My very best wishes

Renzo Piano

Renzo Piano
Architect. Born in Genoa, Italy in 1937. Established a partnership with Richard Rogers from 1970 and with Peter Rice from 1977. Recipient of the RIBA Gold Medal in 1989, the Praemium Imperiale Award in 1995 and the Pritzker Prize in 1998.

過去25年間、グレン・マーカットの果たした顕著な役割について疑うことはできない。彼は、意識的に、オーストラリア版現代建築の開拓を行い、今や世界中からオーストラリア文化として認識されるに至った、明らかに優れた建築をつくりだした。

建築文化の創造において、自明の率先者であったマーカットについて過大に評価しすぎることはありえない。別段の厳しさと繊細さをもった彼の地域に根ざした設計活動は、少なくとも4世代——大学の教育が5年間かそのくらいとして——のオーストラリア建築家たちへの刺激となってきた。これらの世代に教育を受けた者たちは、マーカットの教育者としてのやむにやまれぬ影響を受けた直接的な結果物である。彼の設計活動はゆっくりと、長く引き延ばされた年月をかけて成熟したが、その間ずっと、彼は教育者としての責務を忠実に果たしてきた。

地域の参照という起点をもつマーカットの建築は、たぶん半分は皮肉であろうが、例外なくトレードマークの波板鉄板で葺かれた屋根（時には壁までも）をもつ高床の平屋で、実際的な、高度に美的な「奥地(アウトバック)」方式と言える。しかしながら、彼の建築が年月を経るにつけて、その気候とランドスケープに関連したサスティナビリティに配慮し始めたことについてはきちんと認識されていない。ここ15年ぐらいの、30何軒かの住宅において、彼は自然環境に沿った建築をつくることに集中し、ルーバー、換気塔、樋、縦樋、すべての考えうる構造材、トラス、そして深く跳ね出す日射しを遮る庇の使い方などのマクロなところから、建築のつくり方を根本的に変化させている。

サスティナビリティを実現することは、マーカットの建築を支える基本の倫理的な意志である。自然とともにデザインすることは、単なるかけ声ではない。すべての仕事を通して、例えば、雨水の放流、原生植物の植生の改変、土地の改変、（建築生産プロセスにおける）隠されたエネルギー消費に至るまで、建物が変えてしまう1つ1つの要素が環境にどう影響を与えるか、油断なく気を配っている。このために、マーカットは習慣的に、建築の内外部において自然界の影響を和らげる方法をとっている。冬の寒さを遮断する南の断熱壁と、冬の日射しを採り入れる北の開かれた構造。雨水集水タンク。ランドスケープに開かれた何層かの窓。風力や重力を利用した自然換気(クロスベンチレーション)を可能にする換気窓や換気塔。日中は太陽熱を吸収して夜間には熱を放出する、濃い灰色のタイルで舗装された歩道。これは教育的な、環境保護の原型となる建物の考え方であり、叙情的なものが入り込む余地はない。しかしながらこの態度が、まさに建物を自然と調和を深めるものとしているのである。（自然との調和は）現在の世界の建築界の状況においてマーカットの建築が重要である理由であり、また、（自然との調和は）思慮深い、更なる建築の発展に対する彼の志について確信させるものである。

コロンビア大学
ウェアー建築教授
ケネス・フランプトン

ケネス・フランプトン
建築史家。1930年英国生まれ。AAスクール卒業。コロンビア大学建築都市修景学部ウェア終身教授。1985年アメリカ建築家協会名誉賞、1990年AIA/ASCAトパーズ賞（建築教育への優れた功績）。

There can be no question as to the salient role played by Glenn Murcutt over the last 25 years, particularly with regard to the self-conscious cultivation of a specifically Australian version of modern architecture, the undeniable excellence of which is now being recognized as a significant national culture all over the world.

It is difficult to overestimate Murcutt's unofficial leadership in the generation of this culture. The exceptional rigor and sensitivity of his regional practice has been an inspiration to at least four successive generations of Australian architects, assuming one gets a new crop of graduates coming to their early fruition every five years or so. In many instances they have been a direct consequence of Murcutt's compelling influence as a teacher, for this task he has kept to as a faithful commitment throughout the protracted turbulent years of his slowly maturing practice.

Murcutt's invention of a regionally referential, perhaps partially ironic, but nonetheless practical and highly aesthetic "outback" mode, comprising single-storey houses, elevated off the ground and invariably roofed, if not entirely clad, in corrugated metal, patently made his name, but what has still not been sufficiently recognized is the way in which his architecture has become progressively more concerned with the issue of sustainability in relation to both the climate and the landscape. In the space of some fifteen years he would realize some thirty houses in this genre ringing the syntactical changes at the micro level, in terms of louvers, vents, gutters, down pipes and every conceivable type of frame, truss and over-hanging weather-screening canopy.

The achievement of sustainability is the fundamental ethical intention sustaining his architecture. Designing with nature is not a mere slogan with Murcutt, and in all of his works he has remained extremely aware of the way in which every intervention impacts the ecosystem in which one is working, from the drainage of storm water to the modification of native vegetation, from the erosion of soil to the embodiment of energy in all its hidden aspects. To this end, he has habitually adopted a series of strategies to mitigate this impact both within and without the confines of his architecture; from the provision of southern thermal walls to ward off the winter cold, to the opening of the structure to the north to admit the winter sun; from the provision of storage tanks to collect rainwater, to the screening of windows that open onto the landscape, from the installation of vents and fans to facilitate cross ventilation, to paving walkways in dark grey tiles that absorb the heat during the day and release it at night. This is a didactic, proto-ecological building culture that in no way inhibits the poetic potential of the field. On the contrary, it enhances it by deepening its rapport with nature. It is this that finally bestows on Murcutt's work a relevance for world architecture as a whole and it is also this that assures the profundity and promise of his approach in terms of its further development.

Yours sincerely

Kenneth Frampton
Ware Professor of Architecture
Columbia University

Kenneth Frampton
Architectural historian. Born in UK, 1930. Graduated from the Architectural Association. Ware Professor of Architecture at the Graduate School of Architecture, Planning and Preservation at Columbia University, New York. Recipient of the American Institute of Architects National Honors Award, 1985 and the Topaz Medallion for Excellence in Architectural Education, 1990.

Selected Works

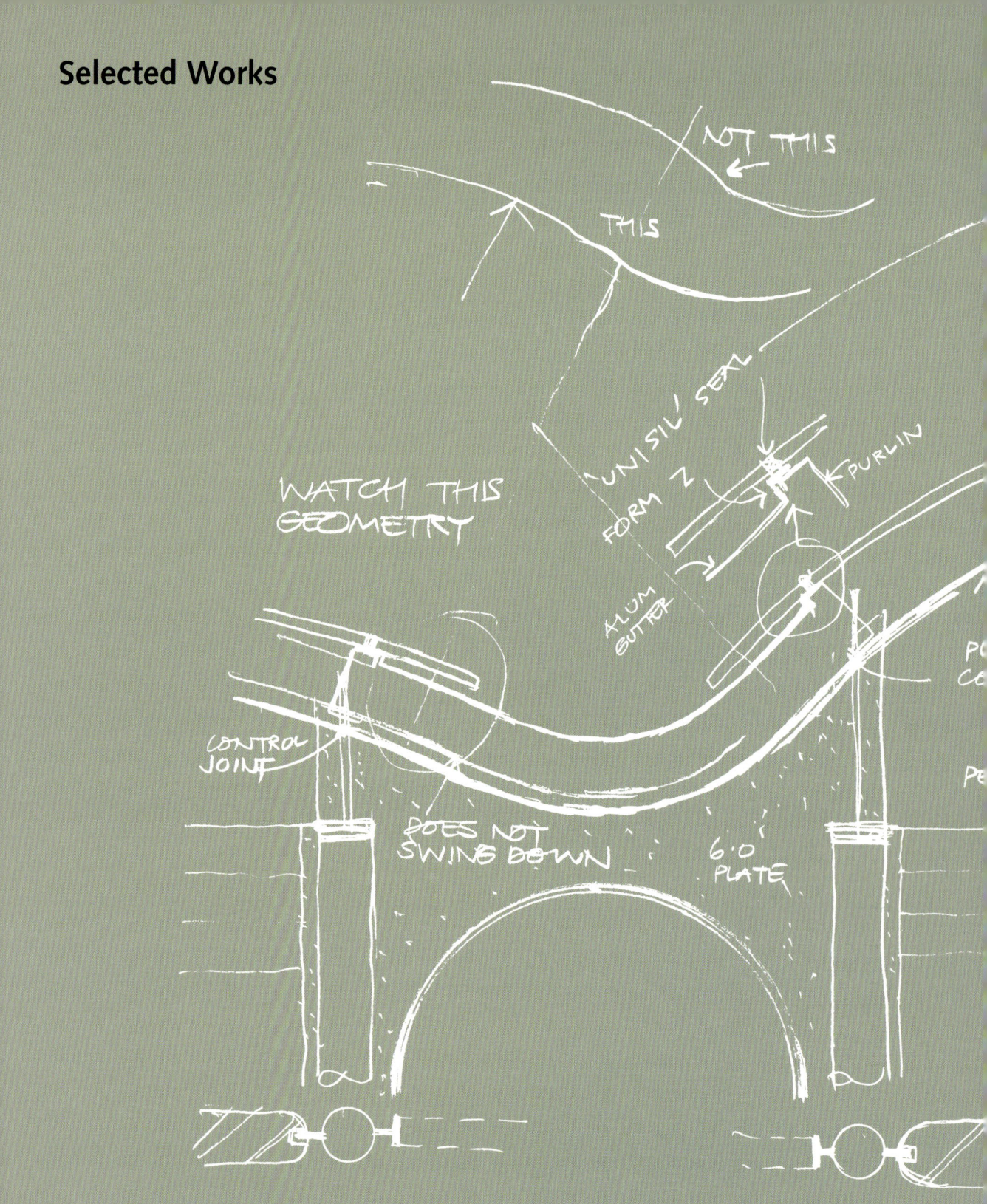

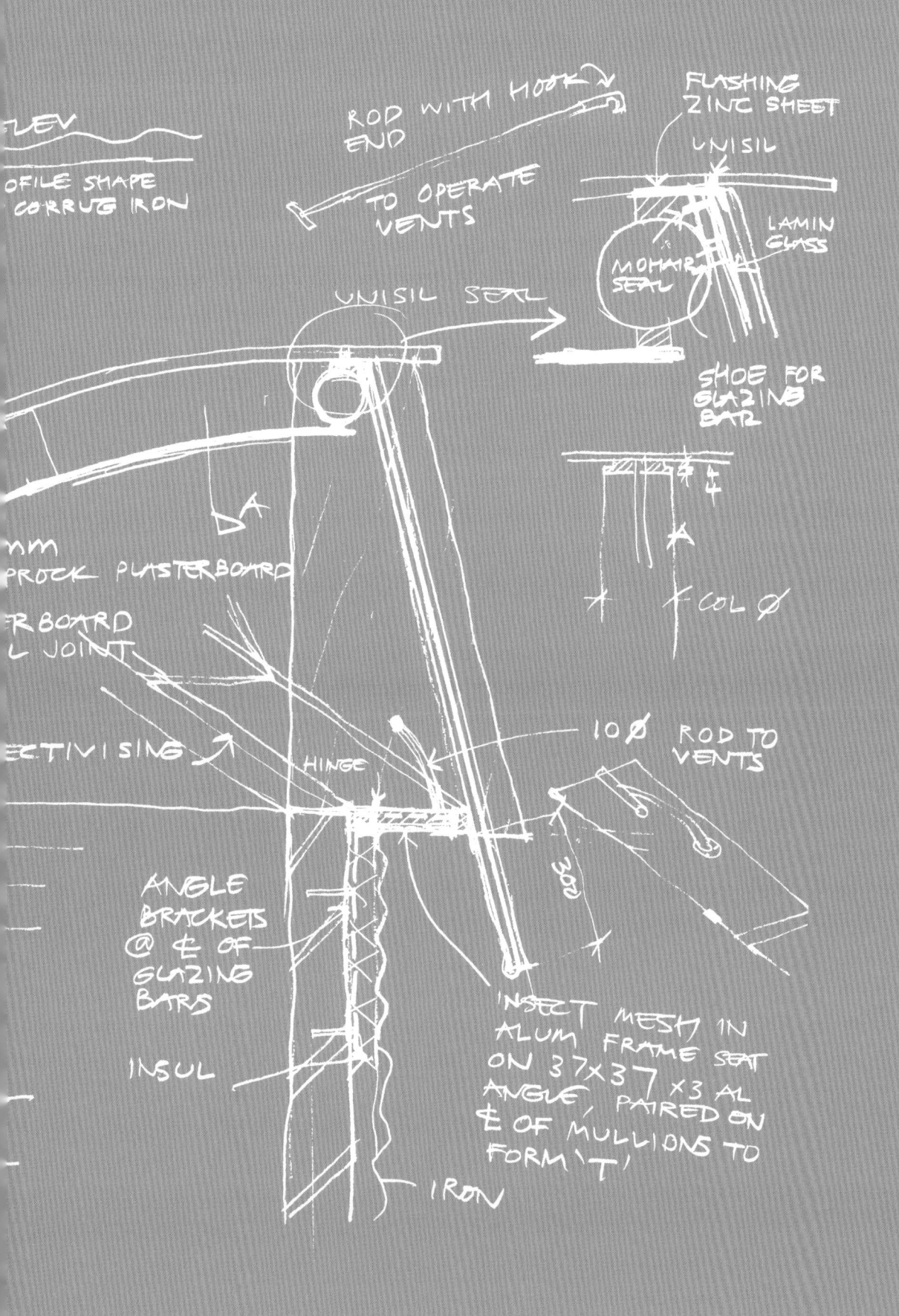

ELEV
OFILE SHAPE
CORRUG IRON

ROD WITH HOOK
END
TO OPERATE
VENTS

FLASHING
ZINC SHEET
UNISIL
LAMIN GLASS
MOHAIR SEAL

UNISIL SEAL

SHOE FOR GLAZING BAR

mm
PROCK PLASTERBOARD
RBOARD
L JOINT

COL ∅

ECTIVISING
HINGE

10∅ ROD TO VENTS

ANGLE BRACKETS @ ₵ OF GLAZING BARS

300

INSUL

INSECT MESH IN ALUM FRAME SEAT ON 37×37×3 AL ANGLE, PAIRED ON ₵ OF MULLIONS TO FORM 'T'

IRON

Douglas Murcutt House

ダグラス・マーカット邸

1969-72 ········ Belrose, Sydney, New South Wales

この初期の住宅は、マーカットのその後の全作品に続く、
自然と建物内部の親密性を予感させる。

This early work prefigures the intimate relationship
between interior and nature that is characteristic of
all Murcutt's subsequent works.

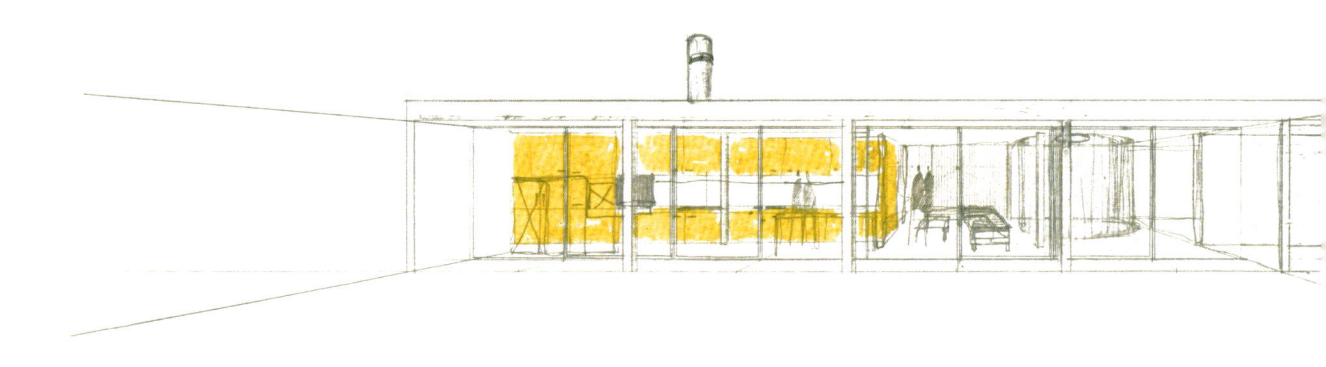

040 | Glenn Murcutt

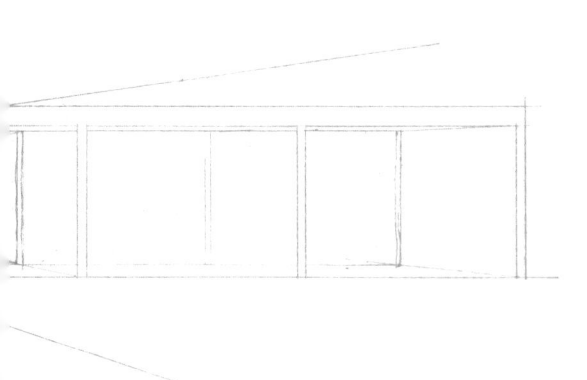

白いセメント塗りの背の高いレンガ壁は、住宅と庭を取り囲み、周辺の郊外住宅から独立させてプライバシーを与えている。

A high, white-rendered brick wall encloses the house and its garden, giving privacy and seclusion from the surrounding suburban houses.

Glenn Murcutt | 041

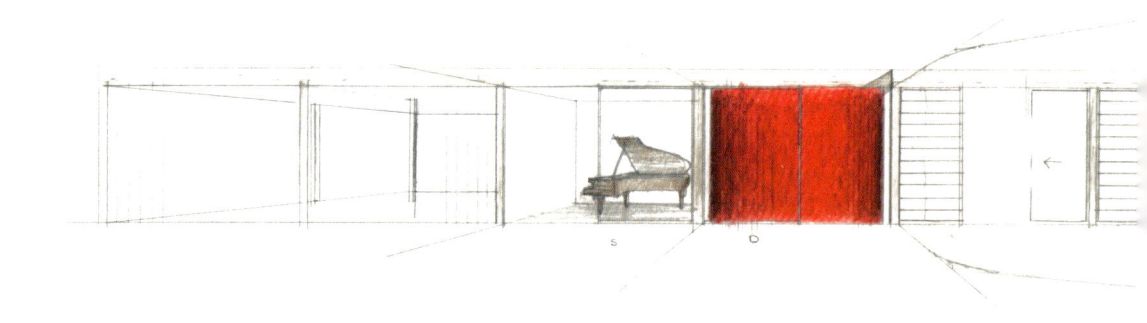

042 | Glenn Murcutt

北向きの部屋は、夏の日射しを遮る深い庇に守られる。南向きの
部屋は敷地境界の白い塀から柔らかく反射する光を採り入れる。

The north-facing rooms are screened from the summer sun by
the deeply-projecting canopy. The south-facing bedrooms receive
soft sunlight, reflected off the white-painted boundary wall.

Glenn Murcutt | 043

Douglas Murcutt House

ダグラス・マーカット邸

マーカット独立後の初仕事であるこの住宅は、夫婦で音楽教師であるマーカットの弟、その妻、2人の子どものために設計された。敷地はシドニー北の郊外住宅地であり、大きな土地の中心に島のように配置される典型的な郊外住宅形態に対する提案として設計された。

住宅は道路に対して90度振られ、北の太陽に向かって開口が大きくとられた。ミース・ファン・デル・ローエのコートヤード形式を試みた住宅の影響を受け、白塗りの高いレンガ壁を用いて周辺環境から私的な部屋を遮蔽している。同じ広さをもつ居間と庭との間には、構造柱から独立した開閉できるガラス面が立つ。それは、外部と内部の仕切りにすぎないことを示し、庭のオーストラリア産の植物と、部屋の間に親密な関係性をつくりだしている。寝室とピアノ・レッスン室は住宅の南側に庭をもち、白い境界壁へ柔らかく反射する光を採り入れる。

ファンズワース邸への参照は、機能を区分けするサービス・コアの採用と、住宅の構造の読みとりやすさに見てとれる。とりわけ柱が、周辺梁に外付けされて梁荷重を受けていることはそう言える。しかしこの住宅は木造であり、その接合部分は、ミースの鉄骨造の原型の擬態ではない。柱の外付けは、垂直・水平部材を簡単にボルト留めできる工法として採用された。この接合方法は、マーカットの父親が自身の家を建てた時に採った方法である。これはまた、シドニーの有名な建築家、アレン&ジャックにマーカットが師事した時に担当した、デヴィット邸(1960-62年)の工法でもあった。

建築工法の簡素化、冬期は日射しを採り入れるが夏は深い庇によって室内への日射しを遮るという注意深い配置計画、庭のオーストラリアの原産植物との親近性など、ダグラス・マーカット邸は、この後に続くマーカットの全住宅がもつ意図と問題性を原型として提示する住宅であると言える。

This is Murcutt's first built work as an independent architect: a house for his brother and his wife—both music teachers—with their two children. It is located in the northern suburbs of Sydney, and is a counter-proposal to the city's typical suburban morphology of houses standing, like islands, each within a large tract of land.

Murcutt placed the house at right-angles to the street, opening to the sun of the northern sky, and—influenced by Mies van der Rohe's experiments with courtyard houses—enclosed it within a high, white-rendered brick wall that screens the private rooms from the surrounding suburban environment. An open-able glass screen, standing independent of the structural columns, runs between the living room and the main garden, creating an intimate relationship between the rooms and the dense indigenous Australian plantings. The bedrooms and piano-teaching room address separate courtyards on the southern side of the house, and receive soft sunlight reflected off the white boundary wall.

References to Farnsworth House may be found in the use of an internalised service core to separate the different activity zones, and in the legibility of the house's structure—particularly in the manner in which the posts of the structure stand proud of the edge-beam that they support. Here, however, the structural frame is of wood, and the joint is not a simulation of Mies' steel original. Instead, it allows a very simple bolting together of the vertical and horizontal members. It was a jointing-method employed by his father in the houses he built, and was used previously by Murcutt, himself, in his design of the Devitt House (1960-62) undertaken while working for the eminent Sydney practice Allen and Jack.

In the simplicity of its structural methods, in the careful orientation and use of a deep overhang to shield the interior from the sun during the summer but admit it during the winter, and in its intimate relationship with the indigenous Australian plantings of its gardens, this house pre-figures intentions and concerns that characterise all of Murcutt's subsequent works.

軒下のテラスとあわせると、居間は面する庭とほぼ同じ広さである。敷地が斜めに狭まる住宅の南側では、寝室とピアノ・レッスン室は独立した庭をもつ。

The living area of the house, with its roofed terrace, is of identical size to the main garden, which it faces. The bedrooms and piano studio open towards separate terraces, created on the southern side of the house in the tapering form of the site.

Glenn Murcutt 045

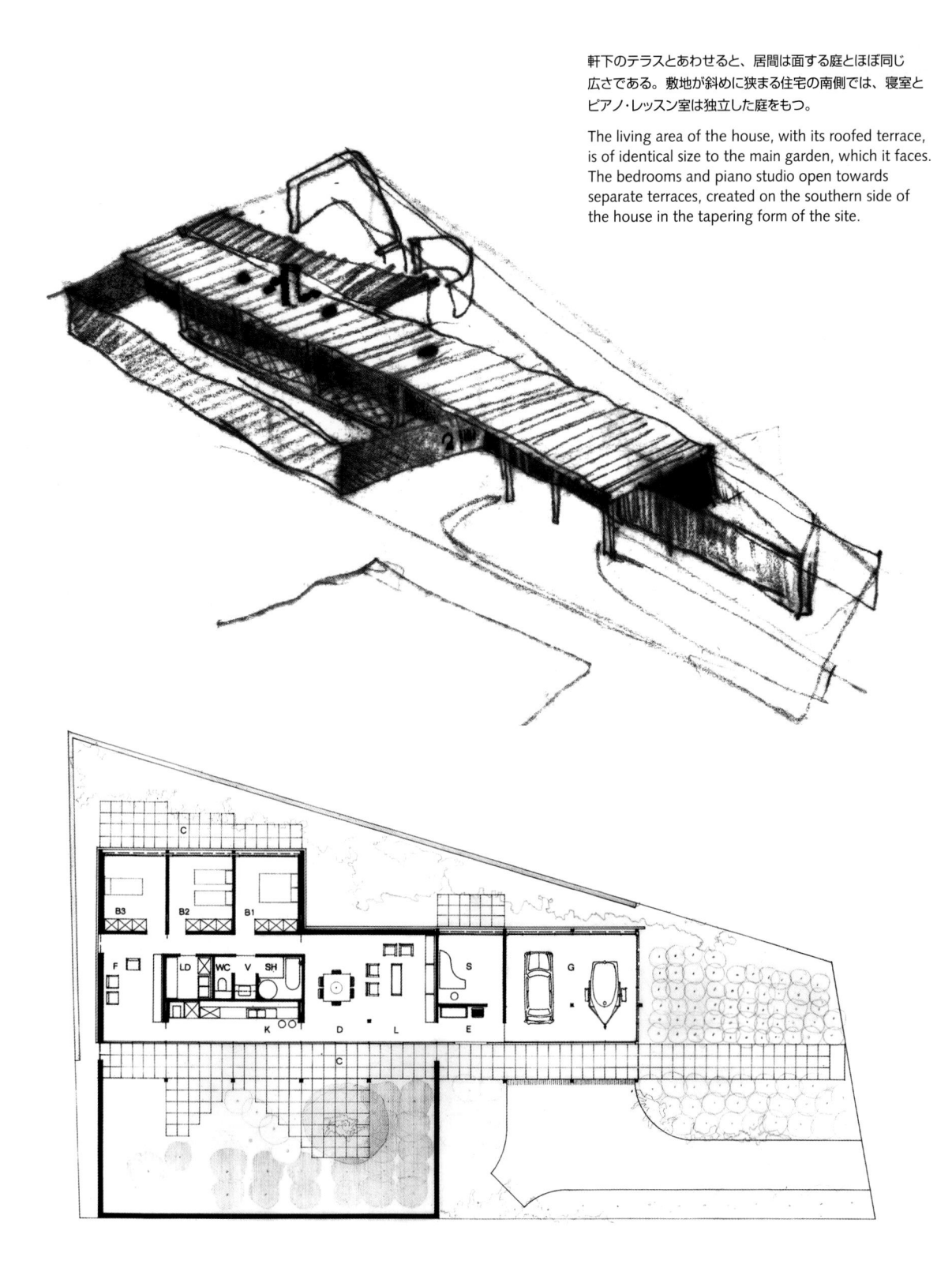

Marie Short / Glenn Murcutt House

マリー・ショート／グレン・マーカット邸

1974−75 / 1980·········· Kempsey, New South Wales

ランドスケープの中の住宅。ほぼ同じ2棟だが、平面は180度
回転してずらしている。端部は別棟への入口で屋外ポーチとなっている。

A house in the landscape. Two almost identical pavilions,
one rotated and slipped, with the last two bays treated as an open
porch for entry into the adjacent pavilion.

梁と柱の木組みを現す工法は、納屋建築や現地技術に拠っている。切妻屋根の抽象的な構成は、浮き床をもつ住宅という建築的コンセプトを強めている。

An expressed post and beam structure draws on farm shed construction traditions and local building expertise. The abstracted treatment of the pitched roof reinforces the architectural conception of the house as a floating platform.

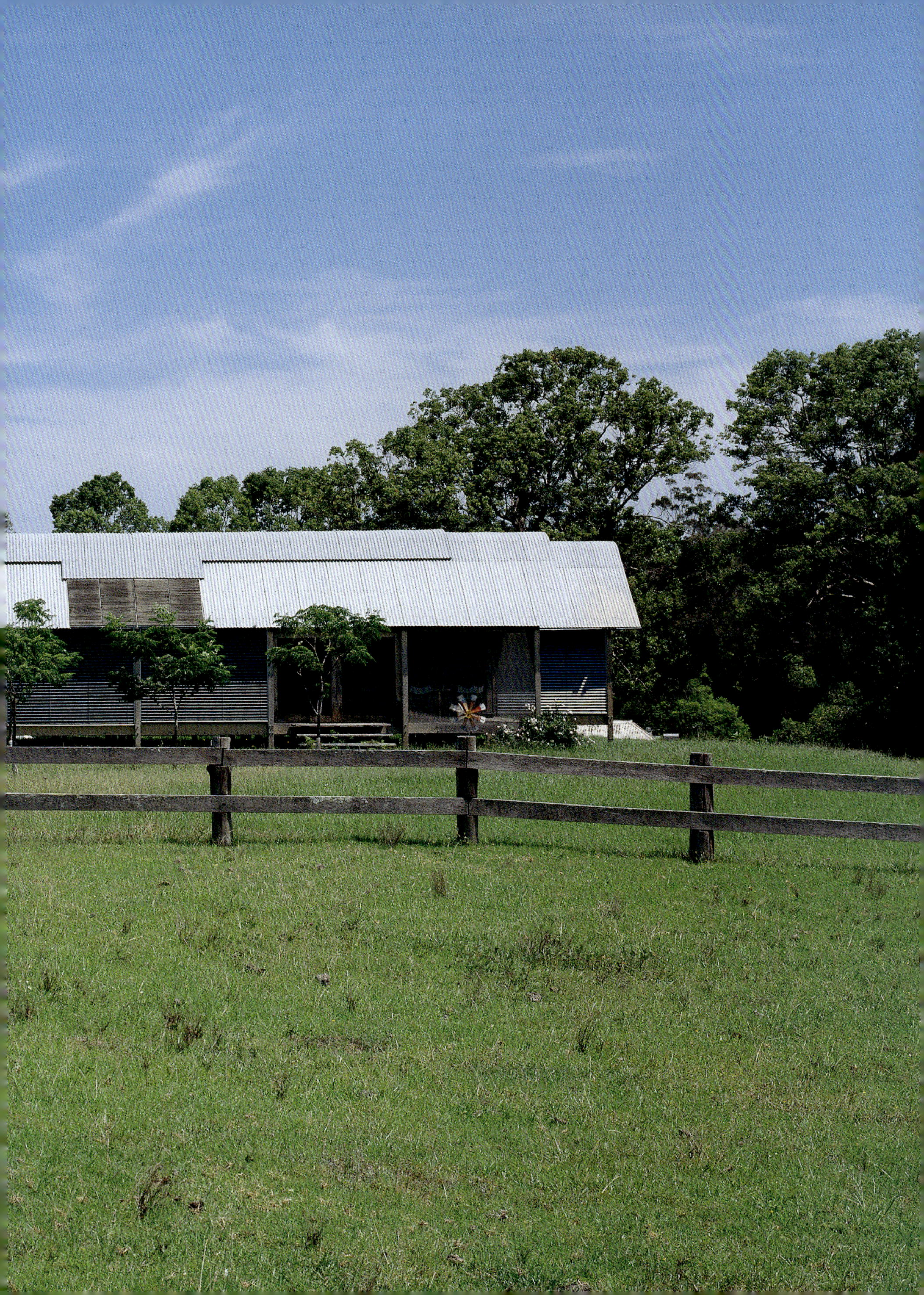

カーブした屋根の棟は二重のシートで強調され、地面からもち上げられた水平性の強い建物であることを示している。シロアリとヘビ除けのためにも高床となっている。

Doubling the roof layers calls attention to the immaterial edge and renders the building as a horizontal floating volume. Murcutt draws attention to the practical advantages of this position where the elevated floor allows for the visibility of termites and the avoidance of snakes.

曲げられた波板鉄板は重ねて小屋裏換気孔としている。屋根の翼形状はよりよい換気を促す。

Curved corrugated metal sheets are overlapped to provide ventilation slots. The aerofoil form of the roof enhances natural ventilation.

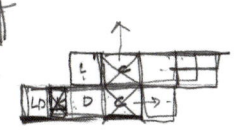

Glenn Murcutt

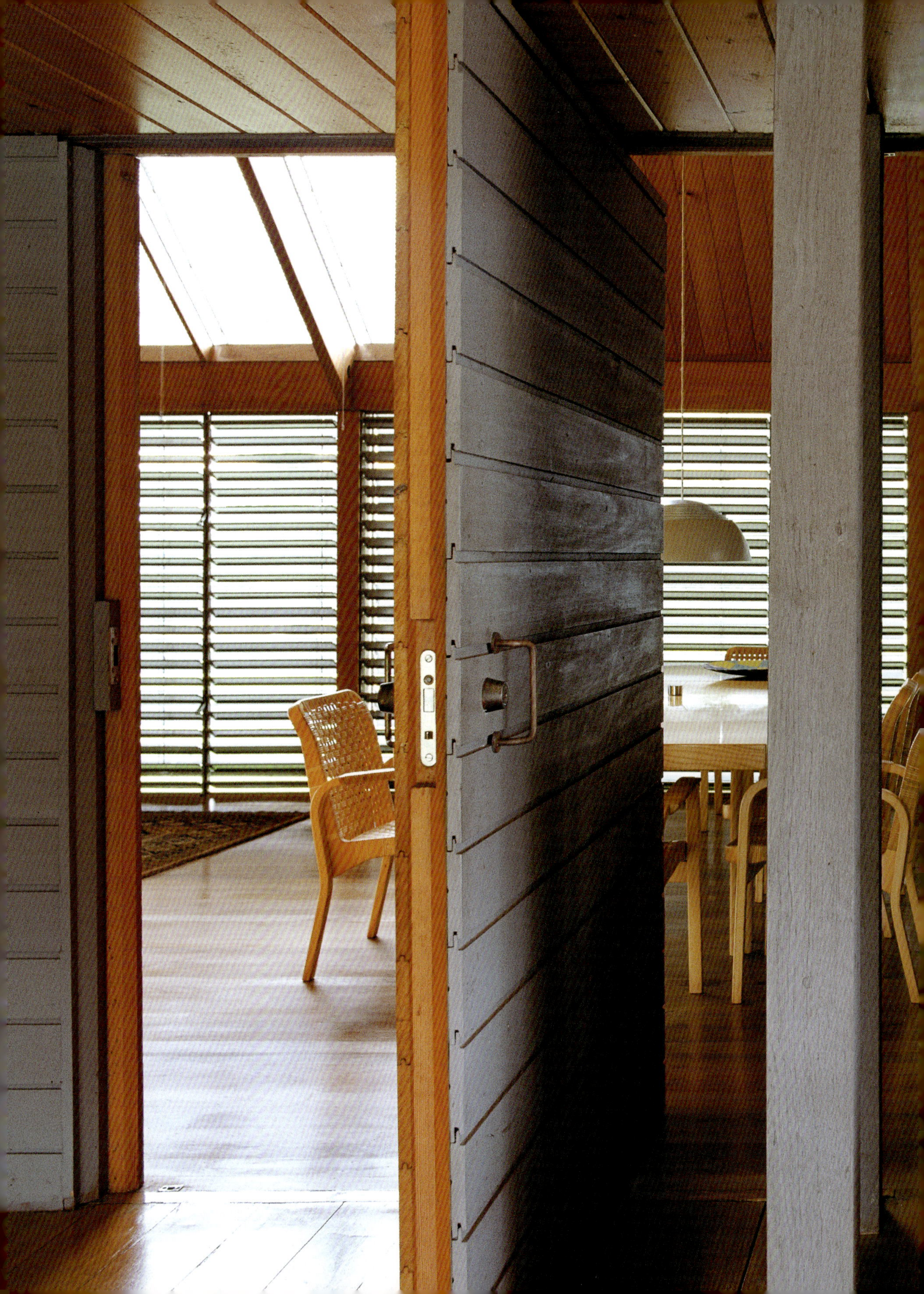

壁のごとく厚い回転扉に見られるように、木材で一色の室内は、機械的な質感をもつ外装との対比においてよい緊張感を生み出している。

The colour and materiality of the predominantly timber interiors, as experienced in the unexpectedly thick pivot doors, is in productive tension with the mechanical quality of the building's exterior skin.

ブラッシュボックス、コーチウッド、ユーカリの一種の
タローウッド、米松など、施主がもっていた木材の量
と寸法を基軸にデザインが発展した。

The house was developed around the precise quantity and dimensions of stockpiled timbers, which included brushbox, coachwood, tallowwood and oregon (pine).

固定ブラインドのある天窓は、夏には日陰を冬には日差しを取り入れる。
立面窓の2層のルーバーは、居間から簡単に操作できる。
この仕掛けは、室内環境とランドスケープへの眺望において、使い手に大きな自由度がある。

A skylight with fixed louvers gives shade in the summer but provides winter sun. A double louver façade allows the building skin to be readily manipulated. This system gives a high degree of personal freedom to orchestrate the building as an environmental instrument, for both climatic comfort and aesthetic experience of the landscape.

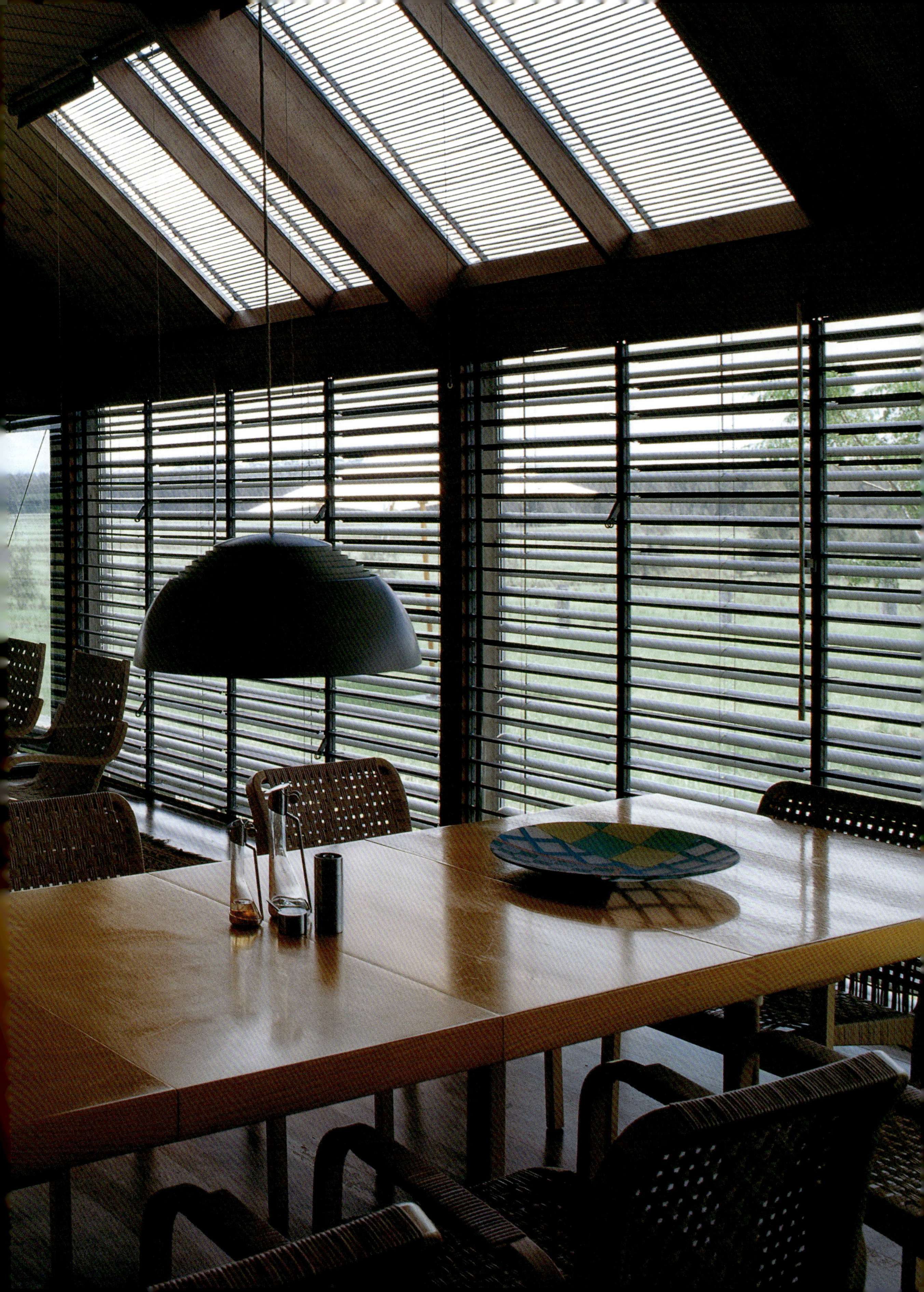

ニューサウスウェールズ州、北部海岸地域の農地にある住宅は、一方の立面を西の川に向け、もう一方を3ヘクタールの広さのある東の潟湖に向ける。

Located within extensive farmland in northern coastal NSW, one end of the house faces west to the river. The other looks east to a 3 hectare lagoon.

MARIA RIVER TIDAL FLOW

← BOUNDARY

EXISTING BUILDING

NEW RESIDENCE ON 655 ACRES.

DAM

GATE TO SHORT FARM

GATE

SCALE

Glenn Murcutt | 059

マリー・ショート邸は、1970年代にニューサウスウェールズ州の北海岸の農地へ建てられた後、80年にマーカットにより購入されて改築が行われた。74年の住宅平面は、無防備なほど簡潔である。ほぼ同じ2棟が、一方を180度回転して雁行に配置され、片棟を寝室、もう片棟は居室とされた。それぞれの棟は6スパンある木構造で、端部の2スパンは屋外ポーチである。2枚の厚い壁の間は、2つのポーチをつなぐ室外動線で、上部は雨水を収集する屋根の谷樋となっている。

形態の繰り返しと、機能による棟の性格分けは、キッチンとバスルームにも及び、水廻りの小部屋としてグループ化されて繰り返されている。サービスと居間空間の大きさの対比は、後者の空間が豊かなことを強く感じさせる。

住宅の配置と各要素は、風土にあわせて決定された。居室棟の長手は北を向き、日中の大半の光を採り入れる。上げ下げできる金属のルーバーは日射しと視線を調整し、ガラス・ルーバーは風量を調節する。建物を最大限まで環境調節の道具として使いこなすように考えられた、この2層の仕掛けは、室内環境の設定や眺望に関して、使い手に大きな自由を与える。

気候に応答する性能は、屋根のディテールにも現れる。曲面の波板鉄板は頂部で重なり、水平に続く棟換気として機能する。二重のシートは、棟材を目立たせず建物の水平性を表出させる。この抽象的な切妻屋根の解法は、この住宅の浮き床（フローティング・プラットフォーム）というコンセプトを強めている。

1974-75年の住宅は、施主が長年かけて集めた木材を利用してつくられた。梁と柱の構造は、農家の小屋の工法に拠っている。工法と接合部のディテールは、将来解体してまた組み直すことができるようにという施主の要望に応えている。保存と部材の再利用というこの念願は、1980年にマーカットがこの住宅を改築した時に実現した。

この住宅において、マーカットは、閉じたセンター・コアという構成を検討しつつ、押出材のような直列性をもつ空間の繰り返しを試みた。現地の建物で見慣れた切妻屋根や玄関ポーチなどの形態が、抽象性と独創性をもって再定義されたことにより、現代オーストラリア建築の発展と遂行において重要な地位を占める住宅となっている。

Marie Short / Glenn Murcutt House

マリー・ショート／グレン・マーカット邸

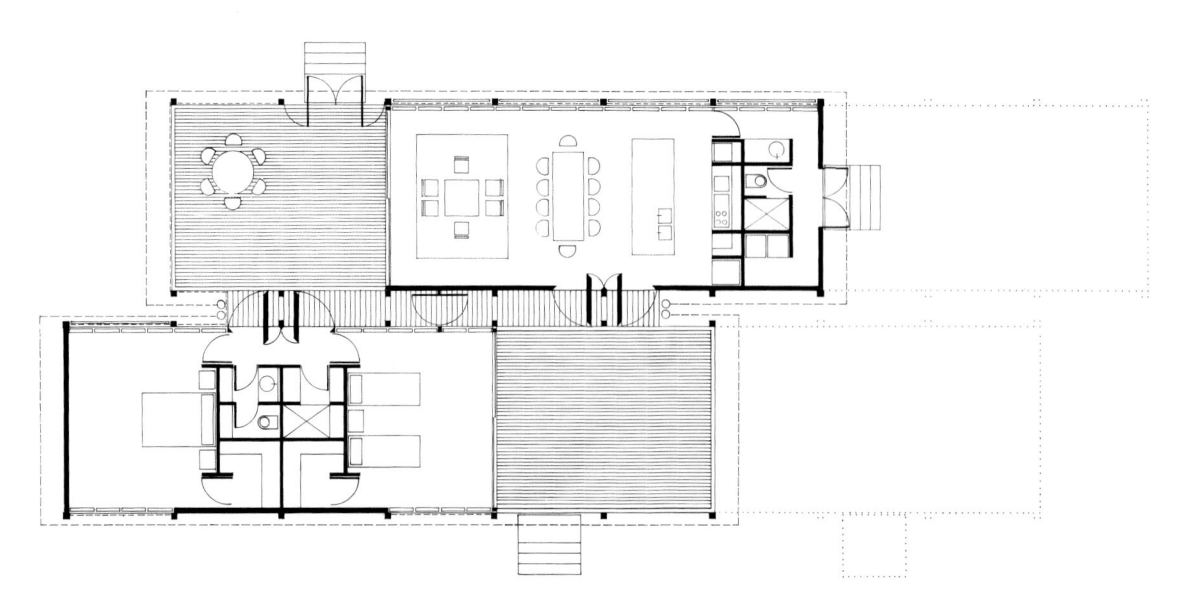

Plan 1974-75

Located on farmland in northern coastal NSW the Marie Short House was designed in the 1970's, later purchased and altered by Murcutt in 1980. The 1974-75 house plan is disarmingly simple with two almost identical pavilions, rotated and slipped; one for sleeping, the other for living. Each pavilion is six, structural timber bays, the last two bays treated as an open entry porch. Between the two, a thickened 'wall' implies an external corridor which links the porches and accommodates the collection of rain water.

The strategy to repeat and distinguish the pavilions by function is extended to the kitchen and bathrooms where each functional component is individuated, repeated and grouped as a cluster of cells. The spatial contrast between the service and living zones heightens a sense of generosity in the larger rooms.

The orientation of the house and its articulation are conceived in relation to climatic considerations. The living pavilion faces north to receive sun for the majority of the day. Retractable metal louvers control levels of light and privacy and the glass louvers allow varying degrees of ventilation. This double layered system gives a high degree of personal freedom to orchestrate the building as an instrument, for both environmental comfort and aesthetic experience of the landscape.

Climatic performance also drives the detailed resolution of the roof. Curved corrugated metal sheets overlap to provide horizontal ventilation slots. Doubling the layers calls attention to the immaterial edge and renders the building as a horizontal volume. This abstract treatment of the pitched roof form reinforces the conception of the house as a floating platform.

The 1974-75 house was conceived in terms of existing timber, stockpiled by the client. An expressed post and beam structure draws on farm shed construction techniques. The assembly system and junction details were developed in order to accommodate the client's wish to pull apart and reassemble the components for future relocation of the house. This ambition for conservation and reuse was realised when Murcutt altered the property in 1980.

In this House Murcutt offers a centred enclosure as well as the spatial repetition and extrusion of a machine. The abstract and original re-presentation of familiar forms such as the pitched roof and entrance porch using local techniques and materials assigns the building an important position within the pursuit and evolution of modernist architecture in Australia.

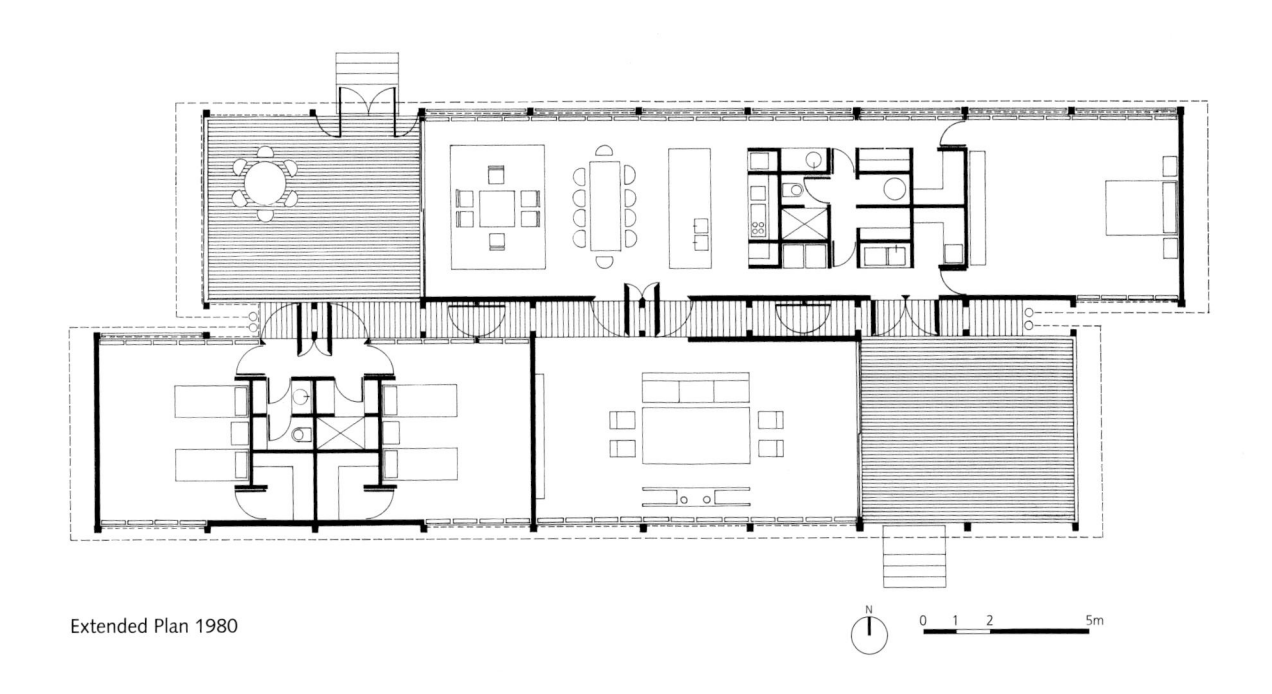

Extended Plan 1980

Fredericks / White House

フレデリックス／ホワイト邸

1981−82 / 2001−04 ········ Jamberoo, New South Wales

北向きに遥かな眺望をもつ住宅と庭は、傾斜地において住まいのつながりをつくっている。

Oriented toward the north and long distance valley views the house and its garden provide a stepped sequence of living platforms.

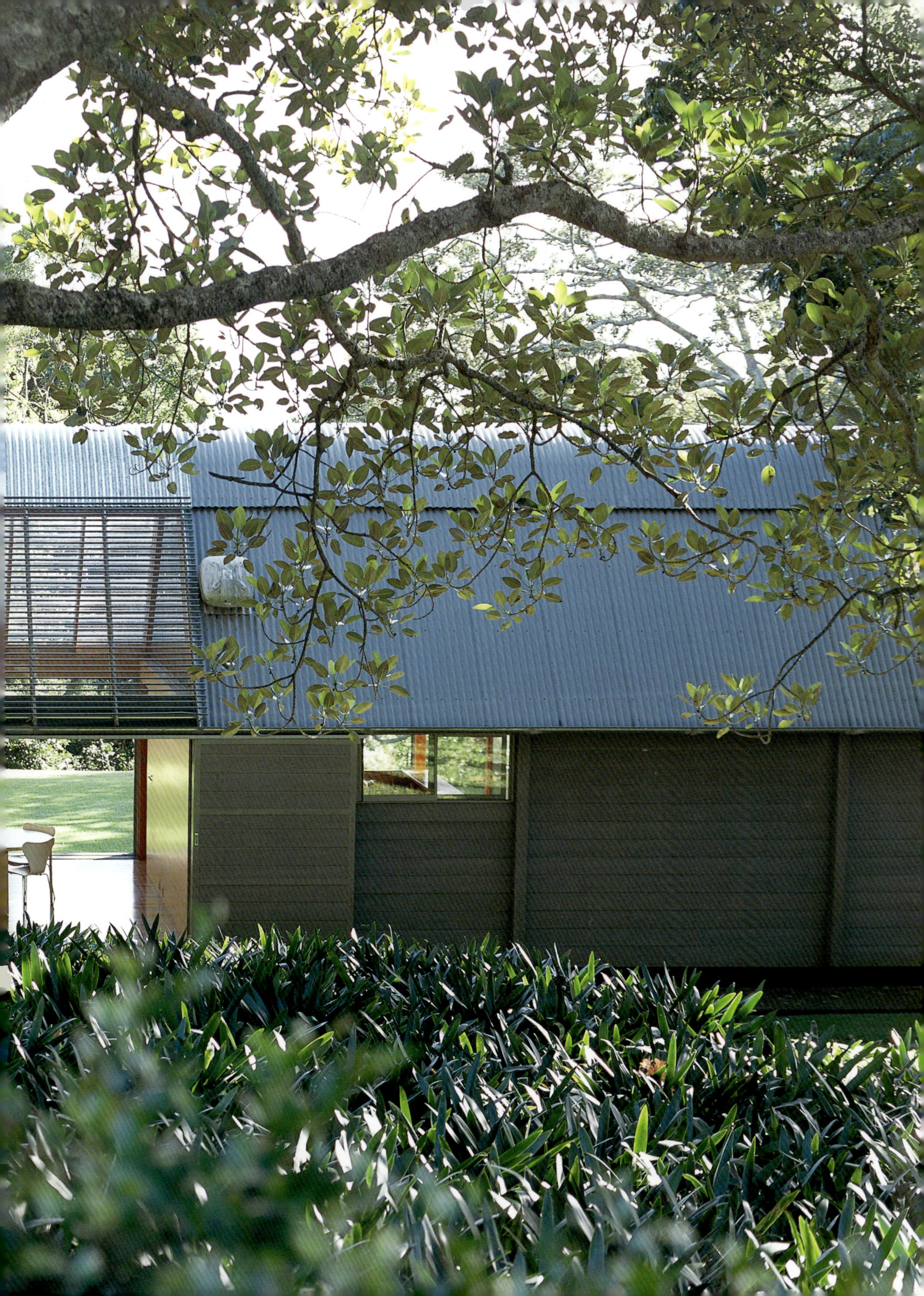

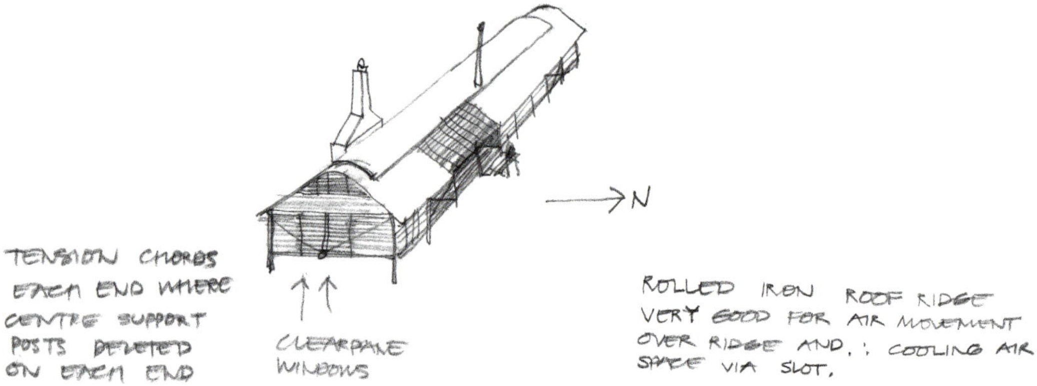

TENSION CHORDS
EACH END WHERE
CENTRE SUPPORT
POSTS DELETED
ON EACH END

CLEARPANE
WINDOWS

ROLLED IRON ROOF RIDGE
VERY GOOD FOR AIR MOVEMENT
OVER RIDGE AND ∴ COOLING AIR
SPACE VIA SLOT.

064 | Glenn Murcutt

住宅は、カーブした波板鉄板の屋根をもつ2棟の
パビリオンで構成された。南の短い棟は、既存の
暖炉脇から入る玄関を定める。

The building is formed by two pavilions each
with a curved corrugated metal roof. The shorter
southern pavilion defines an entry threshold
alongside an existing fireplace.

Glenn Murcutt

天窓に外付けの金属のブラインドは、羽の角度を調整できる。
The angle of external metal blinds at the glazed skylights can be adjusted to allow for personal environmental control.

新たに組み込まれたスクリーン付きのポーチは、住宅の中のヴォイドで
あり、傾斜する敷地の前後をつないでいる。

An embedded open screened porch is a significant void within the
house and connects the building to both sides of the sloping site.

Glenn Murcutt | 069

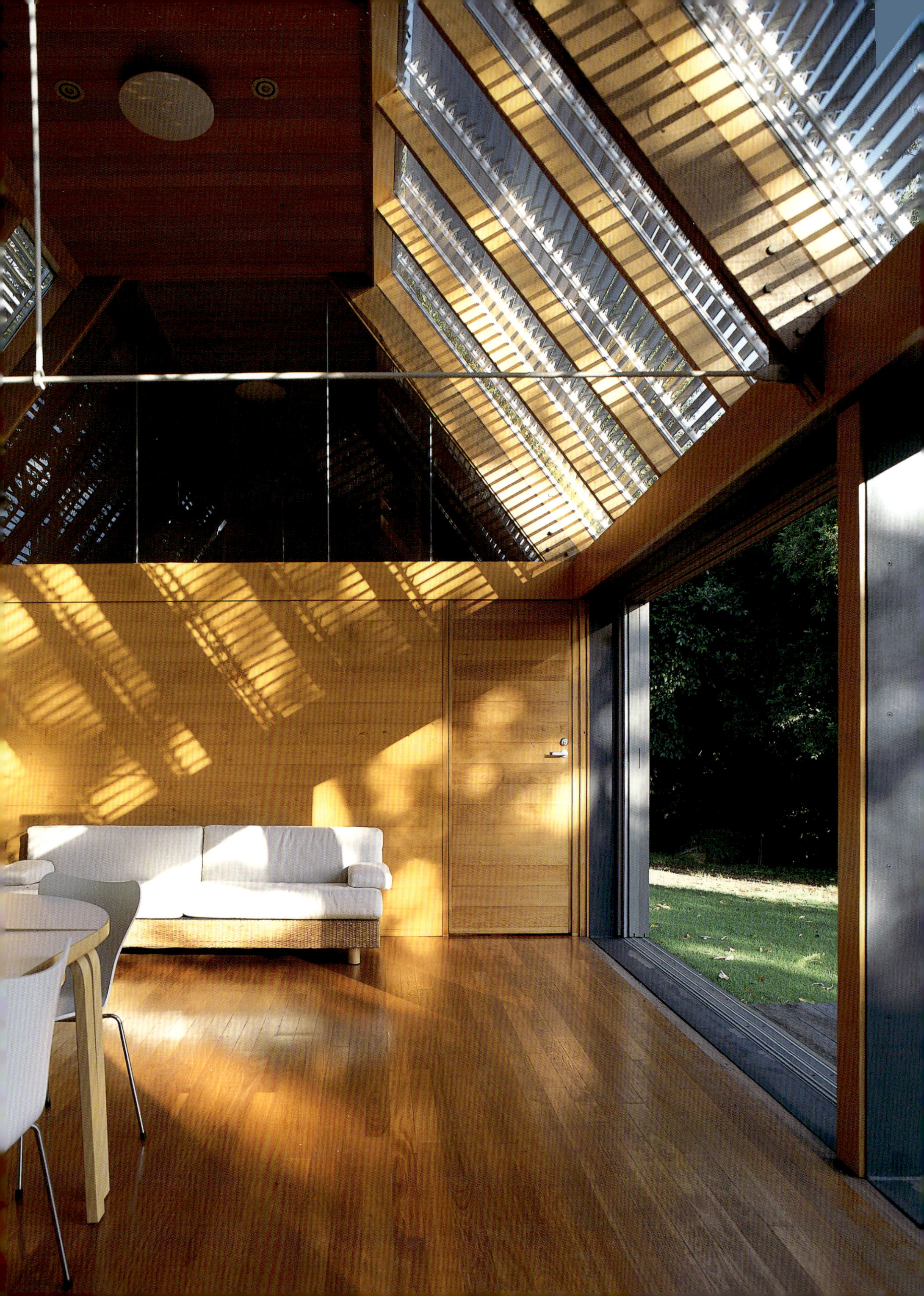

断面形状は、ロフトスペースと階段を確保し、室内の垂直性を強調している。

The section profile allows for a stair and upper loft and gives the internal volume a vertical emphasis.

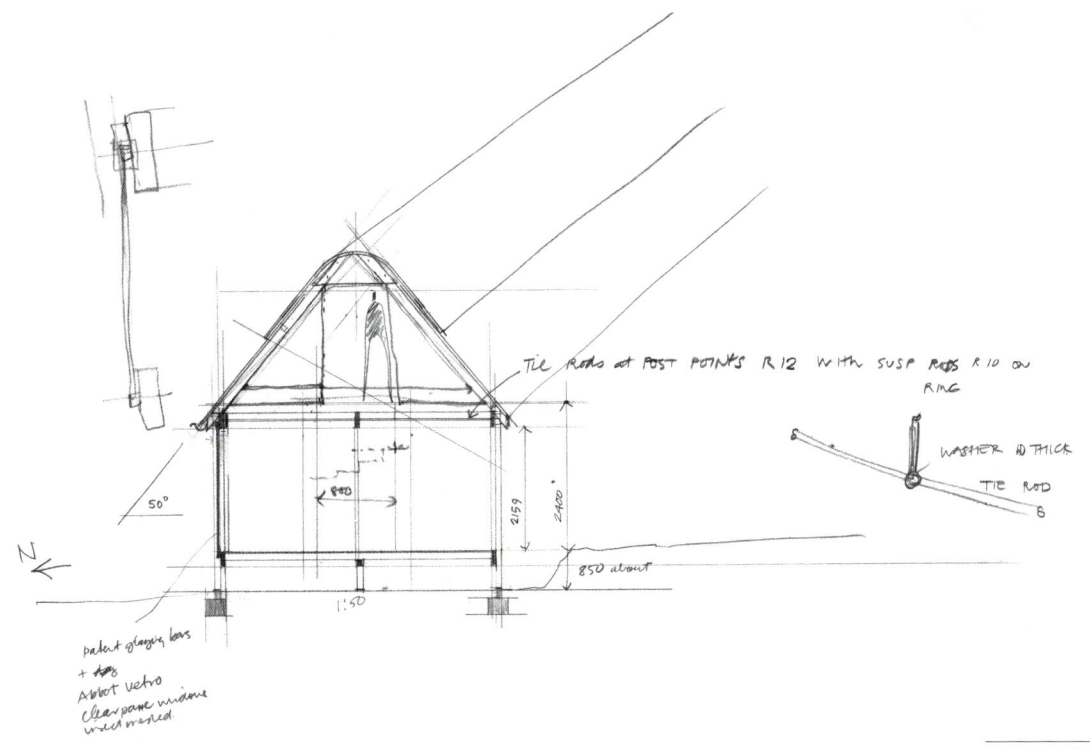

Glenn Murcutt | 071

スパンごとに繰り返される構造は、仕上げの木材とともに、室内でその架構形式をあらわしている。
A repetitive bay structure utilises an exposed timber frame with timber lined interiors.

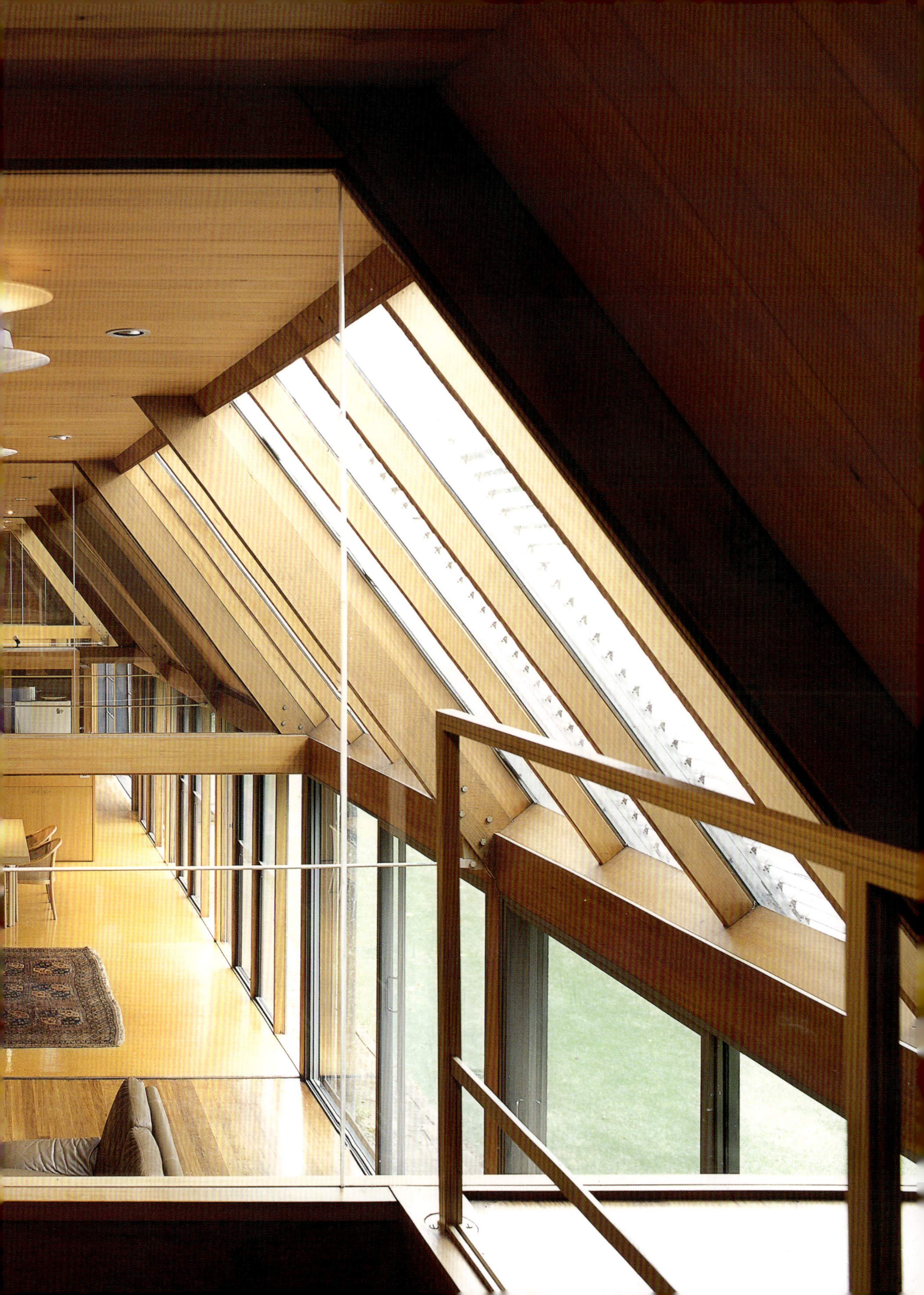

居住空間、バス、キッチンなどの機能のほとんどは北側の棟に収められた。

The domestic program is largely housed in the northern pavilion organised as a sequence of living, bathing and kitchen facilities.

Glenn Murcutt | 075

2001-04年の増築では屋外シャワーが加えられ、
北の棟の端部を開いた。

The 2001-04 additions include an external shower,
providing an open end to the northern living pavilion.

抽象的な北のファサードは、太陽と景色へ向けられた。引戸、上げ下げ窓と、外付け
の金属ブラインドは、木の鎧戸とともに、建物の調節可能な表皮となっている。

An abstracted northern façade is oriented to the sun and views. Sliding/ double hung windows and external metal retractable blinds combine with sliding timber screens to provide an adjustable building skin.

Fredericks / White House

フレデリックス／ホワイト邸

ニューサウスウェールズ州の南海岸にあるこの住宅は、熱帯雨林(レインフォレスト)に囲まれ、谷へ向かう眺望を得ている。フレデリックス邸（1981-82年）は、古い農家の暖炉を中心に設計された。さらにこの住宅は、新しいオーナーの与件を組み入れるため、マーカットの設計により2001-04年に増築された。

明らかにここでは、ケンプシーのマリー・ショート／グレン・マーカット邸で試された多くのアイデアを再度試みている。カーブした波板鉄板屋根をもつ棟は、ずらして配置され、似た素材を選択している。どちらも東西の軸に配置され、リビング棟は北側にある。木造であり、室内も木材で仕上げている。木架構フレームは、相似した柱間で立てられた。

ケンプシーの住宅で組織立てられたアイデアは、この敷地の豊かさと、施主の与件に応えるため新たに整えられた。入口へ繊細なアプローチをとるように棟の配置は考え直された。南の棟は長さを切り詰められて、既存の暖炉脇から入る玄関を定めている。断面形状は、階段とロフトスペースを確保するために垂直方向に伸ばされた。抽象的な北立面ではショート邸の遮光装置が変化している。より寒い気候に対応するために、ガラス・ルーバーではなく引戸か上げ下げ窓にして、冷気を入れない配慮がなされ、外付けのブラインドは、羽の角度を調整できるように変更された。北面のガラス・スクリーンが太陽と景観に向かうのに対して、南の壁は「裏」である。1棟に近い、正面性のある建物となったことは、この住宅がケンプシーの繰り返しでなく、注意深い再解釈であることを証明している。

2001-04年の増改築は、この平面形が改築に対応できるものであることを示した。ここでマーカットは、オリジナルのデザインでは実現されなかった、網戸で囲われた屋外ポーチを実現する機会を与えられた。増築において虚空間(ヴォイド)となったポーチは、前後の敷地を結び、傾斜地における住宅と庭の、住まいのつながりをつくりだしている。

Located on the south coast of New South Wales, this house is surrounded by rainforests and oriented toward long distance valley views. The original building (1981-82) was designed around an existing fireplace remaining from an old farmhouse. It was extended by Murcutt in 2001-04 in order to accommodate the new owner's additional requirements.

The design is an explicit reworking of many of the ideas initially tested in the Marie Short House in Kempsey. The building is a staggered double pavilion with curved pitched corrugated metal roofs and employs similar materials as the house at Kempsey. In both projects the pavilions are located on an east/west axis with the 'living' pavilion on the northern side. Timber is used as a structural frame and to line the interiors. The repetitive structural bay is similarly proportioned.

The systems developed in the Kempsey house are here adjusted in specific response to the particular qualities of this site and differing requirements. Murcutt's reworking of the double pavilion is evident in his subtle treatment of the entry sequence. Here a substantially truncated southern volume defines an entrance threshold alongside the original fireplace. The section profile is manipulated to allow for a stair and upper loft and gives the internal volume a more vertical emphasis. An abstracted northern façade uses the sun shading devices employed in Kempsey but with variations. Sliding and double hung windows rather than louvers provide a better seal in the colder climate and external metal retractable blinds tilt to allow for greater adjustability. The northern glazed screen is oriented to the sun and views whilst the solid southern wall implies a 'back'. This articulation of the building as a single pavilion with a dominant orientation confirms that the house is no simple repetition of the Kempsey design but is a careful translation.

The 2001-04 reconfiguration and extension illustrates the flexibility of the plan type. It also provided Murcutt with the opportunity to realise an embedded open screened porch, an unrealised component of his original design. In the new house this significant void provides an important opportunity to connect the building to both sides of the sloping site and registers the house and its garden as a stepped sequence of living platforms.

Glenn Murcutt

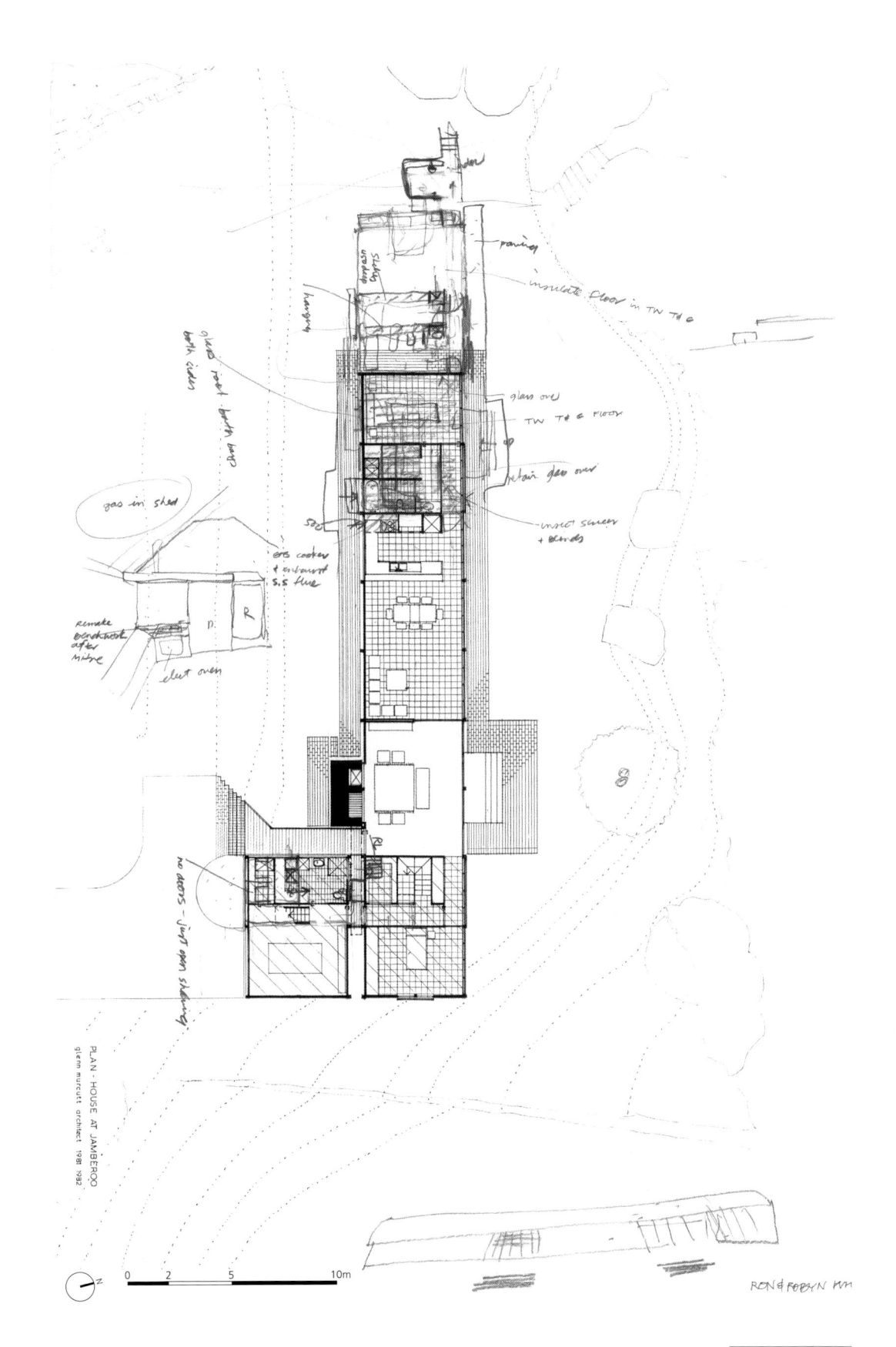

Glenn Murcutt | 081

Magney House

マグニー邸

1982−84 / 1999·········· Bingie Point, New South Wales

印象的な屋根形状は、正面と背面の性格が違うことを示している。
北の開かれた立面は、冷たい南風の当たる閉じられた背面と対照的である。

The striking roof form registers a pavilion type with a distinct front and back. An open northern face is contrasted with the largely closed rear wall facing harsh southerly winds.

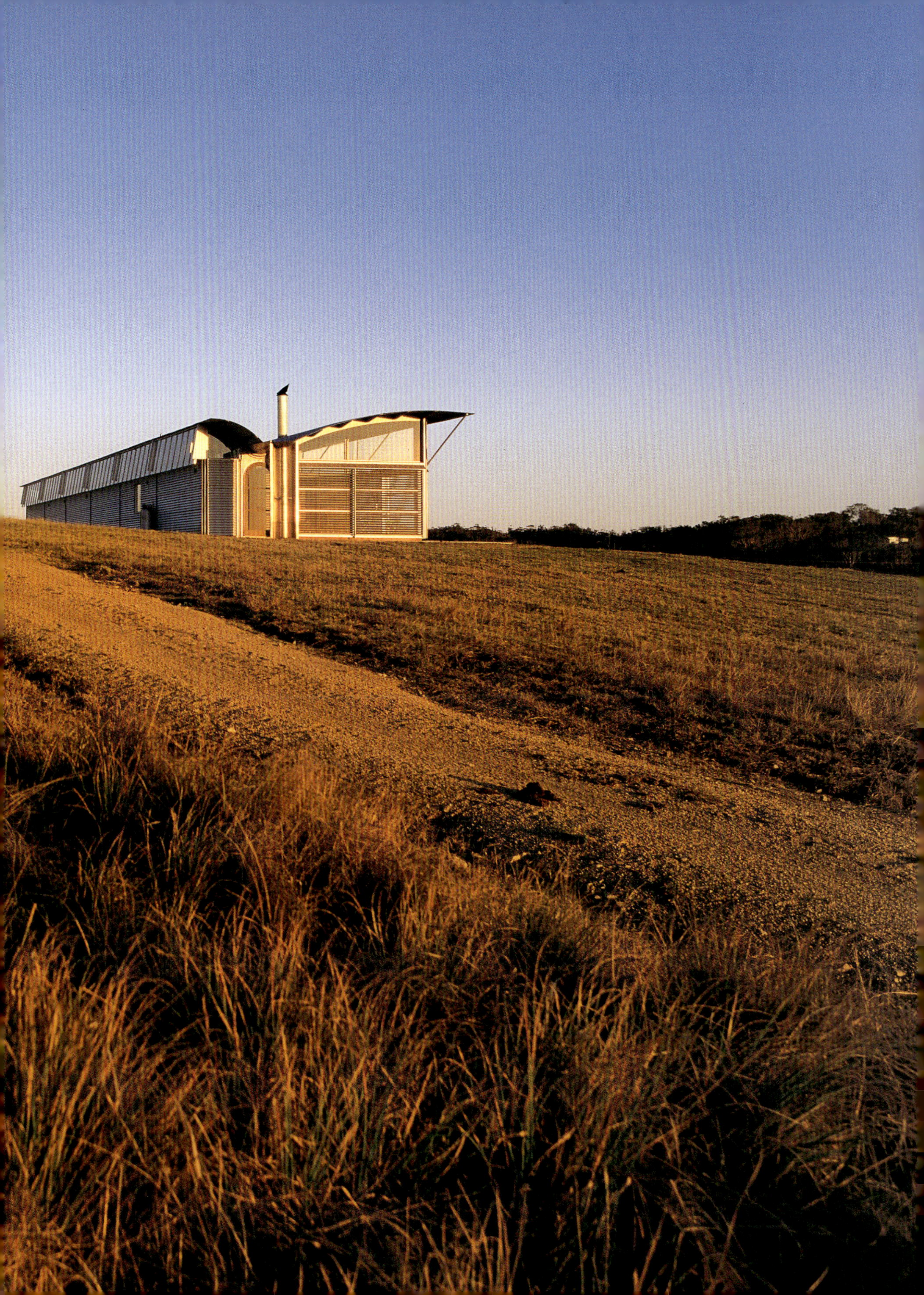

中庭を挟んで、それぞれ独立したキッチンとバスルームをもつ。片方は両親のため、もう一方はゲストやファミリー用となっている。

The building is a single pavilion divided by a central court and can operate as two self contained suites, one for the parents, the other for guests or family.

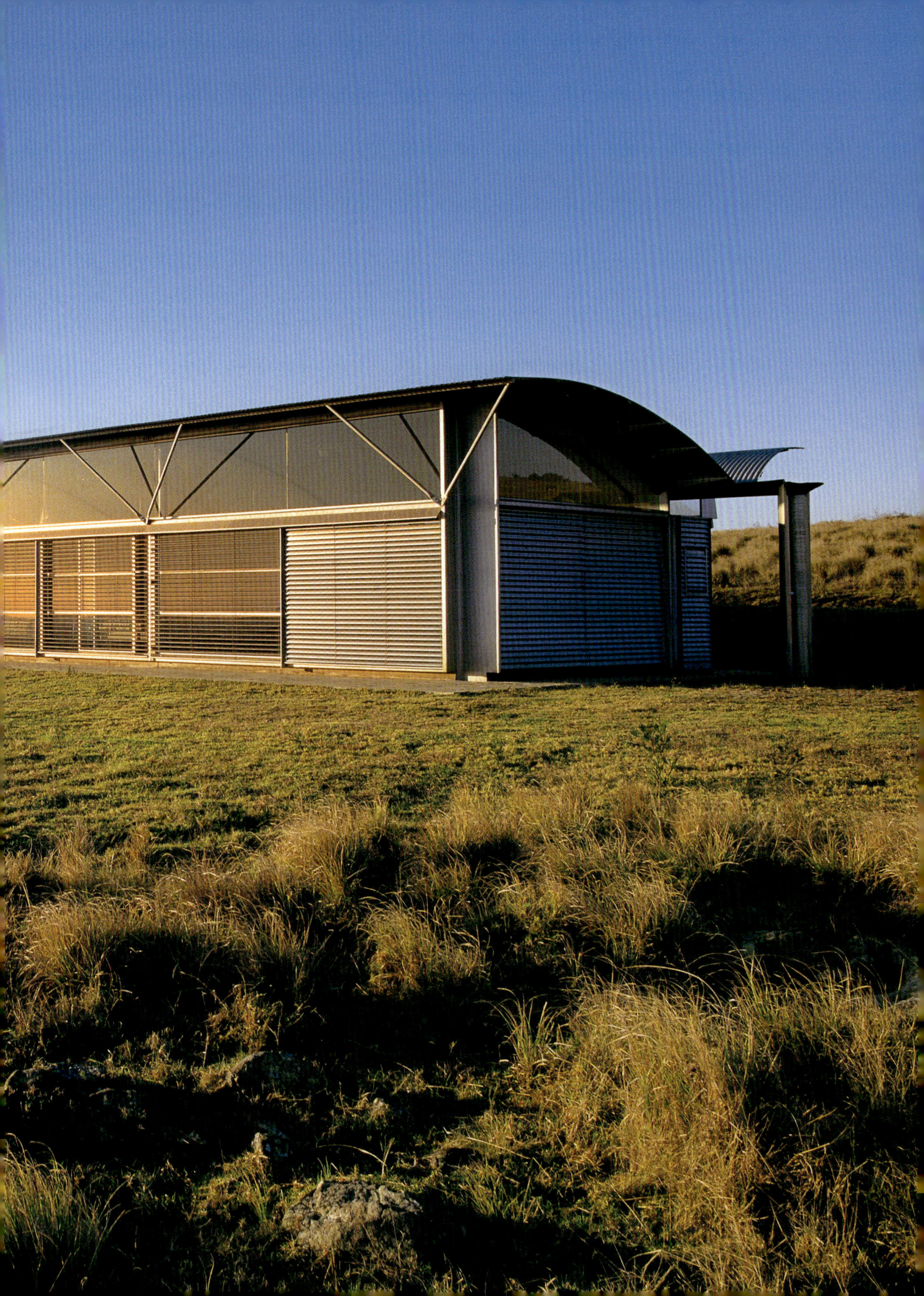

住宅の両端では径の大きな縦樋が通常よりも大きな屋根樋を受ける。東西の立面では、建物の雨水収集能力は象徴的に表現されている。

An unexpectedly large single downpipe is linked to either end of an oversized gutter. The building's capacity to collect water is given formal and symbolic representation in the east and west elevations.

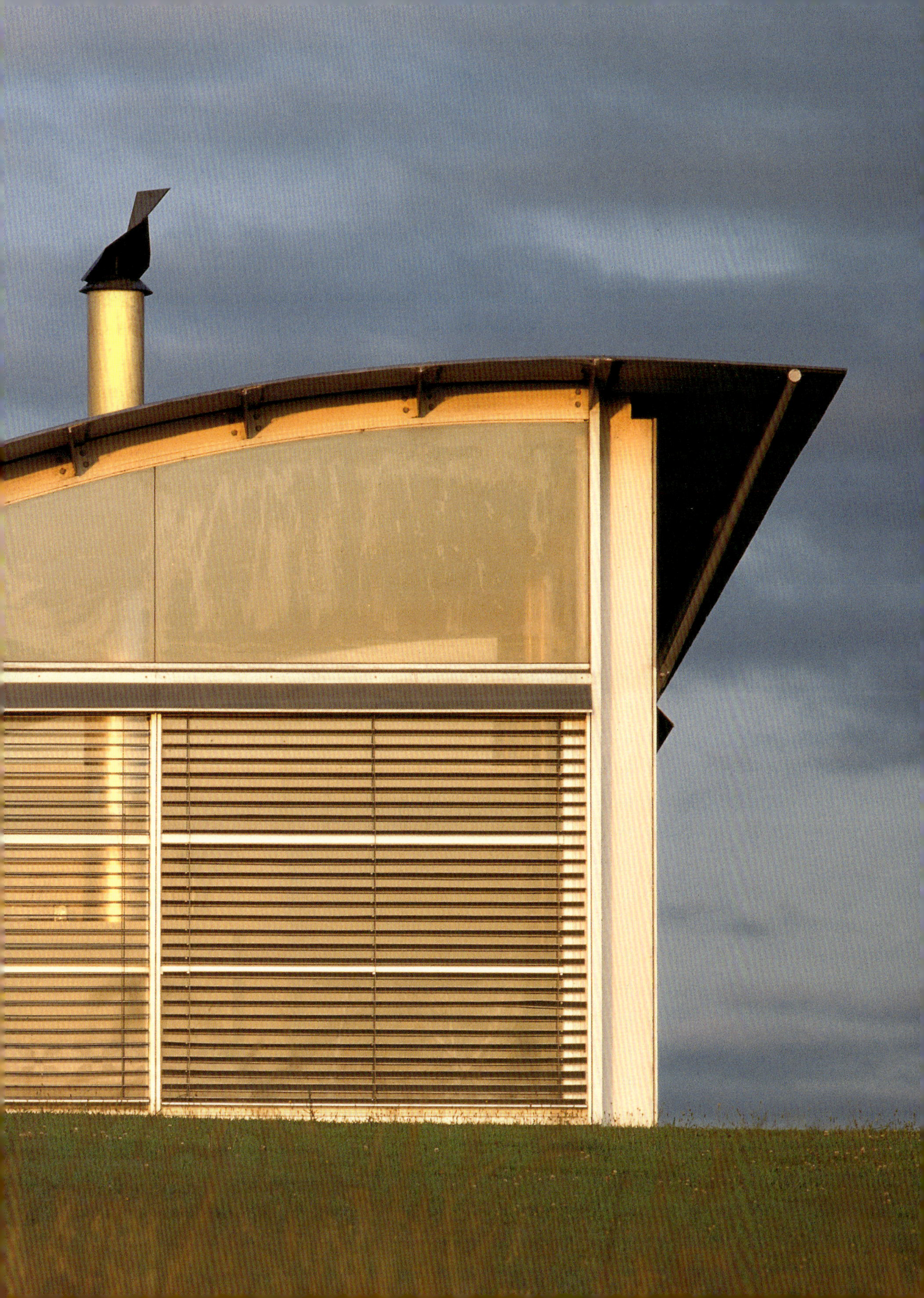

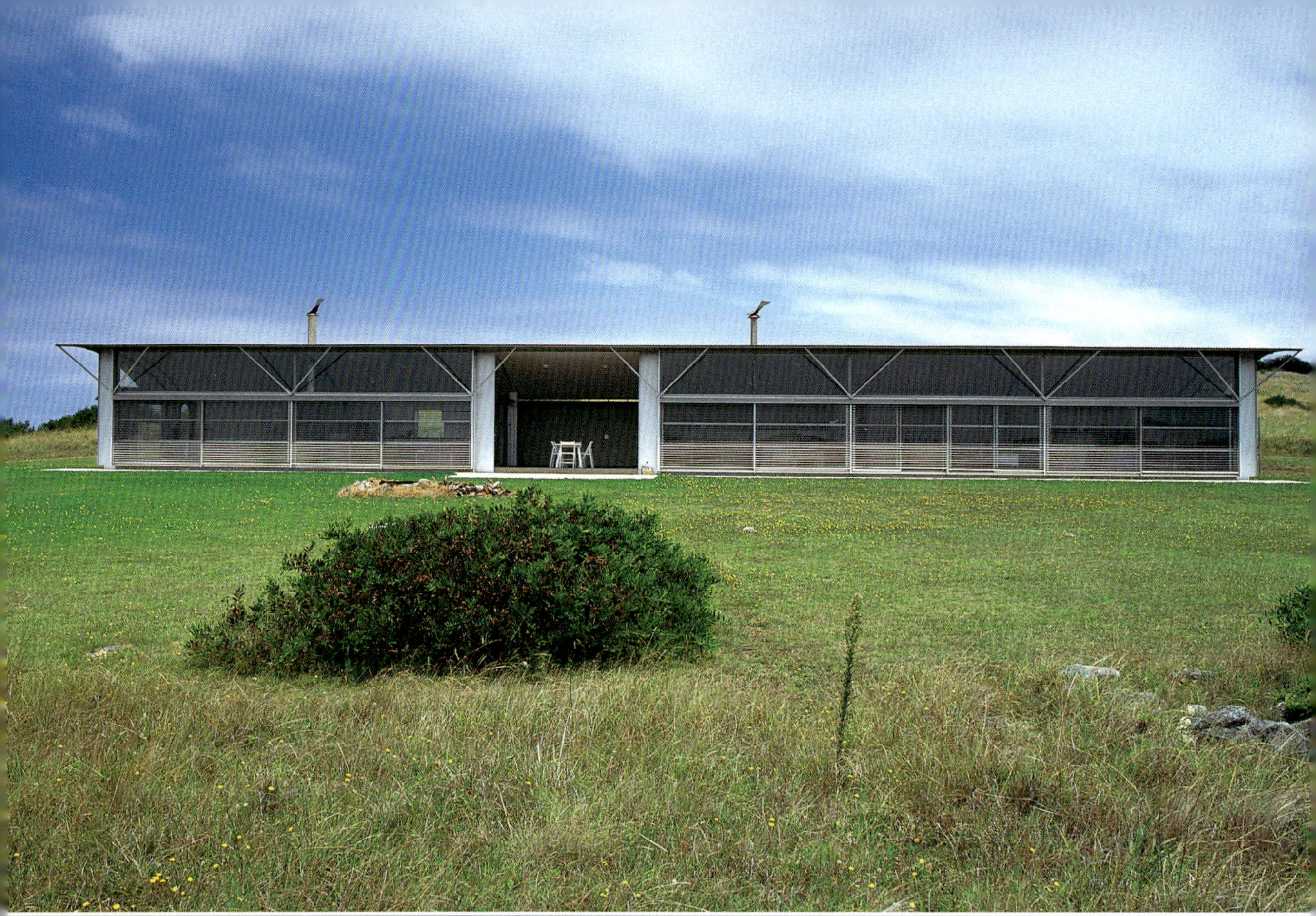

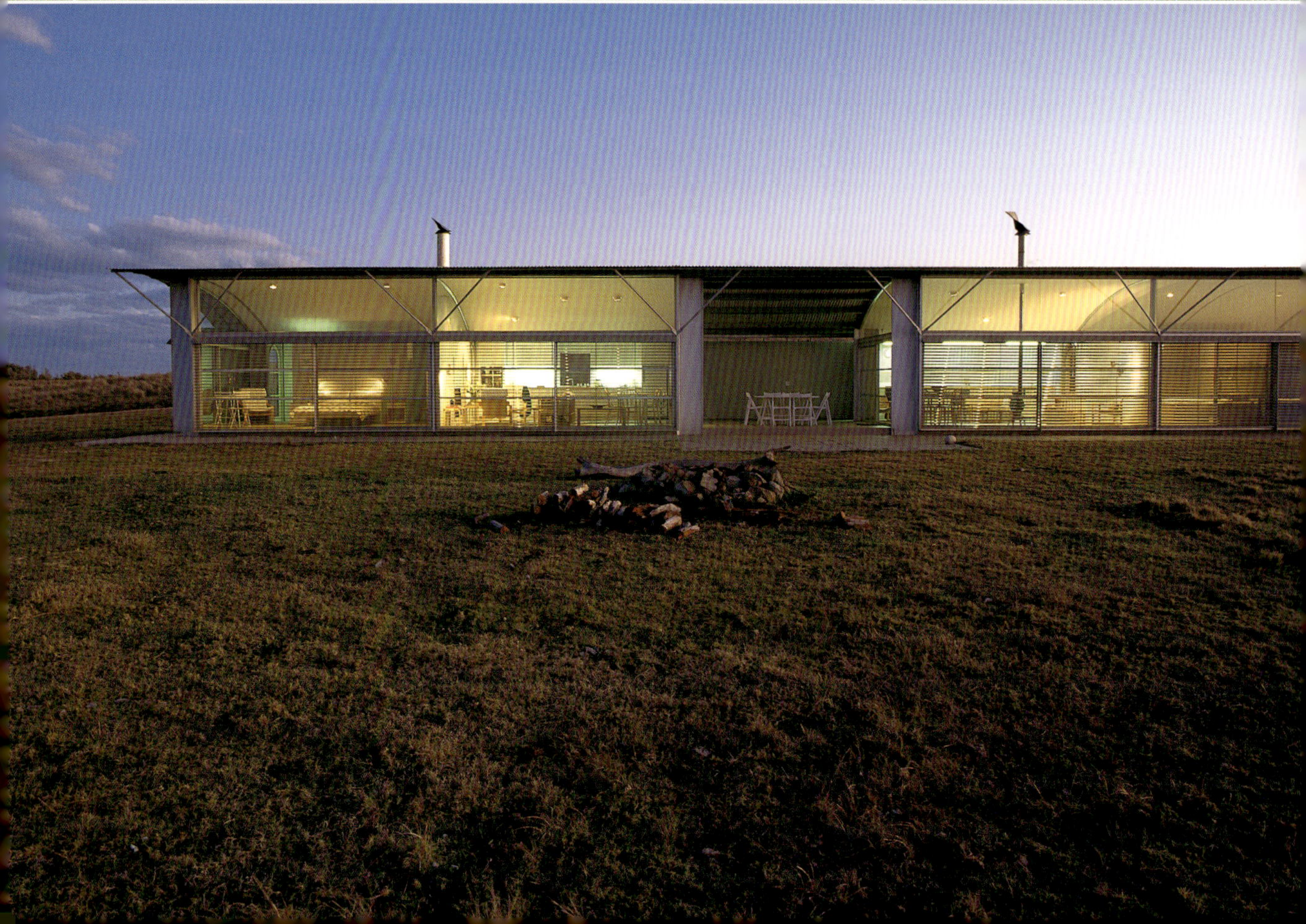

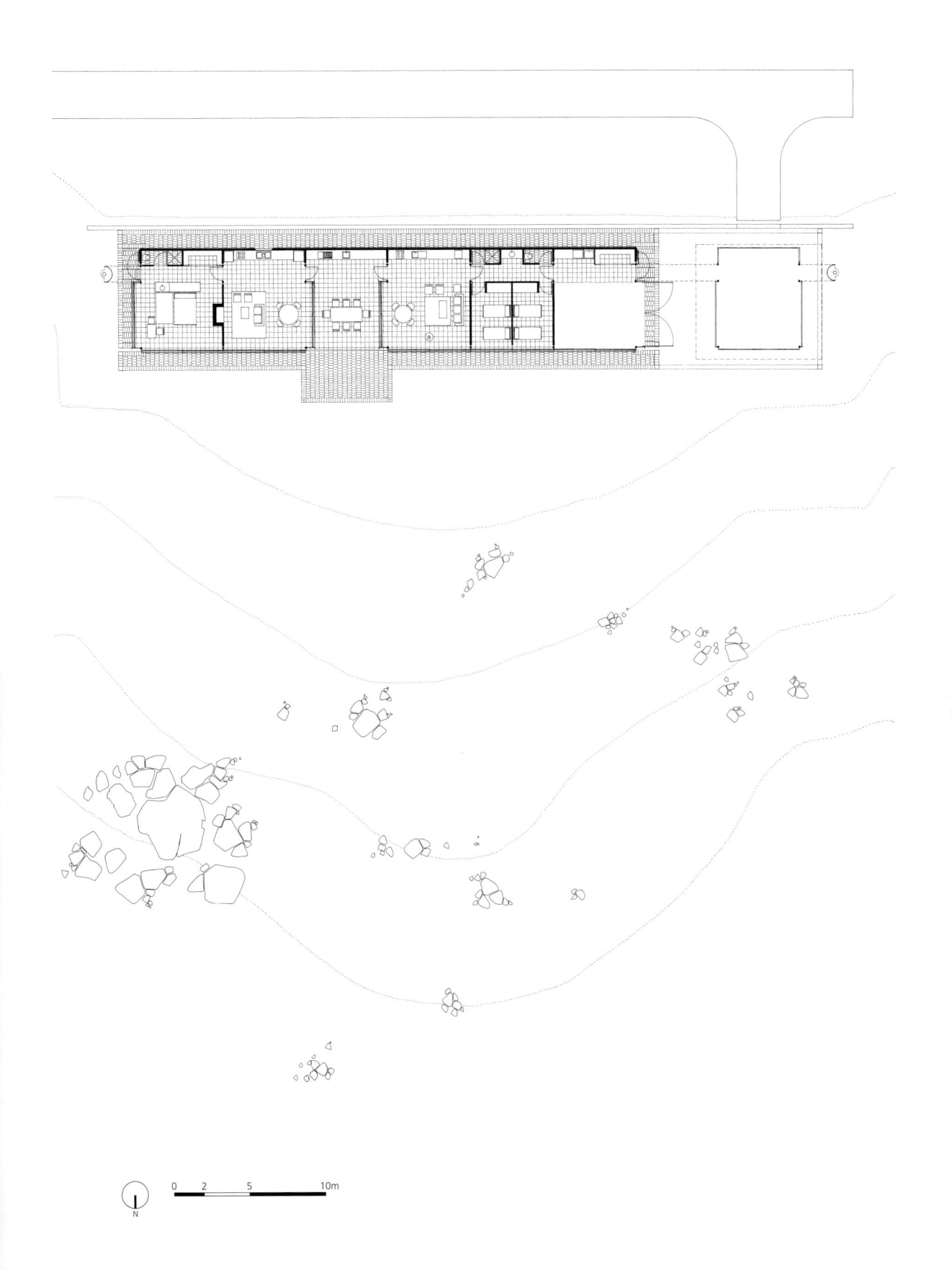

Glenn Murcutt 089

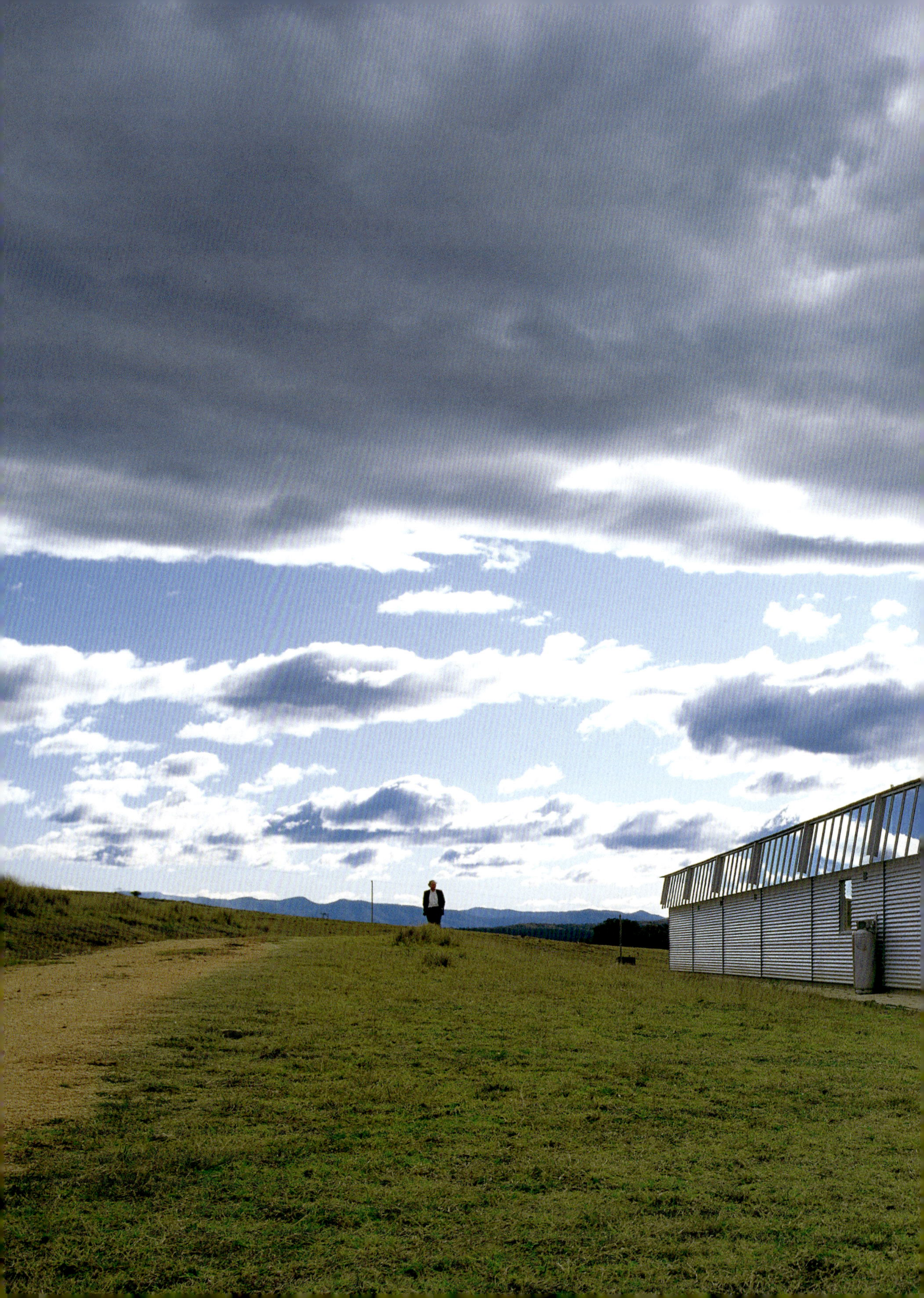

南面の一連の高い嵌め殺し窓は、ブラインドがなく、光と空への眺望を確保している。ガラス・パネルは、ドア高さに設定された水平の通気孔を内包している。

Continuous upper fixed glazing along the southern façade has no external louvers and admits light and sky views. These glass panels accommodate continuous adjustable horizontal vents set at door head height.

敷地は自然環境に露にされ、風にさらされた荒野である。
The site is exposed, windswept and rugged.

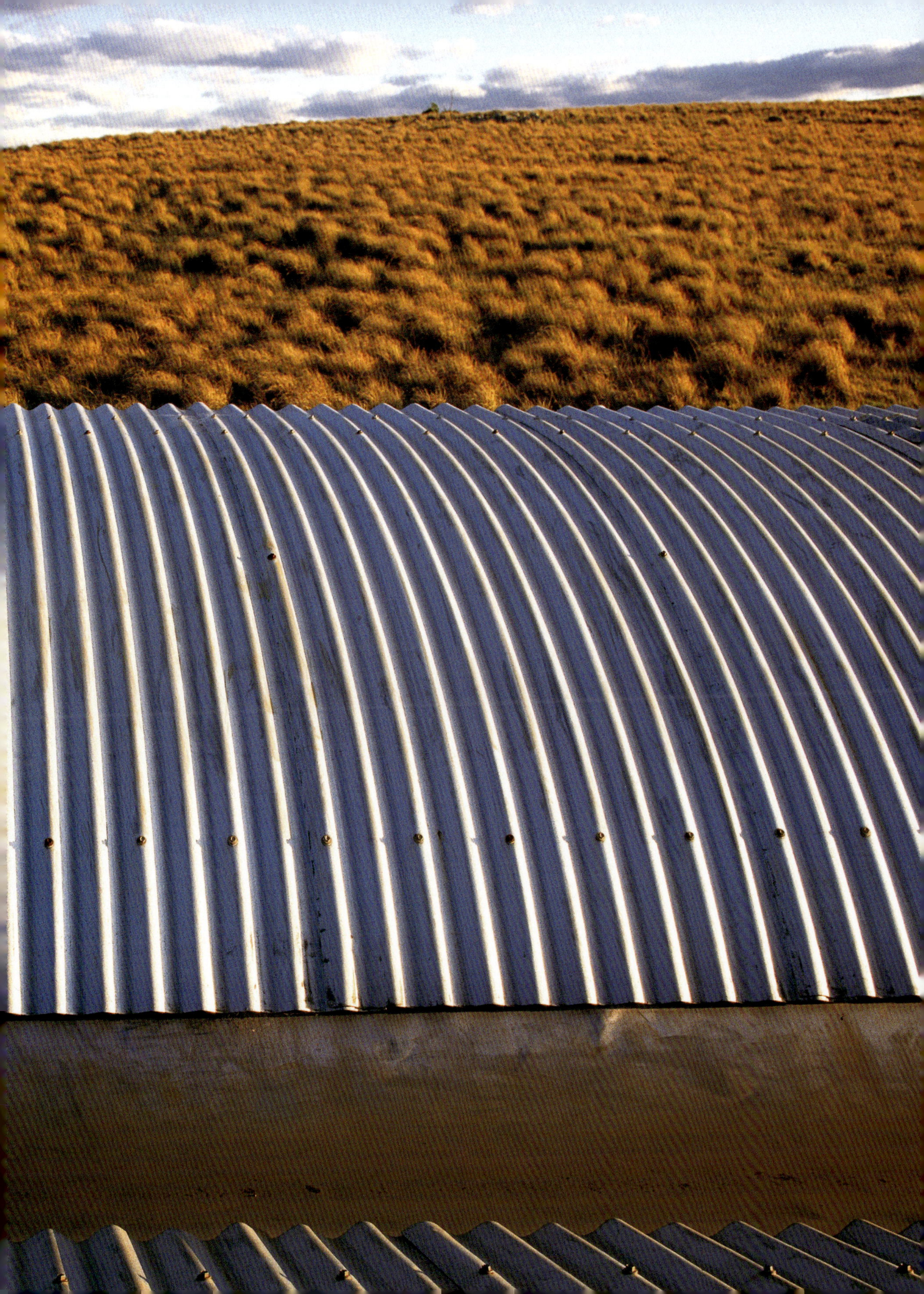

住宅は太平洋と西方の山々に挟まれて、北には湖が近い、
壮観なランドスケープの中にある。

The house is located in a spectacular landscape in between the ocean and the western mountains with a nearby lake to the north.

Glenn Murcutt

住宅の北はガラスの引戸で構成され、部屋ごとに調整できる可動ブラインドが外部に付けられている。

The north façade is treated as a series of glazed sliding screens with individually adjustable and retractable external louvers.

0 1 2   5m

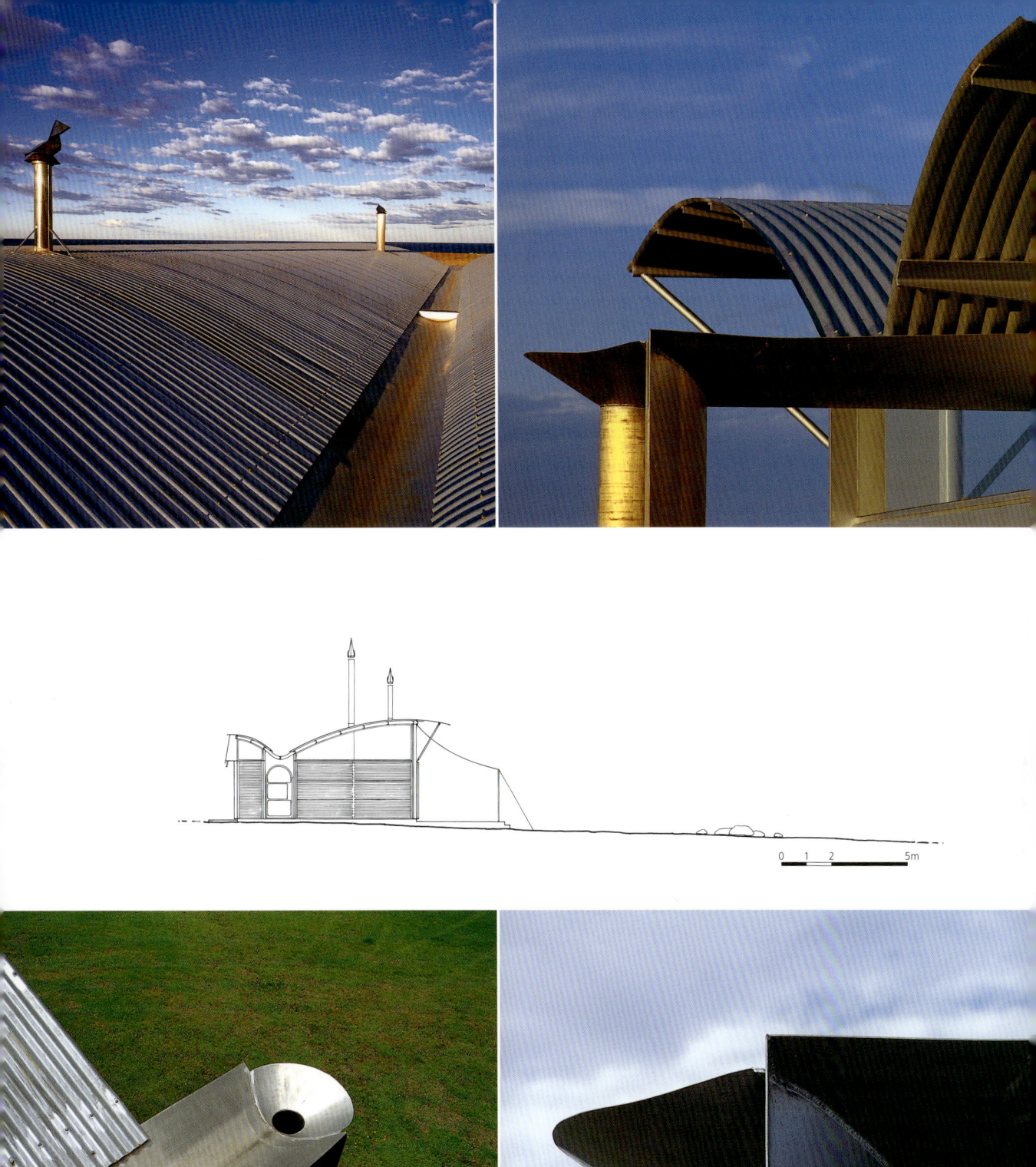

気候と形態に関する野心的な試みは、構造システムに明らかである。丸鋼のフレーム構造は経済的な少部材の骨組みであり、北面屋根のオーバーハングの部材の薄さに表れる。屋根材は支柱と一体に働いて、余分な構造材を省いている。

The climatic and formal ambitions of the building are evident in the resolution of the structural system. The design of the tubular steel frame achieves an extremely economical and light structural skeleton, visible in the fine edge of the northern roof overhang. The roofing skin acts structurally with the tensile struts and eliminates an additional supporting steel member.

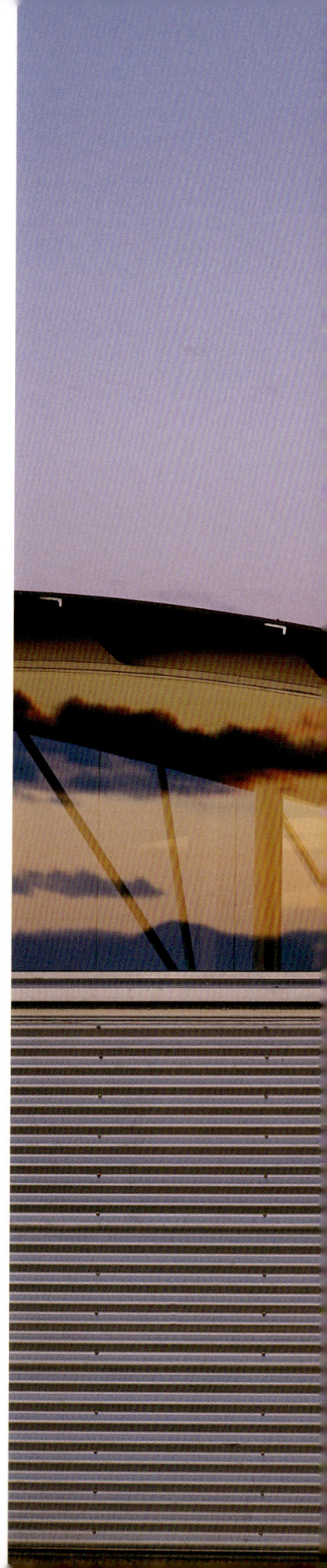

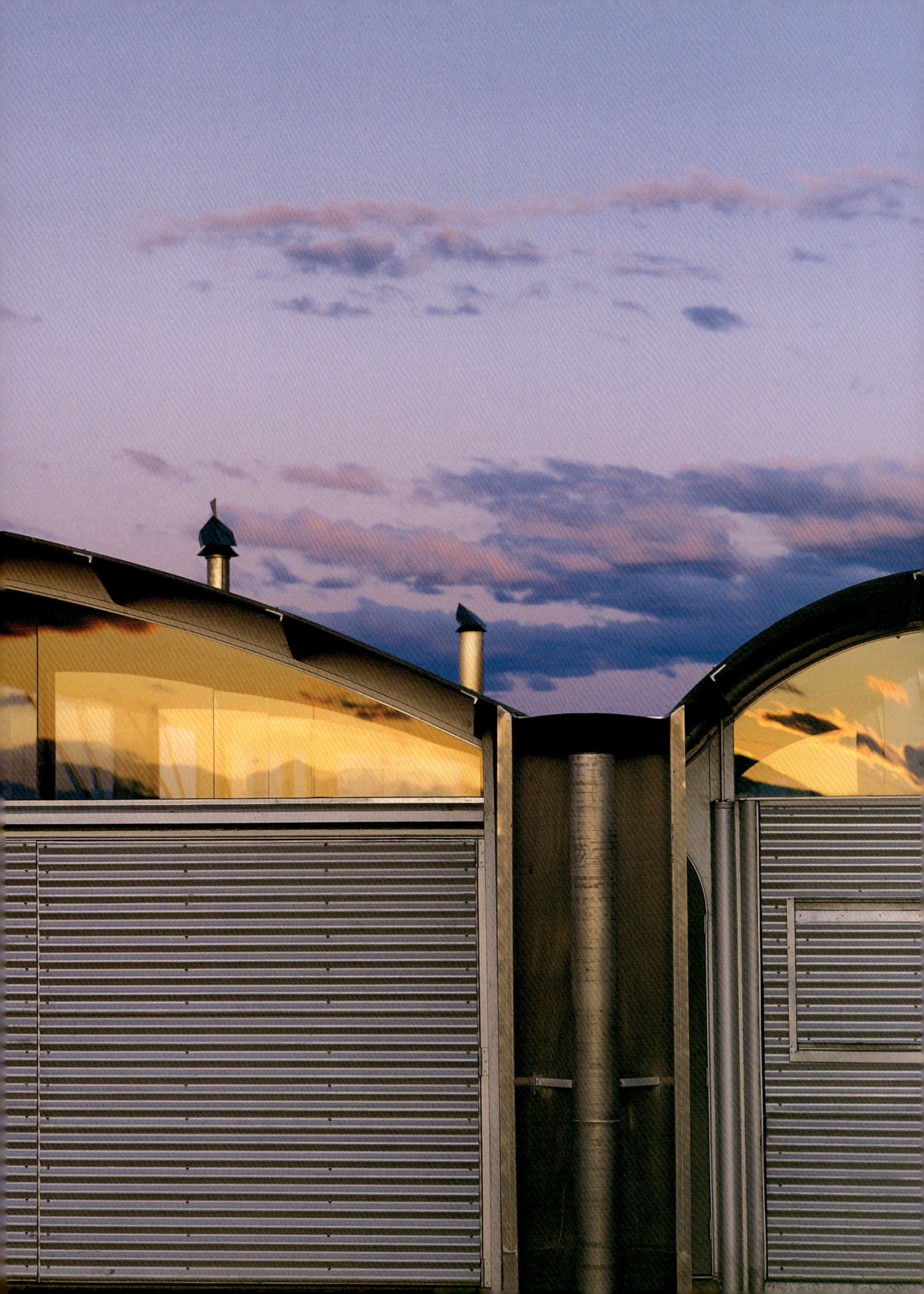

機能による秩序立てが、典型的な平面ユニットを構成している。
背面に水廻りのサービスをもつ大きな部屋は動線部により分割される。
動線は廊下を示唆し、機能分割は屋根断面に明確に見てとれる。

A functional hierarchy structures the organization of each bay. Typically, a large room with rear service facilities is divided by a circulation zone. The latter collectively forms an implied corridor and this division is clearly registered in the bipartite section.

0 1 2 3m

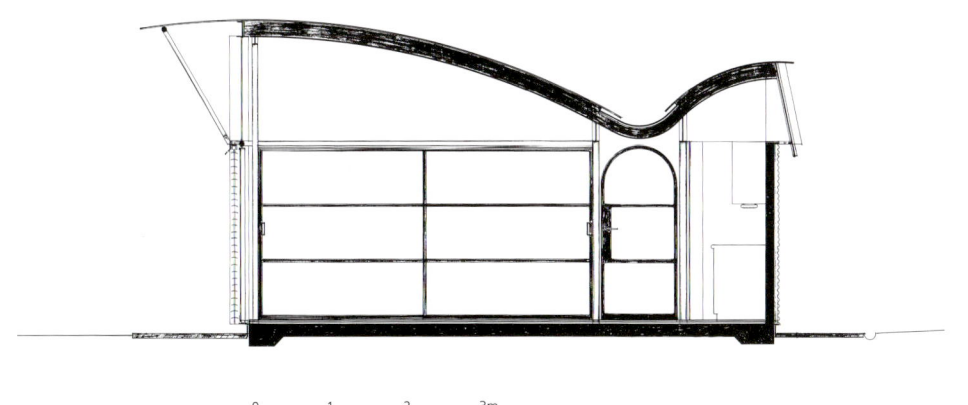

Glenn Murcutt | 101

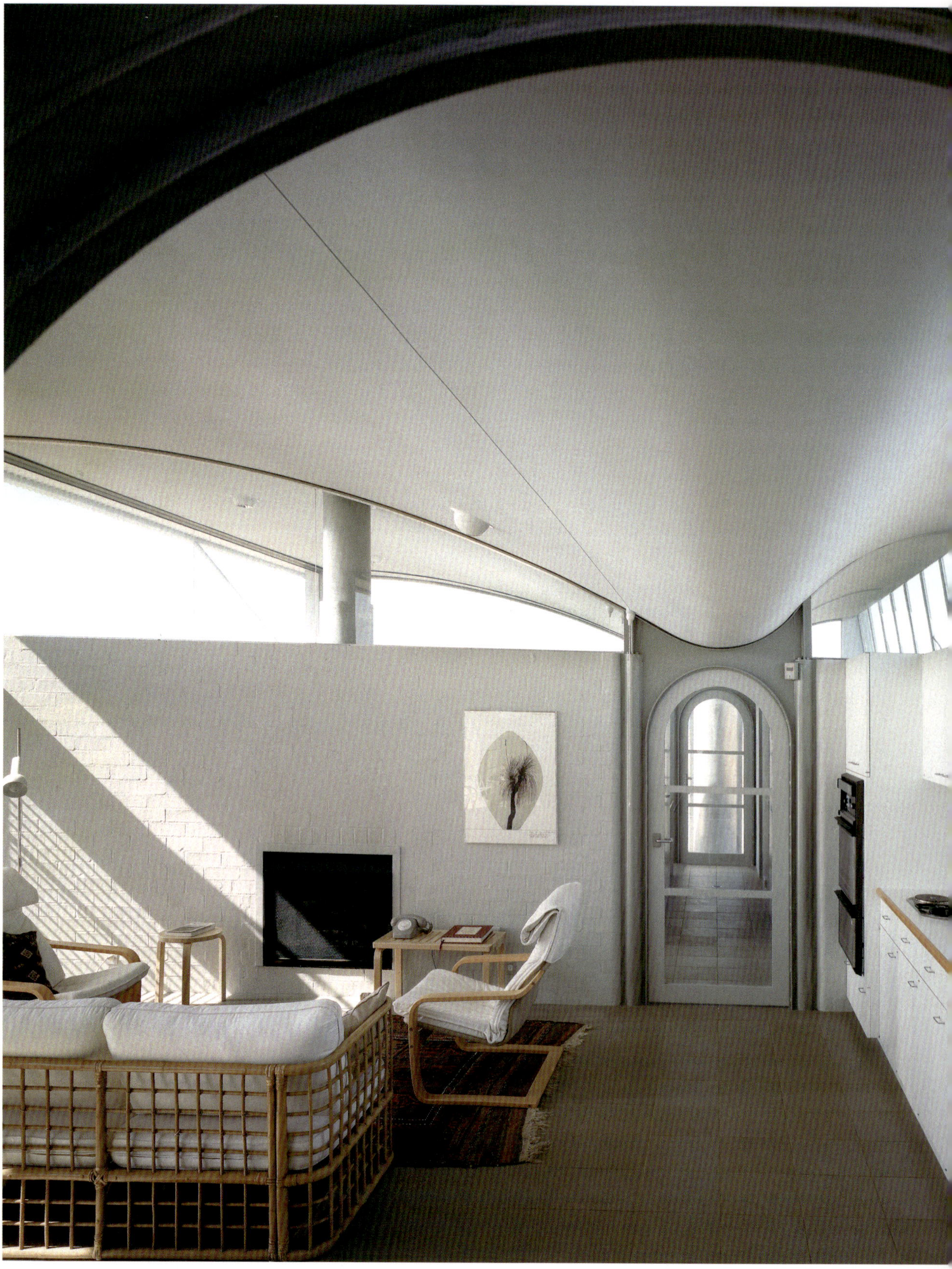

室内のレンガ壁はキッチンやバスルームの用途に適するとともに、コンクリートの床と一体に蓄熱層として機能する。

Inner brick walls accommodate kitchen and bathroom elements and together with the concrete floor provide the building's thermal mass.

傾斜屋根の深い庇は、夏は日陰をつくるが、冬の日射しは採り入れている。

The large angled roof overhang shades the building from the summer sun and allows winter sun access.

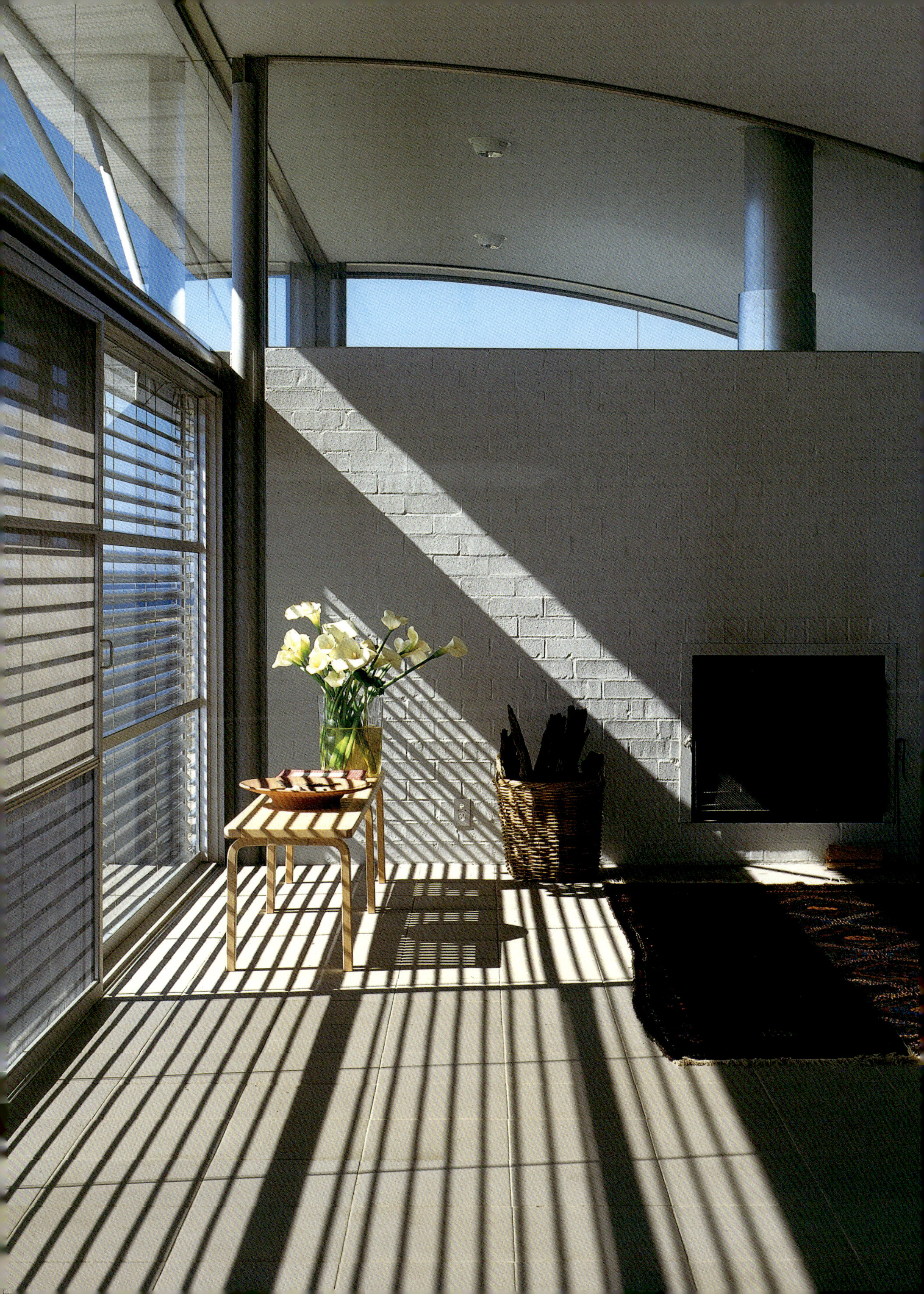

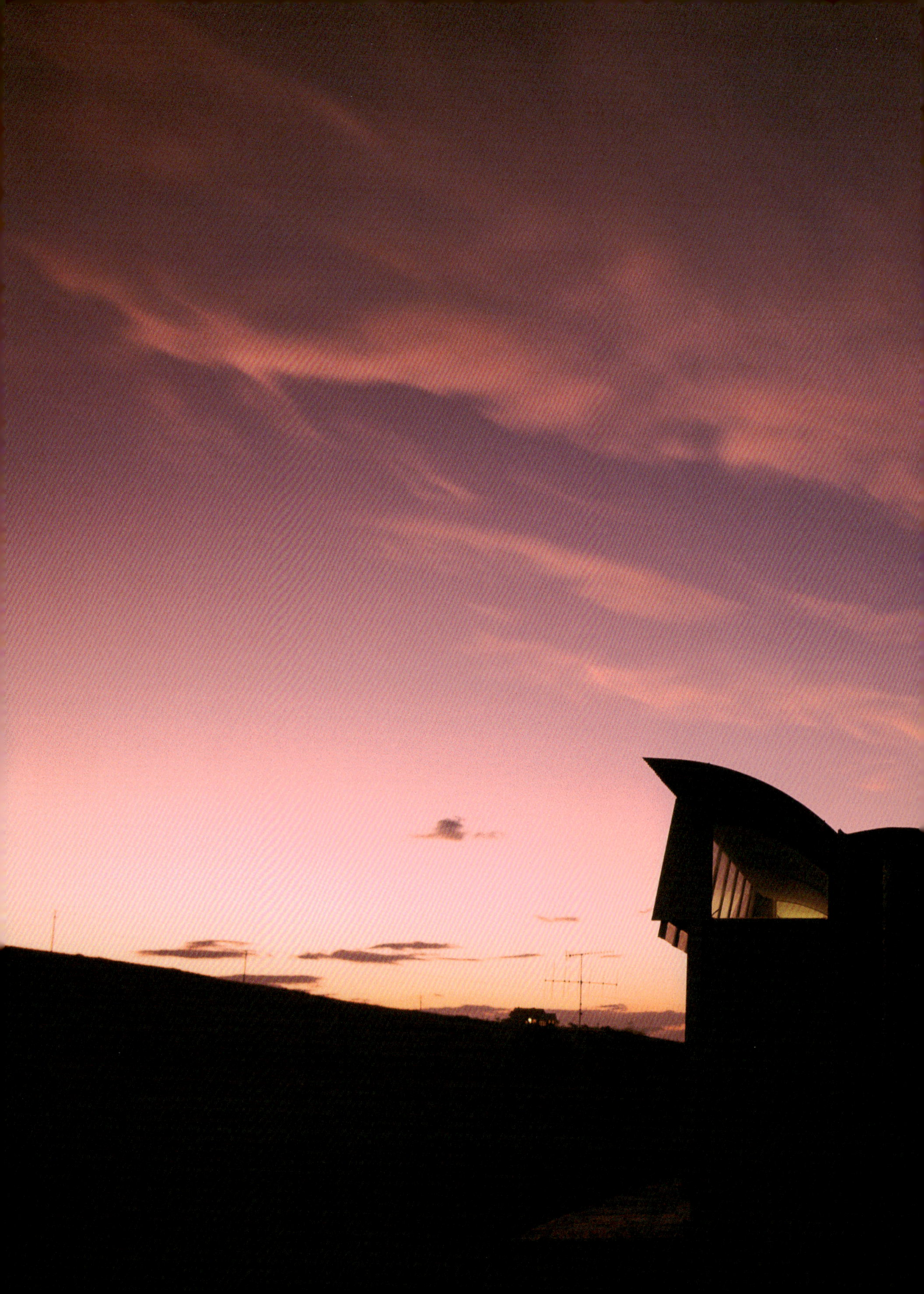

屋根は明らかに軽く浮き、テントのような空間という施主の要望を、明るく移動可能とさえ感じる住宅に昇華させたマーカットの答えを象徴している。

The apparently floating roof is symbolic of Murcutt's translation of the client's interest in tent-like enclosures into a house which feels unexpectedly light, almost transportable.

Magney House

マグニー邸

ニューサウスウェールズ州の南海岸にあるこの敷地は、太平洋と西方の山々に挟まれ、北には湖が近くにある壮観なランドスケープをもつ。自然環境に露にされ、風にさらされた荒野である。施主はこの土地を長年所有し、キャンプを張って休暇を過ごしてきたことから、テントのような利点をもつ住宅がよいのではないかと考えていた。

住宅は1棟のパビリオンで、中庭を挟んで、それぞれキッチンとバスルームをもった部屋に区分され、片方は両親のため、もう一方はゲストやファミリー用となっている。2つのリビングルームは共有する中庭に開かれて、スペースが関連していることを示している。母屋から離れて計画された車庫は実現しなかった。平面では、構造が繰り返されている。典型的な平面ユニットは、背面に水廻りのある大きな空間が、天井の低い動線部分により分割されている。廊下による機能の分割は屋根断面に示される。住宅の両端では大きな縦樋がオーバーサイズの谷樋を受ける。このように住宅の機能的な秩序と、建物の雨水収集能力は、東西の立面で象徴的に表現された。

印象的な屋根形状は、マーカットが正面と背面の違いをつけた住宅形を発展させたことを示しており、その空間配置は気候条件に拠っている。北の窓は部屋ごとに調整でき、完全に巻き上げられる外ブラインドが付けられたガラス引戸である。傾斜した屋根の深い庇は、夏は日陰をつくるが、冬の日光は採り入れる。まったく対照的に、南の冷たい卓越風に向かう低い住宅背後の壁は外断熱のレンガ造である。南面の高い一連の嵌め殺し窓は光と空への眺望をとっている。このガラス・パネルは、壁より離れるように傾斜して、ドア高さにある水平の通気孔を確保している。

気候と形態に関する野心的な試みは、構造システムと建物の素材に明らかである。丸鋼のフレーム構造は、過去のプロジェクトから洗練されて、至極少ない部材で構成している。部材の最少化は北面屋根のオーバーハングの部材の薄さに見てとれるが、金属屋根は引張材の支柱とともに働いて、余分な構造材を省いている。この信じがたく薄い屋根は、移動可能と感じるほど軽く見える住宅を象徴している。

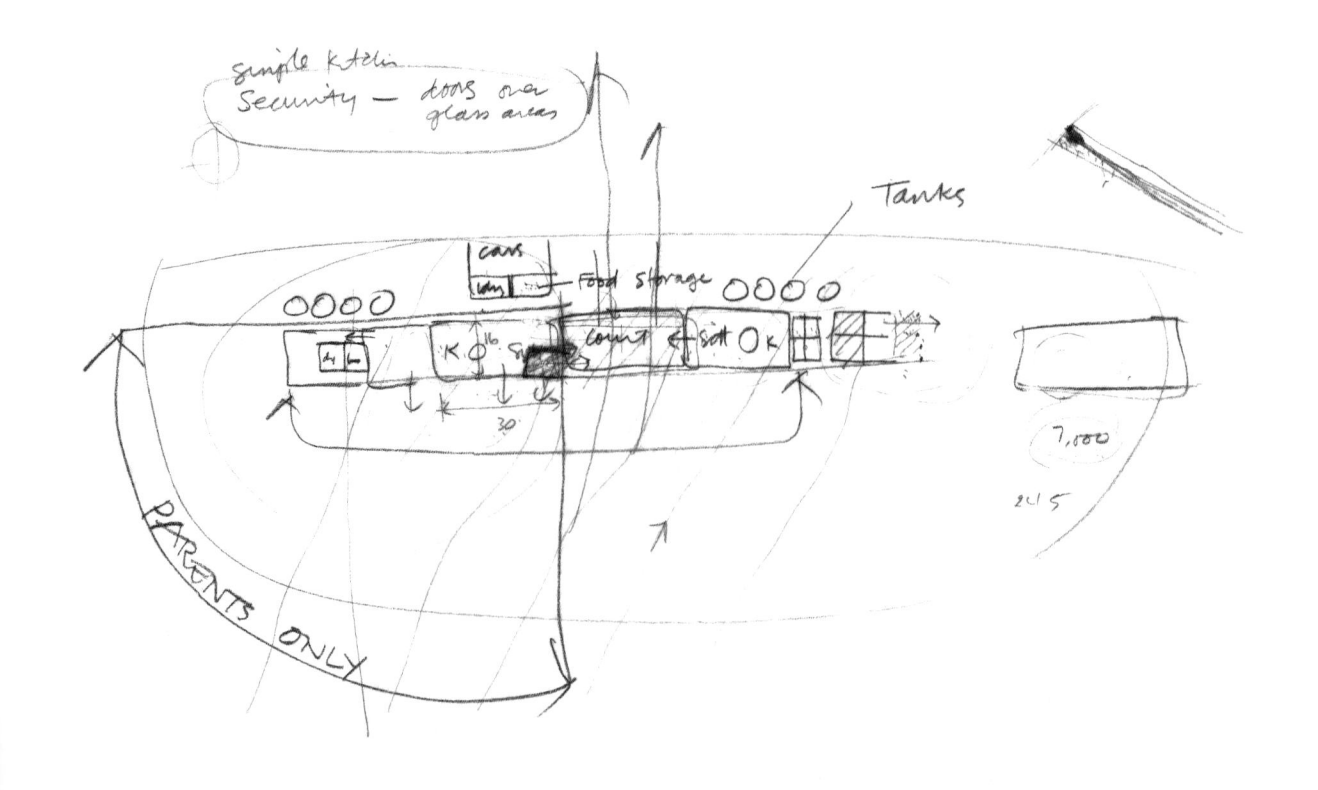

Situated on the southern coast of NSW, the site is a spectacular landscape between the ocean and western mountains with a nearby lake to the north. It is exposed, windswept and rugged. The clients had owned the land for many years using it for camping holidays and were interested in a house with tent like qualities.

The building is a single pavilion divided by a central court and can operate as two self contained suites, one for the parents, the other for guests or family. Living areas open onto the shared court and a connection is implied between these adjacent spaces. The separate proposed garage bay in the plan illustrated was never realised.

A repetitive bay structure is employed. Typically, large rooms with rear service facilities are divided by a lower circulation zone rendering a functional distinction in the bipartite section. The implied internal corridor supports an oversized gutter which connects at either end to two large single downpipes. In this way both the functional hierarchy of the house and the collection of rainwater are given symbolic representation in the east and west elevations.

The striking roof form also registers the architect's development of a pavilion type with a distinct front and back and this dominant spatial orientation is primarily developed in relation to climatic considerations. The open northern face is treated as a glazed sliding screen with individually adjustable and retractable external louvers. The large angled roof overhang shades the building from summer sun and allows winter sun access. In sharp contrast, the lower rear wall facing the predominant southerly winds is largely closed and is constructed of reverse brick veneer. Continuous upper fixed glazing along the southern façade admits light and sky views. These glass panels slope away from the wall to accommodate continuous adjustable horizontal vents at door head height.

The climatic and formal ambitions of the building are evident in the development and material resolution of the structural system. The design of the tubular steel frame refines experiments from previous buildings and achieves an extremely light skeleton. This material reduction is visible in the fine edge of the northern roof overhang where the metal skin acts with the tensile steel struts and eliminates additional supporting members. The improbably thin roof is symbolic of a house which feels unexpectedly light, almost transportable.

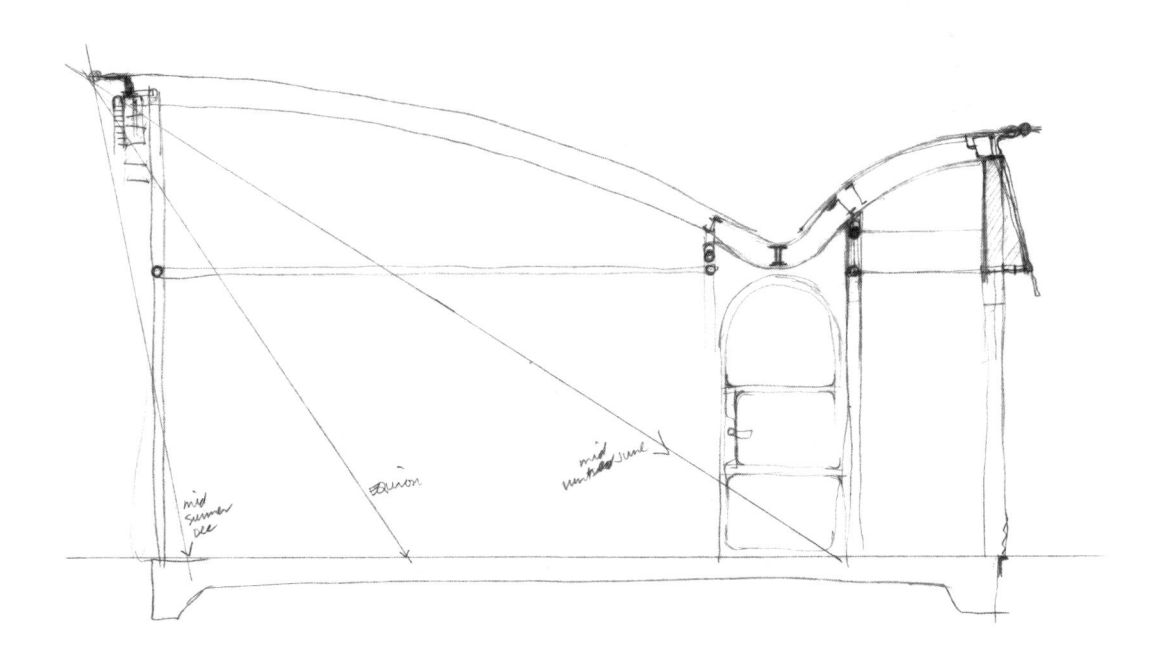

Magney House

マグニー邸

1986–90 ·········· Paddington, Sydney, New South Wales

北立面では、両袖壁に固められた大きなガラス窓が、内部のボイド空間を予感させる。袖壁は両隣からの視線を遮り、庭のランドスケープの中で屋外ダイニングを形作る。

The north façade is dominated by two blank walls framing a glazed implied void. They provide privacy from adjacent neighbours and define an outdoor dining area within a constructed landscape.

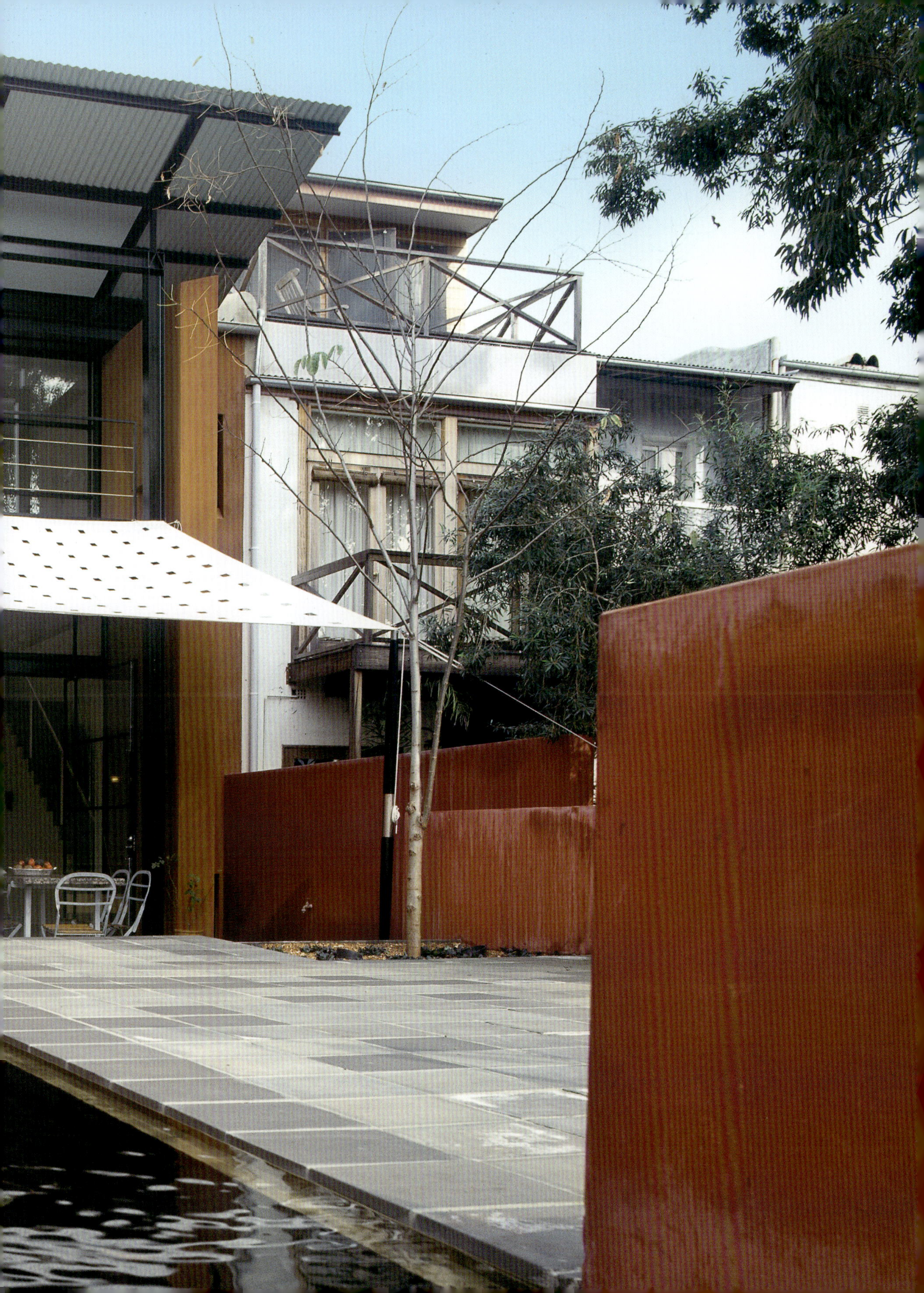

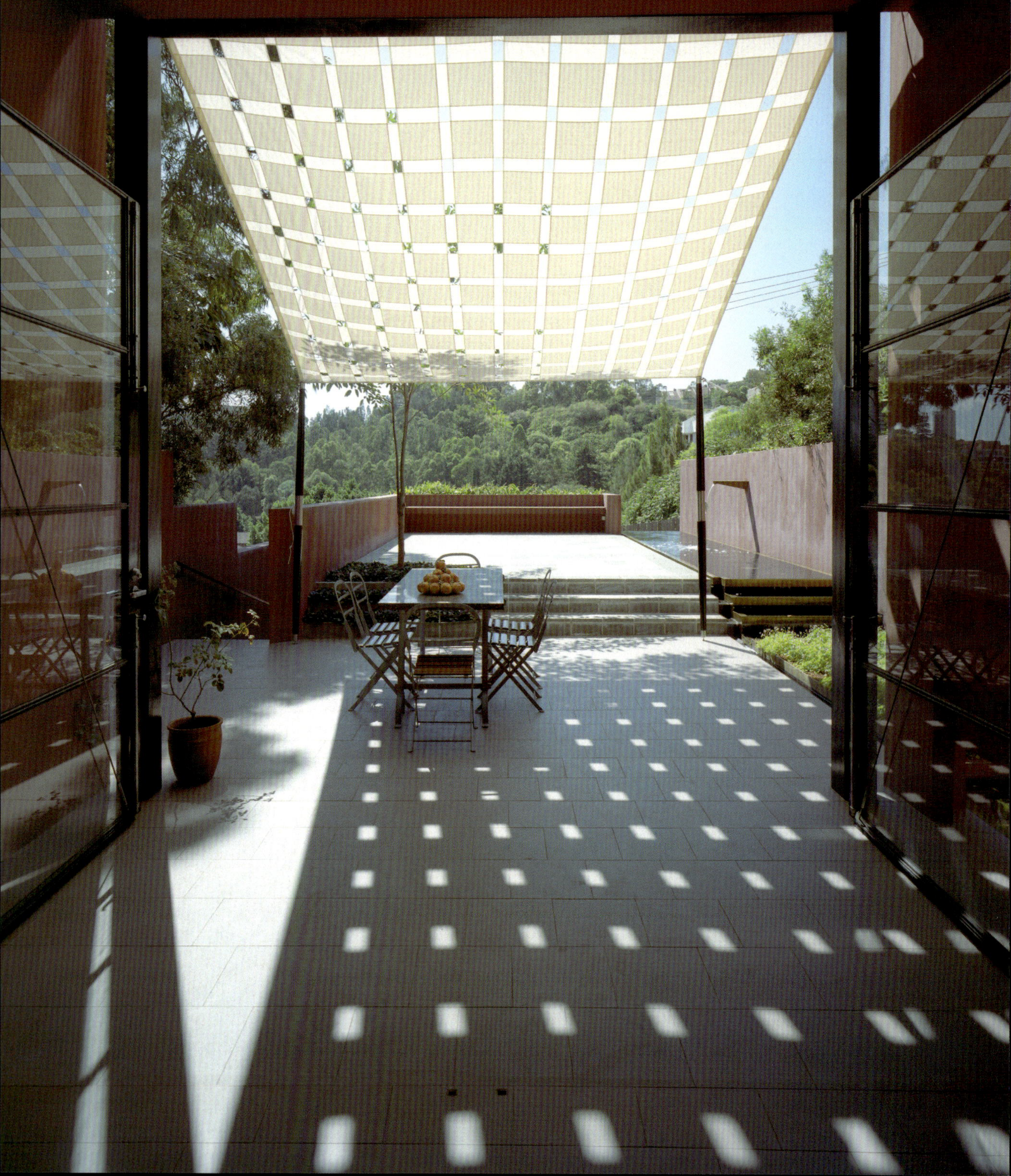

屋外ダイニングエリアの上部には日除けの布がかけられた。宙に浮かんだ庇のごとく、繊細な織布はそよ風をとらえ、斑模様の陰をつくりだしている。

A piece of shade cloth is held over an outdoor dining area. The delicately woven fabric registers the movement of the breezes and offers dappled shade in the manner of a floating canopy.

リビング、ダイニングは大きな1部屋として下階に計画された。北の庭に向かってスチール枠の大きなガラス回転扉を開くと、内部と外部が一体となる。

The living spaces are all accommodated at the ground floor in a large single room which opens to the north facing garden via full height glazing.
Very large steel framed doors pivot open to allow for the desired spatial connection.

Glenn Murcutt

既存の組石造の外殻の中に、
精美な鉄骨が設置された。
上階の新しい寝室と小さなバス
ルームを支え、北の庭へ大きな
開口をつくっている。

The fine steel frame sits within a large void formed by the original masonry shell. It supports a new upper bedroom with small bathroom and frames very large north facing openings.

Glenn Murcutt | 117

新しい部屋は、縦横の光と空気の中に浮かぶヴォリューム
として玄関から見える。西の界壁に沿った階段は
縦長の吹き抜けをつくり、トップライトから入る光は家の間口
いっぱいに広がる。

A new room is visible from the entrance as an apparently floating volume, vertically and horizontally surrounded by light and air. A stair to the lower level along the western wall forms one vertical void and a skylight across the width of the house forms another.

鉄のプレートによる階段と柱のミニマルな構造。

Planar steel elements form an extremely minimal structure at the stair and columns.

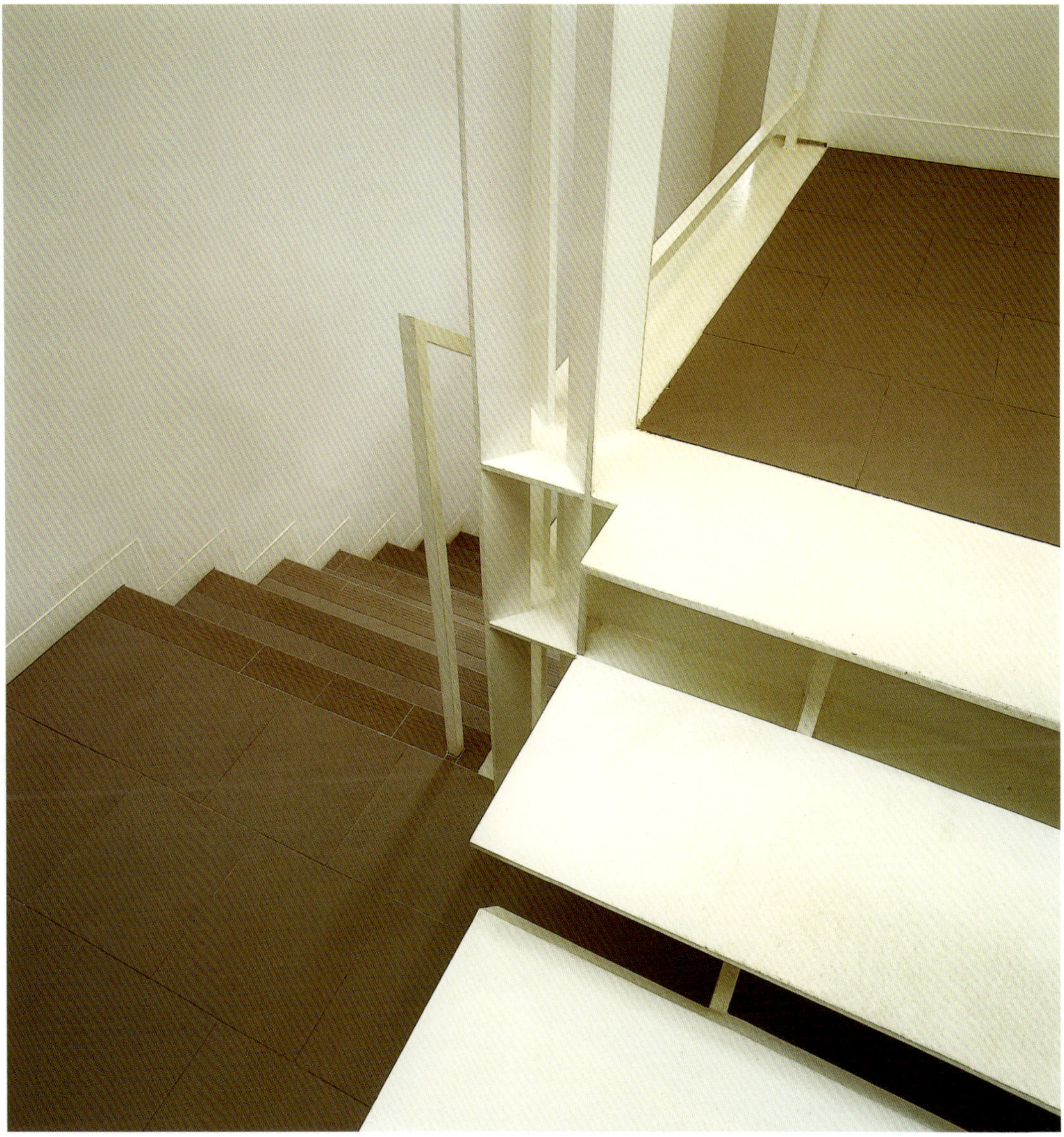

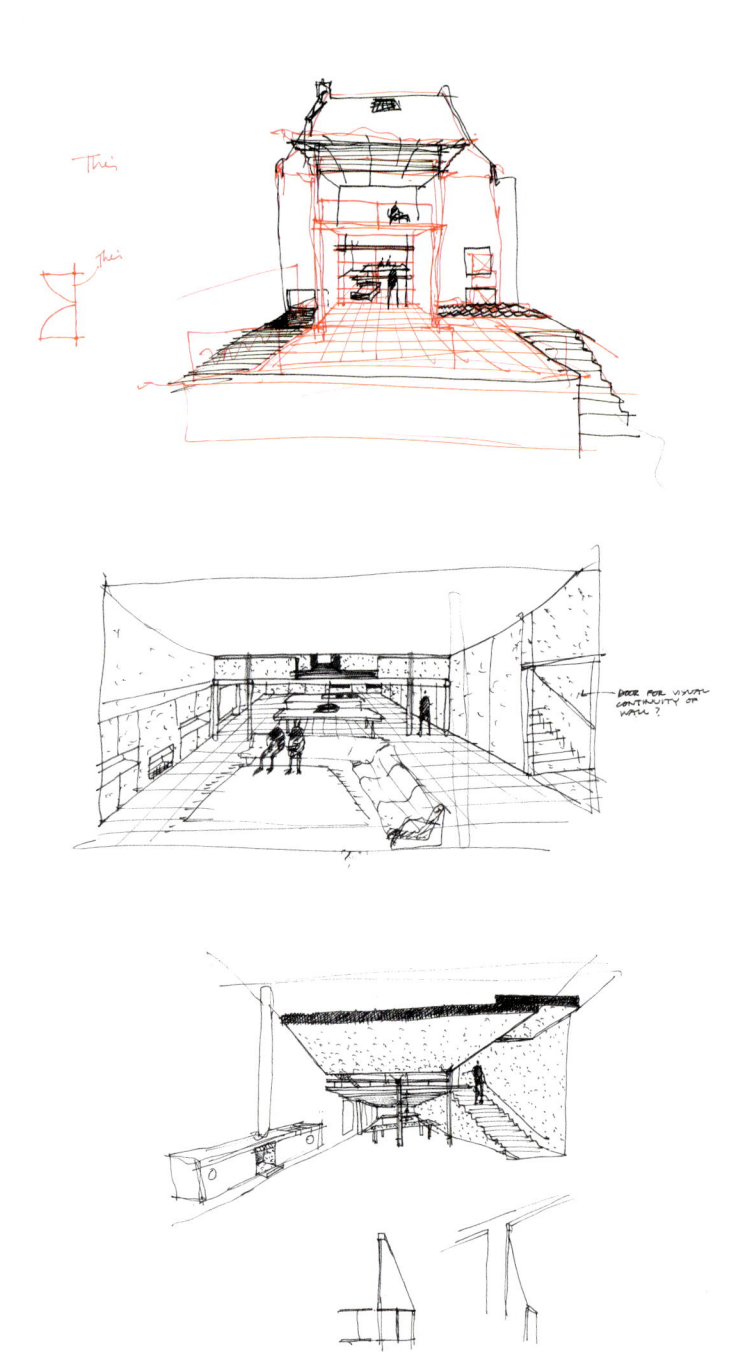

シドニー市内の住宅地、パディントンの特徴的な住居形態の1つであるテラスハウスに大々的な改築を行ったのが、この住宅である。庭側の立面の両脇の石壁は、近隣の住宅の寸法を示している。

The project is a substantial reworking of a 'terrace' house, an urban dwelling type characteristic of the inner Sydney residential suburb of Paddington. Two vertical masonry walls in the rear façade proportionally describe the typical dimensions of neighbouring houses.

Glenn Murcutt

Magney House

マグニー邸

この住宅では、シドニー市内パディントンの特徴的な住居形態の1つであるテラスハウスへ大々的な改築が行われた。19世紀の都市構造がよく保存されていることから、地区内の建築計画には厳しい規制が適用される。マーカットは敷地選定にも関わり、北へ向かっての急な傾斜、ゆとりのある間口、そして大きな木やランドスケープへの眺望と近さを理由に敷地が選ばれた。既存家屋は中央廊下と両側の部屋と階段という平面だったが、入口脇の部屋とバスルーム以外はすべて取り除かれた。2通りの案が提出され、屋根裏を新しい上階とする初期案は、後により経済的な計画に変えられた。2案とも既存の街路立面と界壁は保存されている。

テラスハウスといえば、部屋が繰り返され、暗い室内が定番の住居形態だが、この家は光が満ち溢れて空間が広がり、庭や周囲の木々を近くに感じる。既存の組石造の外殻の中に、精美な鉄のフレームが設置された。これは上階の新しい寝室と小さなバスルームを支えて、北の庭への開口を形づくっている。寝室は、周囲から切り離された光と空気の中に浮かんだヴォリュームとして、エントランスホールからすでに認めることができる。西側界壁に沿った下階への階段は縦に長い吹き抜けをつくり、トップライトから入る光は家の間口いっぱいに広がっている。通常は最も暗くなる場所が予期せず明るい効果がよく活きている。

リビング、ダイニングは、高いガラス扉を開くと庭に出られる、大きな1部屋として下階に計画された。スチール枠の大きな軸回転扉が空間の連結を果たす装置となっている。リビングの床は外の庭へと広がりをもち、そこから数段昇ったステップフロアが周辺の樹木の上に浮いている。北立面は、両脇にある縦長の、窓のない石壁で開口を枠組みしている。壁はプライバシーを確保し、両隣の住宅の背面と調子をあわせる。屋外ダイニングエリアの上部には日除けの布がかけられた。繊細な織布はそよ風をとらえ、遠くの木陰のように斑模様の日陰をつくりだしている。

This building is a substantial reconfiguration of a row 'terrace' house, an urban dwelling characteristic of the inner Sydney suburb of Paddington. With a substantially conserved 19th century urban fabric, all development in this area is tightly controlled. Murcutt was consulted in the building site selection and the block was chosen for its steep fall from the street to the north, a generous width and adjacency and outlook toward established trees and landscape. The original building had rooms located either side of a central corridor and stair most of which was demolished excepting one bedroom and bathroom at street level. Two designs were prepared; the first with an additional upper level which was later revised in favour of a more economical solution. Both schemes retained the original street façade and flanking masonry party walls.

In a building type normally experienced as a sequence of interiors and darker rooms, the house is striking for its sense of light and spaciousness and inclusion of the external landscape. A fine steel frame sits within a large void formed by the original masonry shell. It supports a new upper bedroom with small bathroom and frames openings to the north facing garden. This new room is visible from the entrance as an apparently floating volume, vertically and horizontally surrounded by light and air. A stair to the lower level along the western wall forms one void and a skylight across the width of the house forms another. An unexpected lightness is found in what would typically be the darkest part of the house.

The living spaces are accommodated at the ground floor and extend to the garden. Very large steel framed glazed doors pivot to allow for the desired spatial connection. The exterior landscape is defined as a series of horizontal planes, stepped up to a platform which appears to float over the adjacent trees. The north façade is rendered as two vertical blank masonry walls framing a metaphorical void. The walls provide privacy from adjacent neighbours and proportionally describe the typical dimensions of neighbourhood houses. A piece of shade cloth is held over an outdoor dining area. The delicately woven fabric registers the movement of the breezes and offers dappled shade in the manner of a floating canopy, an abstract register of the landscape beyond.

Section

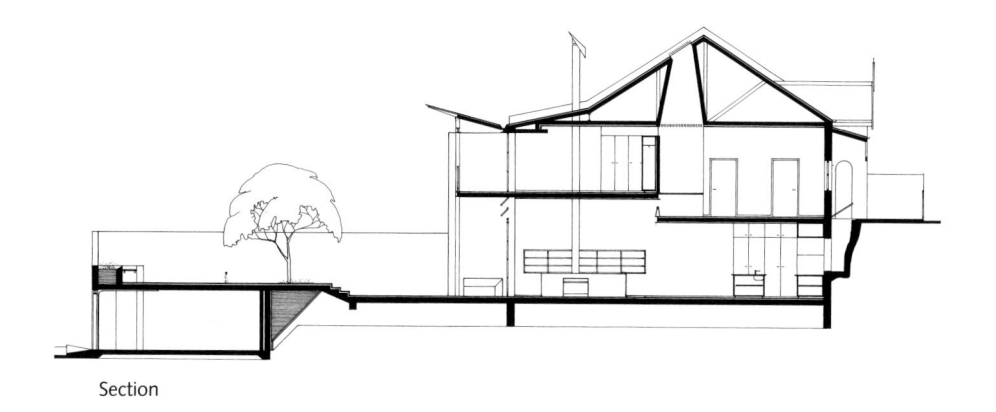

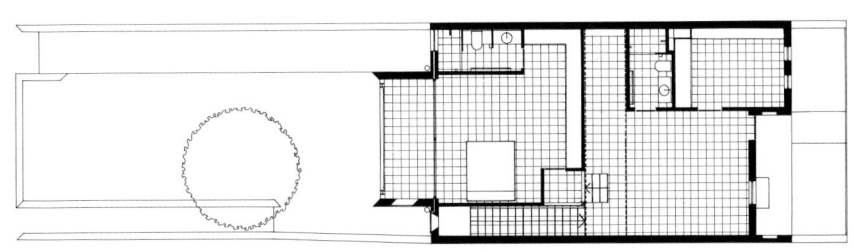

Second floor

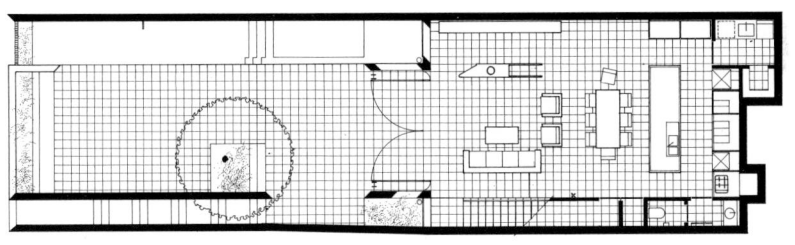

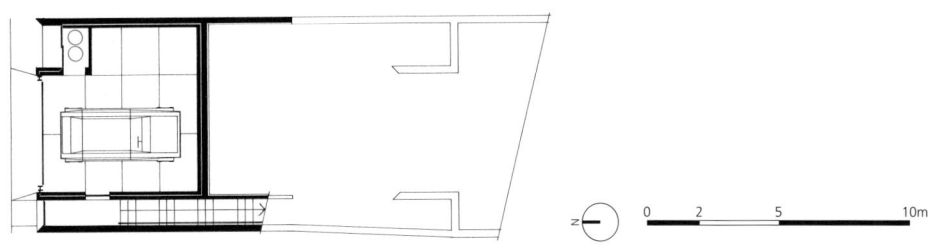

First floor

Basement

0 2 5 10m

Glenn Murcutt | 125

Simpson-Lee House

シンプソン=リー邸

1988–93 ……… Mount Wilson, New South Wales

池は山火事に備えて要求される防火水槽の詩的な回答である。その大きさは、母屋の居間の大きさを予感させる。
The pool is a lyrical treatment of the storage of water required for fire prevention. It proportionally anticipates the living area of the major pavilion.

鉄骨の梁と柱は至極軽く、金属屋根の庇を支える2本の斜材は、ビンジーポイントの住宅からさらに繊細になった。

The steel skeleton is extremely light and the angled double strut support to the metal roof edge further refines the awning detail of the Bingie Point House.

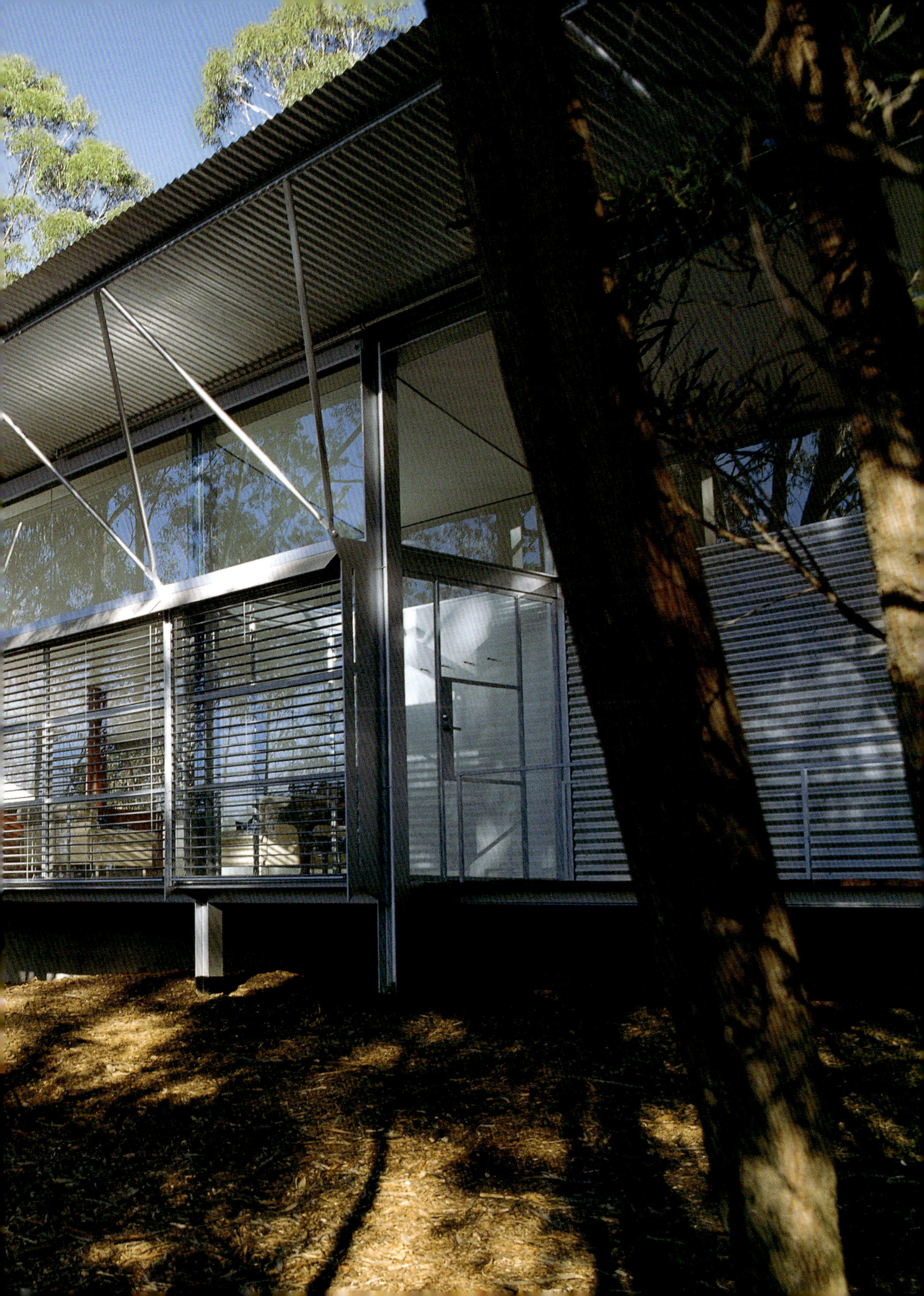

リビングの開口を挟む、両端の風除室。アプローチデッキは、このガラスの玄関に続く。

The timber bridge enters the house via a glass vestibule, one of two which bracket the glazed opening of the living areas.

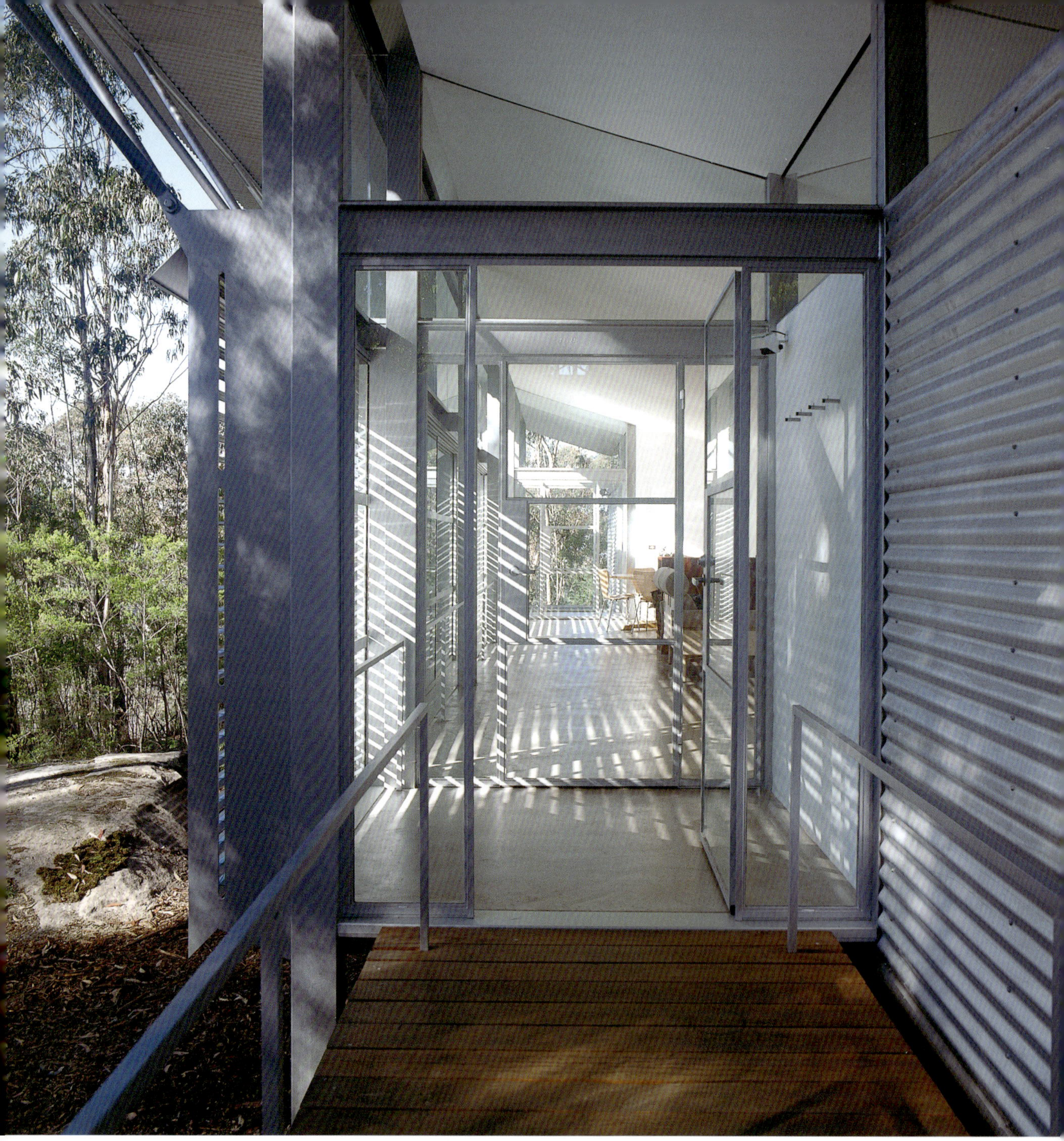

敷地に存在したアボリジニの旧道を辿った動線計画。スタジオを
兼ねる車庫と、住居棟の2棟のパビリオンをつないでいる。

The circulation strategy is an acknowledgement of an
existing aboriginal path. This linear movement connects two
pavilions, a garage/studio and the major living spaces.

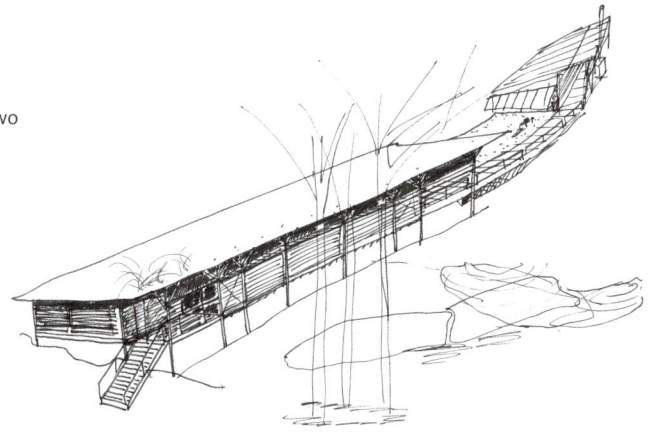

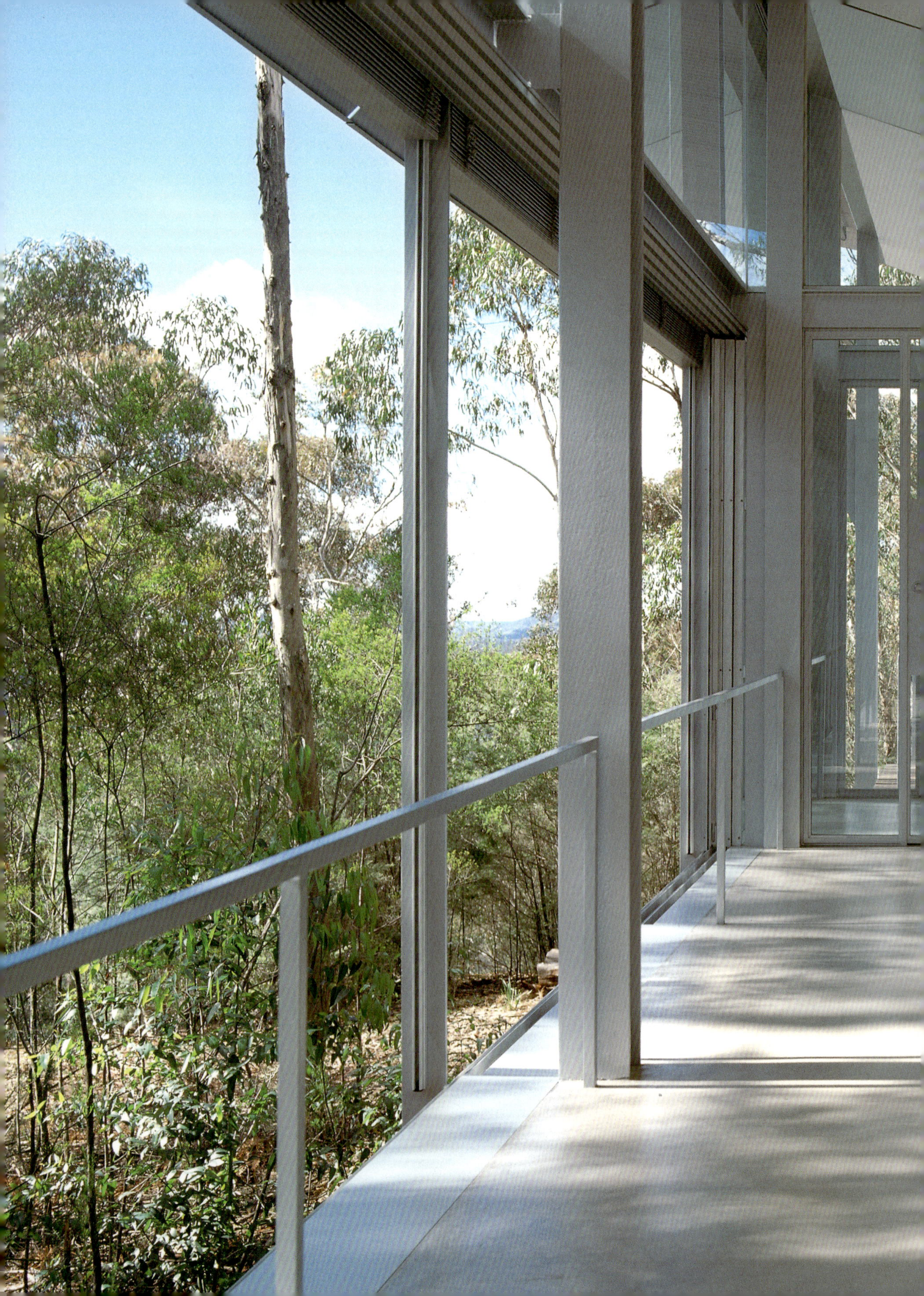

ガラスの玄関の奥行きは、居間のすべての窓を引き残さずに収納する。
ガラスがないことで、居間はオープンベランダとして感知される。

The glass vestibules accommodate a series of sliding screens allowing the glazed wall to completely disappear. This uninterrupted connection to the landscape allows the room to be experienced as an open veranda.

住宅背面の荒い漆喰仕上げのレンガ壁は部屋を
囲み、ガラス・ファサードへつながる。

Painted bagged brick walls at the rear
of the house wrap to form rooms and connect with
the frontal glazing.

南のガラス面は押し出されて、キッチンカウンターを広げている。水平窓で自然換気量を増減できる。

Glazing at the south façade spatially extends the kitchen bench.
Adjustable horizontal vents can be used to promote or reduce natural ventilation.

リビングの床は、先にある深い谷へ下る斜面の上に浮かぶ新しいプラットフォームとなっている。渓谷はユーカリの高枝越しに眺めることができる。

The living spaces form a new platform over a fall in the landscape which anticipates a much larger valley beyond. This is viewed through a screen of upper branches of eucalyptus trees.

背後の壁は水廻りの部屋をつくり、住宅の正面は渓谷へ開かれる。
A rear wall accommodates services; the front of the building opens towards the valley.

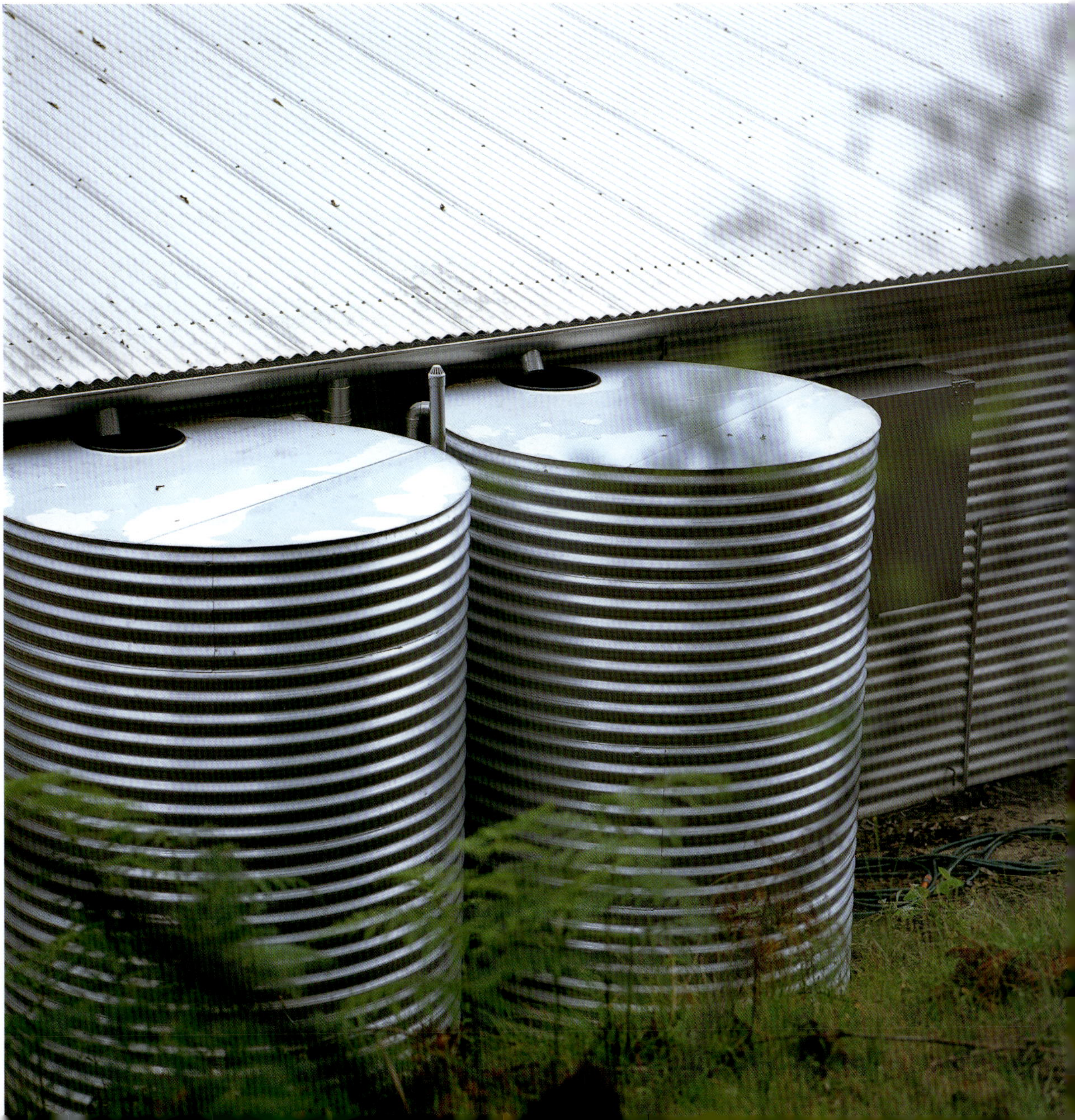

SITE PLAN

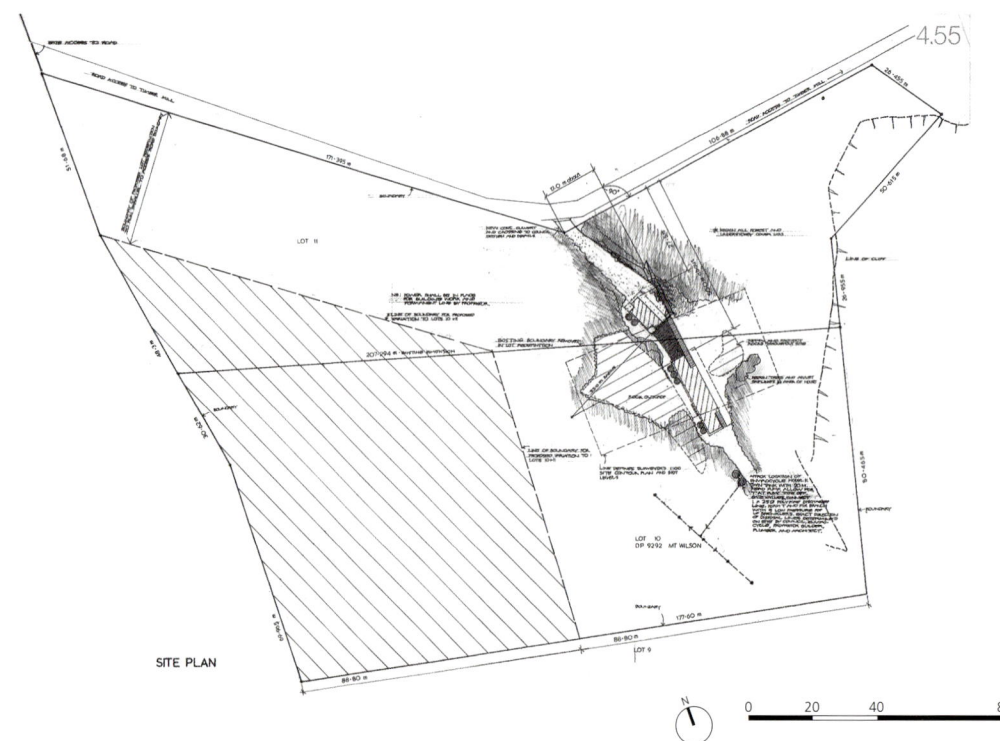

142 | Glenn Murcutt

守られた背面と開かれた前面の構成は、隆起岩に対して低い水廻りの壁が地面に固定するように、敷地の地形を読むことで再度理由づけられている。

The protective back and open front organisational strategy is reinforced by the site topography where the low service wall is grounded against an existing ledge.

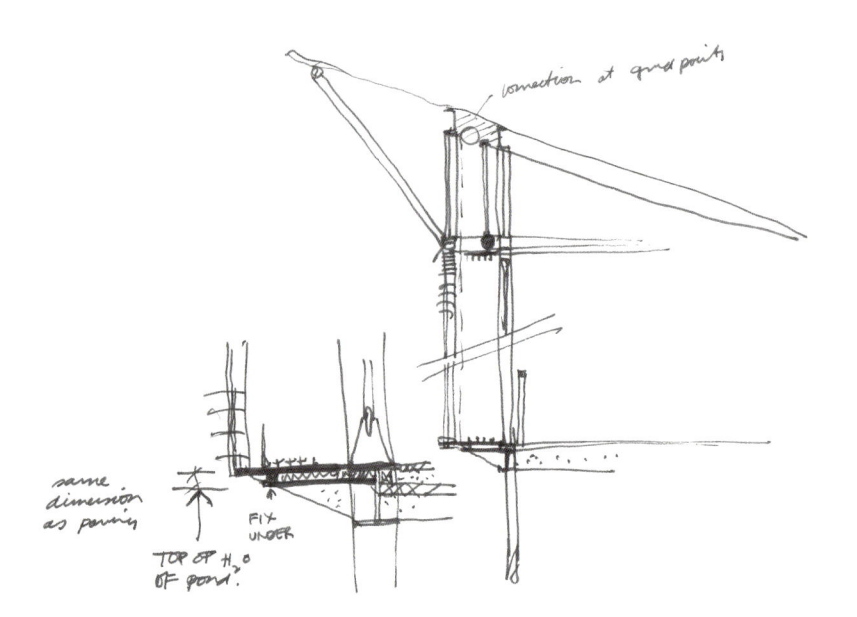

アプローチデッキは、抽象性をもつランドスケープとしての池を、住宅の構成要素に採り入れている。

A timber bridge, passing an external pond, includes this abstracted landscape within the built extent of the house.

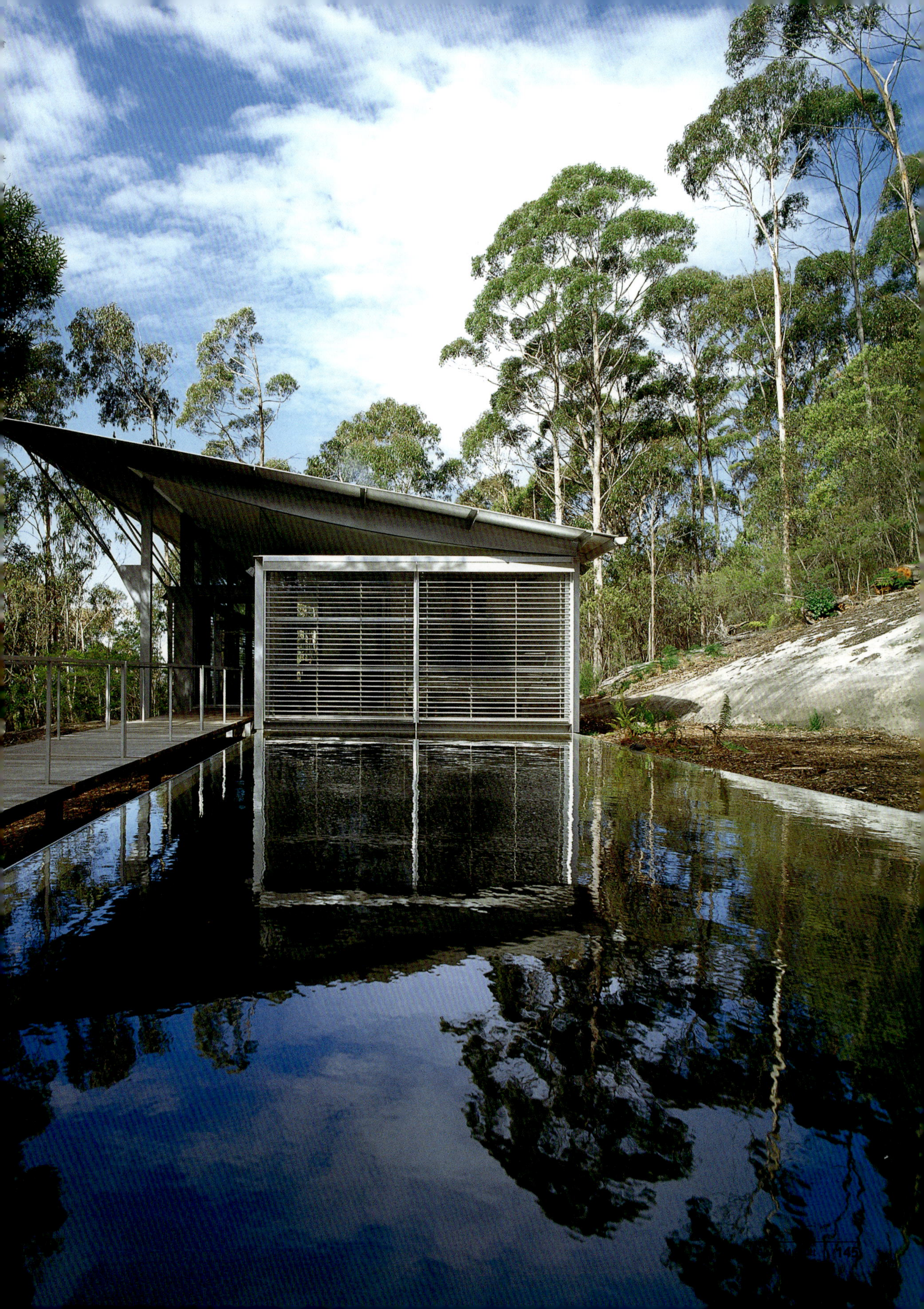

すでに広く称賛されているように、この住宅は、グレン・マーカットの建築が展開した中で重要な作品と位置づけられている。シドニーの西のブルーマウンテンにある。ここで応用された数々のアイデアはビンジーポイントのマグニー邸から発展しているが、それが集約され洗練された結果、より質実な、より抽象的なものとなった。施主は長い設計期間と申請過程のすべてに関与し、彼らの個人的な美学観と倫理観がデザインを左右した。施主との間にあった緊張感と連携は、マーカットの規律だった手法をさらに研ぎ澄ました。その結果について、彼は、「この住宅のディテールは私の仕事の中でも最高のものだ」と満足したことが伝わってくる。

与件では、素材に対しても制約を強いる「宗教色のない、修道院的な静けさ」が求められた。磨きあげられたコンクリートの床、荒い漆喰塗りのレンガ壁、鉄構造と波板鉄板という質実剛健な素材は、必要不可欠な抽象性を帯びるところまで削られた。平面は、マグニー邸の開かれた前面と守られた背面という構成の援用である。それは、敷地の特徴である隆起岩に対して、背後の低い水廻りの壁が地面に固定されることで再度理由づけられている。リビングの床は、先にある深い谷へ下る斜面の上に浮かぶ新しいプラットフォームとなっている。マグニー邸の厳密な「前後」のある平面計画に比べると、シンプソン＝リー邸は、バスルームを構成するコアが正面のガラス・ファサードを挟むように、より進化したものであると言える。

スタジオを兼ねる車庫と、住居棟の2棟のパビリオンをつなぐ長い軸に沿う動線は、敷地に存在したアボリジニの旧道を認識したものであるとマーカットは説明している。抽象性をもつランドスケープとして、アプローチにある池は住宅を構成する要素の一部であり、リビングの大きさを予感させるものである。その脇のアプローチデッキは、母屋のガラスの玄関に続く。この両端にある風除室は、リビングルームの開口を挟んでいる。その奥行きは、リビング、ダイニングのガラス戸を引き残さずに収納できる長さに決定された。その窓が開かれた時、室内はランドスケープと一体的になり、オープンベランダとして感知されるようになっている。

Simpson-Lee House

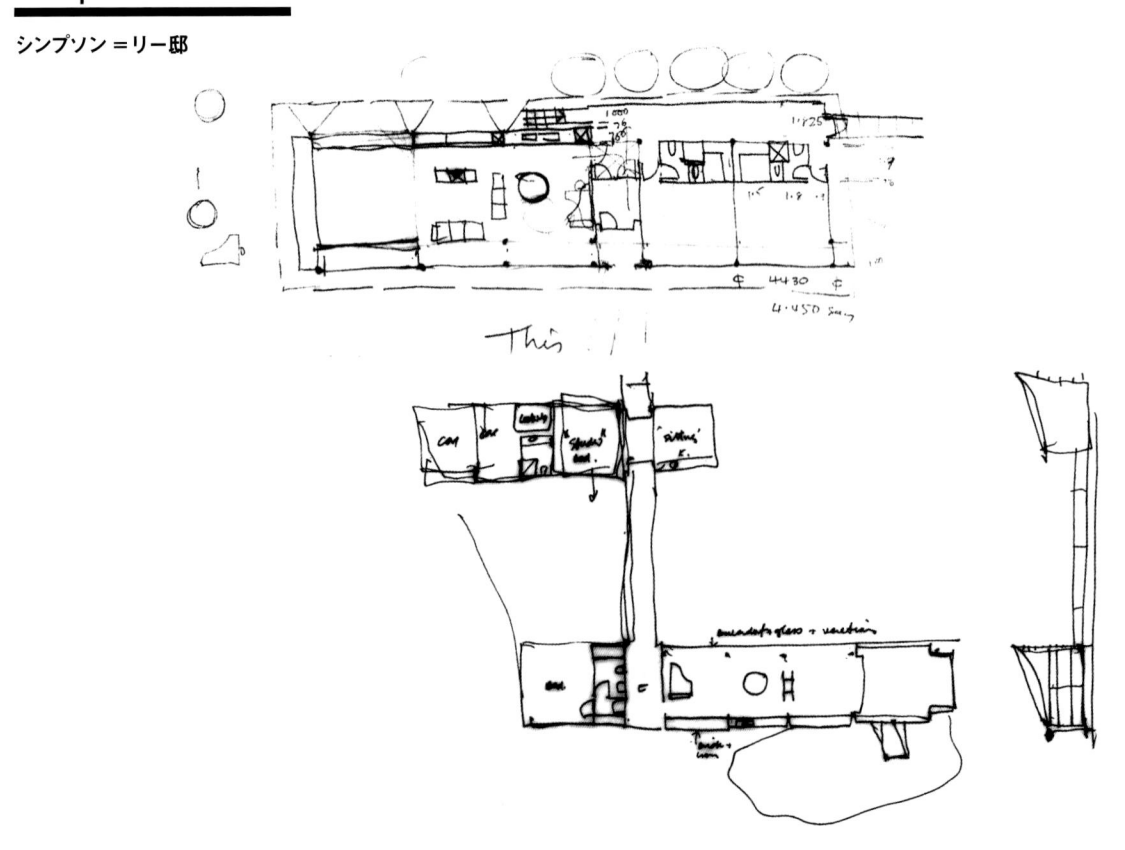

シンプソン＝リー邸

Critically acclaimed, this house has been acknowledged by many as a significant project in the evolution of Glenn Murcutt's work. Located in the Blue Mountains west of Sydney. It is a development of many of the ideas employed in the house at Bingie Point but concentrated and refined and the result is more austere and abstract. The clients were engaged at every stage of the lengthy design and approval process; the decision making affected by their personal ethics and aesthetics. Alignments as well as tensions intensified the architect's disciplined approach. Murcutt's descriptions of the building reveal satisfaction with the results suggesting that "the detailing in this house is as good as I've ever done."

The clients requested a house with a "secular monastic quality" with an insistence on restraint. Simple, hard wearing materials; polished concrete floors, bagged painted brickwork, steel structural frame and exterior corrugated metal sheeting are here reduced to a point of elemental abstraction. The plan follows the protective back and open front organisational strategy employed at Bingie point. This emphasis is reinforced by the site topography where the rear low service wall is grounded against an existing rock ledge. The living spaces form a new floating platform over a fall in the landscape which anticipates a much larger valley beyond. In tension with this implied strict back/front hierarchy is a more complex spatial configuration in which the rear bagged brick walls wrap to form rooms containing the services and connect with the frontal glazing.

Murcutt describes the circulation strategy as an acknowledgement of an existing aboriginal path. This linear movement connects two pavilions, a garage/studio and the major living spaces. A timber bridge, passing an external pond, includes this abstracted landscape within the built extent of the house. The pool reads as an implied platform which dimensionally anticipates the living area of the major pavilion. The timber bridge enters the house via a glass vestibule, one of two which bracket the glazed opening of the living areas. The vestibule dimension accommodates a series of sliding screens allowing the glazed wall to completely disappear. This uninterrupted connection to the landscape allows the room to be experienced as an open veranda.

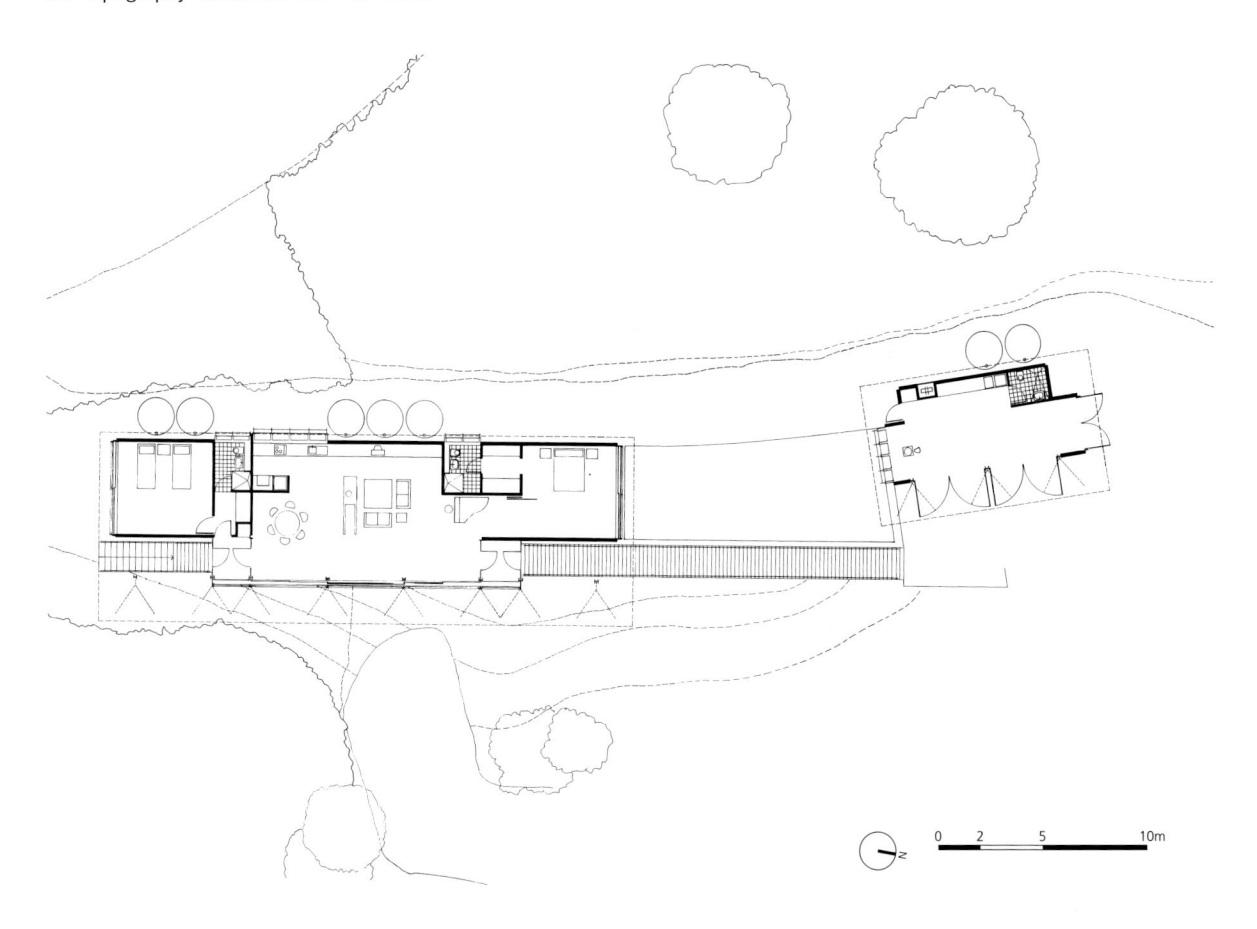

Marika-Alderton House

マリカ＝アルダートン邸

1991−94 ·········· Eastern Arnhem Land, Northern Territory

この住宅では建築要素が明らかである。切妻屋根、乾いた木材の床、開閉可能な外皮がそれぞれに関連している。南側はさまざまな深さの合板の仕切り壁が飛び出て、出窓に仕込まれたさまざまな大きさの家具を示している。

The building is elemental. A pitched roof, dry timber platform and operable skin float in relation to each other. Vertical plywood blades of varying depths project out from the steel column line along the southern façade. These register the dimensions of different built-in furniture elements.

外壁はガラスのない建具として扱われている。下部の隙間は、水平な床から出窓が浮かんでいることを強調している。

The exterior wall is treated as finely crafted infill panels with no glazed openings. Gaps under the bay window structures confirm the sense of suspension above a horizontal floating floor.

Glenn Murcutt | 151

合板と鎧戸は引くか押して開けられて、卓越風で自然冷房する。天井に溜まった
余剰熱は棟頂部の換気塔で逃がし、熱帯低気圧時の内気圧を外気と同圧にする。

Plywood and slatted timber screens slide or pivot open allowing prevailing breezes to naturally cool the house. Additional built up heat is discharged via wind driven vents which also equalise internal and external air pressures during cyclones.

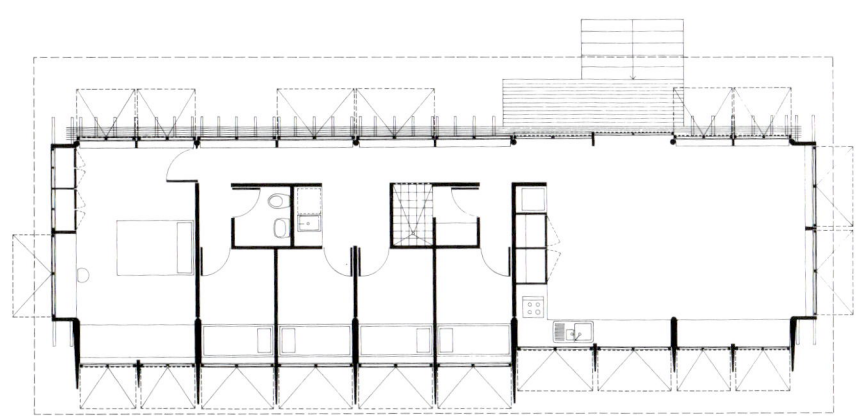

Glenn Murcutt | 153

1枚の鉄の屋根は立面を支配し、深い庇で夏の日射しを遮る。

The fine sheet metal roof is dominant. Deep eaves protect the interior from summer sun.

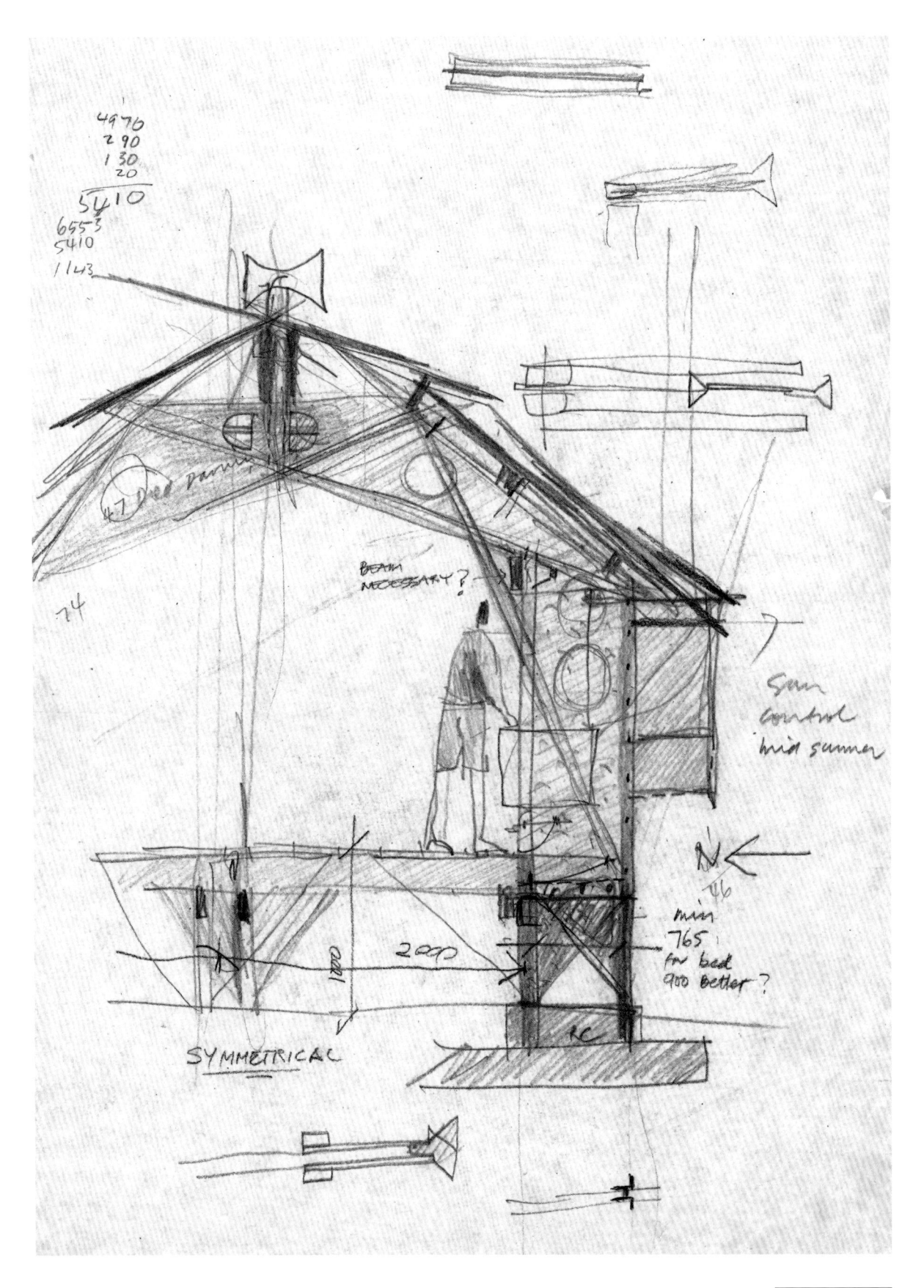
4970
290
130
20
5410
6553
5410
1143
BEAM NECESSARY?
Sun control mid summer
min 765 for bed 900 better?
2000
RC
SYMMETRICAL

アルミペイントの鉄骨造と、オーストラリアの硬木の混構造で、プロトタイプとしてつくられた。部材は切り出され、コンテナ2つに納められて、セミトレーラーと船便によって運ばれた。現地においてボルトとネジで組み立てられた。

Conceived as a prototype, the structural system is comprised of a steel frame finished in aluminium paint and Australian hardwoods. Prefabricated, all components were packed in two shipping containers and transported to site via semi-trailer and barge. The house was bolted and screwed together on site.

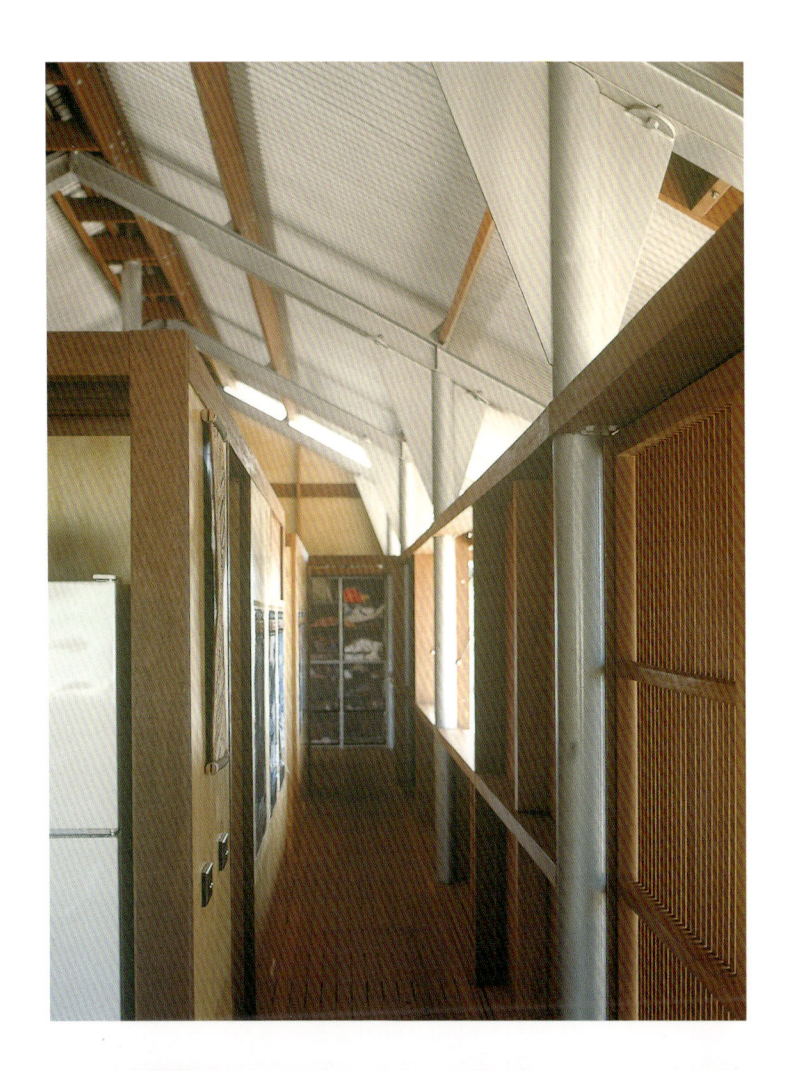

Glenn Murcutt 157

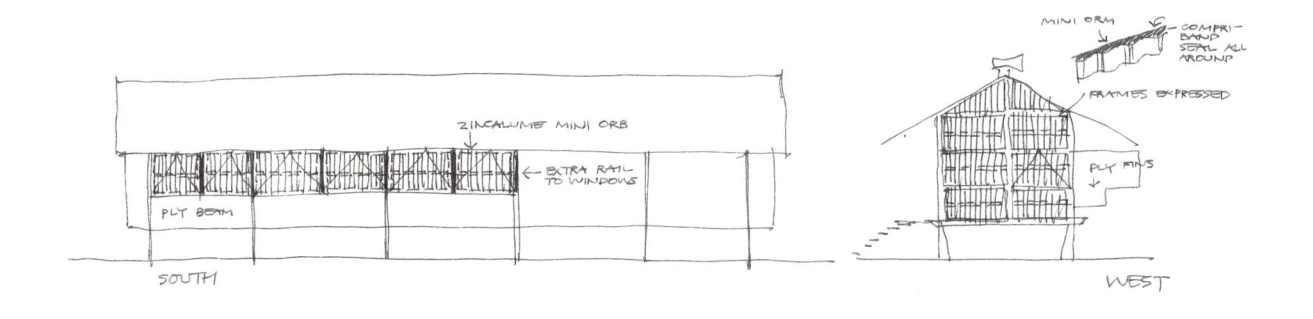

158 Glenn Murcutt

Glenn Murcutt

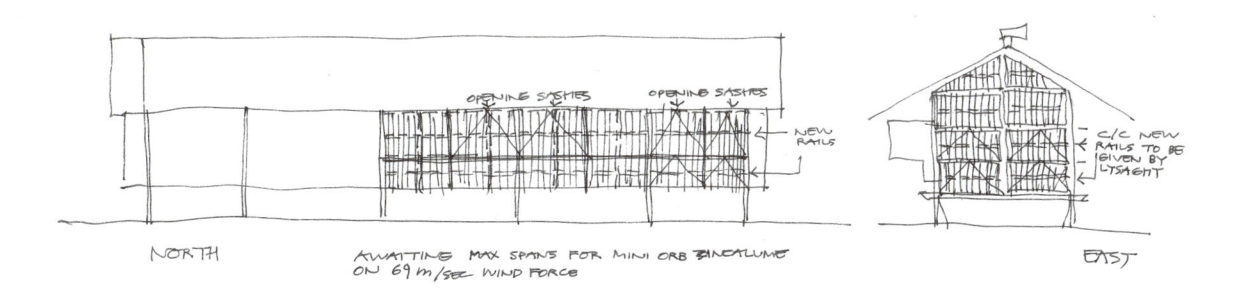

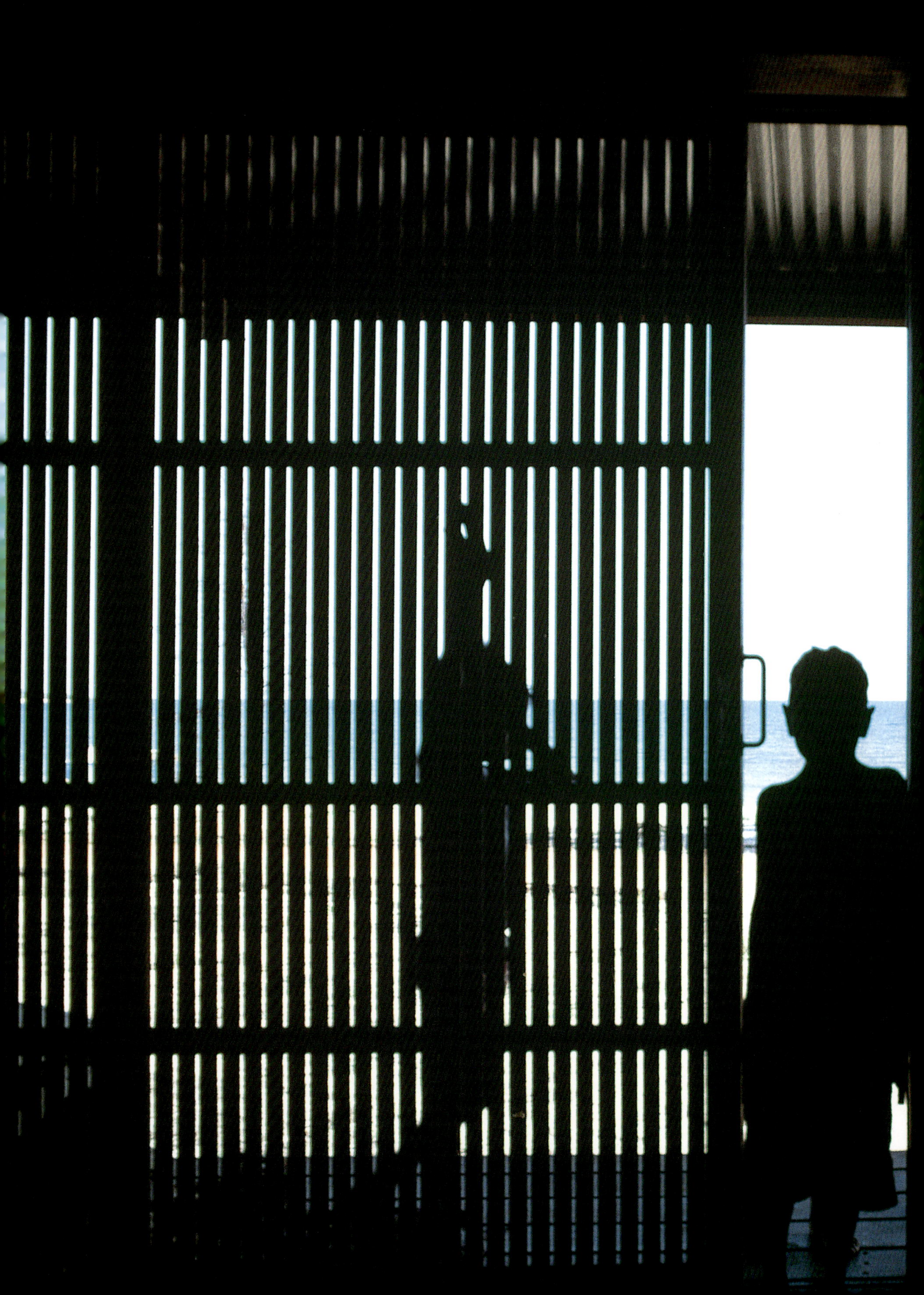

日除けのある高床としての住宅。水平線や、天気の移り変わり、人々や動物の動き、子どもたちが遊ぶ様子を眺められる場所である。

The building is experienced as an elevated shaded platform. The inhabitants can observe the horizon, changes in the weather patterns, the movement of people and animals and the playing of children.

アボリジニのリーダーであるブンダック・マリカと彼女のパートナーのマーク・アルダートンにより、マリカー族の住むイルカラ集落に建てられた。この住宅は、オーストラリアの最北部で、特有の気候と文化を建築で実践する稀な機会となった。アラフラ海、カーペンタリア湾に面する敷地は熱帯低気圧が強い風と激しい雨をもたらす熱帯気候にある。浜辺、河口、淡水池が周囲にあることから、建て込んだ居留地とは少し距離をおいて建てられた。

住宅は、施主が住んでいた小さな窓があるレンガ造の典型的なアボリジニのための公共住宅にとって代わるプロトタイプとしてつくりだされた。シドニー北部のゴスフォードで建物の部材が作成され、2つのコンテナに納められて、セミトレーラーと船便によって現地まで運ばれた。家はボルトとネジで組み立てられ、全工程は4カ月であった。

建物は、1つ1つの要素がはっきりしている。切妻屋根、乾いた木材の床、開閉できる表皮がそれぞれに関連している。構造は、鉄骨造と、オーストラリアのハードウッドの混構造である。屋根の1枚の鉄は、何にもまして存在感があり、深い庇が夏の日射しを遮っている。外壁はガラスのない建具パネルとして扱われている。この合板と鎧戸は、引くか押して開けられて、卓越風によって自然冷房している。

建築として力強い表情を見せているのが南の立面であり、合板の仕切り壁が、鉄の柱が並ぶ線上からいろいろな長さで飛び出している。壁は違う大きさの造作家具を示唆している。キッチンカウンター、収納やベッドなどが出窓に組み込まれて、床からわずかに浮かんでいる。この仕切り壁は、視線を遮り、また、夏の早朝と午後の日射しを遮る覆いである。出窓の下の隙間は、水平な床から出窓が浮かんでいることを強調している。ここでマーカットは、水平線や、天気の移り変わり、人々や動物の動き、子どもたちが遊ぶ様子を眺められるような場所をつくった。この建物は、日除けに守られた高床(プラットフォーム)として機能するように考えられている。

Marika-Alderton House

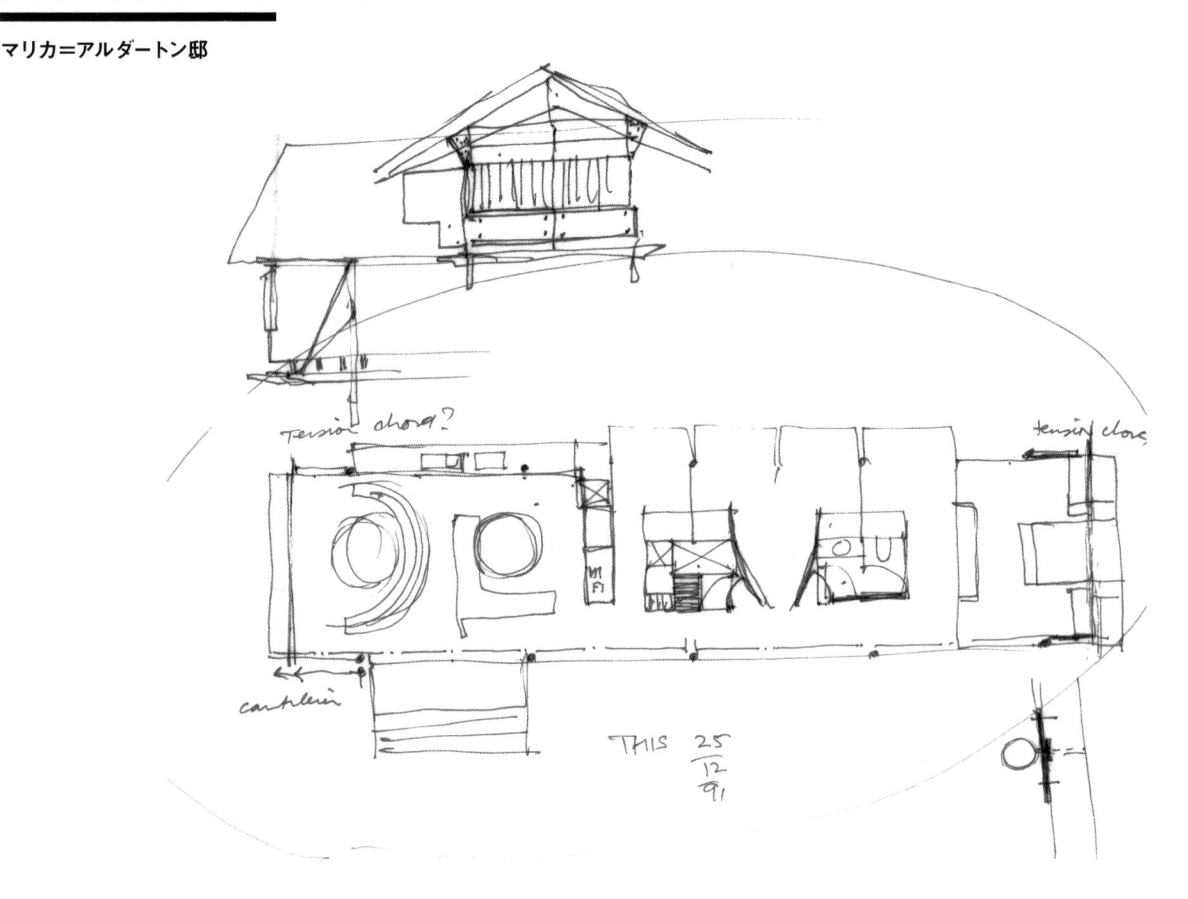

マリカ＝アルダートン邸

Commissioned by the aboriginal leader Banduk Marika and her partner Mark Alderton this project is in Yirrkala on land associated with the Marika clan. The project presented a rare opportunity to design a house in Australia's extreme north and to architecturally address the inherent climatic and cultural conditions. Facing the Arafura Sea and the Gulf of Carpentaria the site has a tropical climate with cyclonic conditions, high winds and very heavy rainfall. Surrounded by a beach, estuary creek and freshwater lagoon, the building is slightly removed from a generally suburban settlement.

It was conceived by Murcutt as a prototype and as a viable alternative to the house then occupied by the clients, a brick building with small windows typical of aboriginal public housing in this context. Prefabricated in Gosford, north of Sydney, all components were packed in two shipping containers and transported to site via semi-trailer and barge. The house was bolted and screwed together on site, the entire process taking four months.

The building is elemental. A pitched roof, dry timber platform and operable skin float in relation to each other. The structural system is comprised of a steel frame and Australian hardwoods. The fine sheet metal roof is dominant, deep eaves protecting the interior from summer sun. The exterior wall is treated as finely crafted infill panels with no glazed openings. These typically plywood and slatted timber screens slide or pivot open allowing prevailing breezes to naturally cool the house.

One of the most striking aspects of the architecture is the southern façade, where vertical plywood blades of varying depths project out from the steel column line. These register the dimensions of different built-in furniture elements; a kitchen bench, timber joinery or beds, framed as floating window bays. The fins provide both visual privacy and shade from the summer sun in early morning and late afternoon. Voids under the bay structures confirm the sense of suspension above a horizontal floor plane. In this house Murcutt creates a situation from which the inhabitants can observe the horizon, changes in the weather patterns, the movement of people and animals and the playing of children; a building which is experienced as an elevated shaded platform.

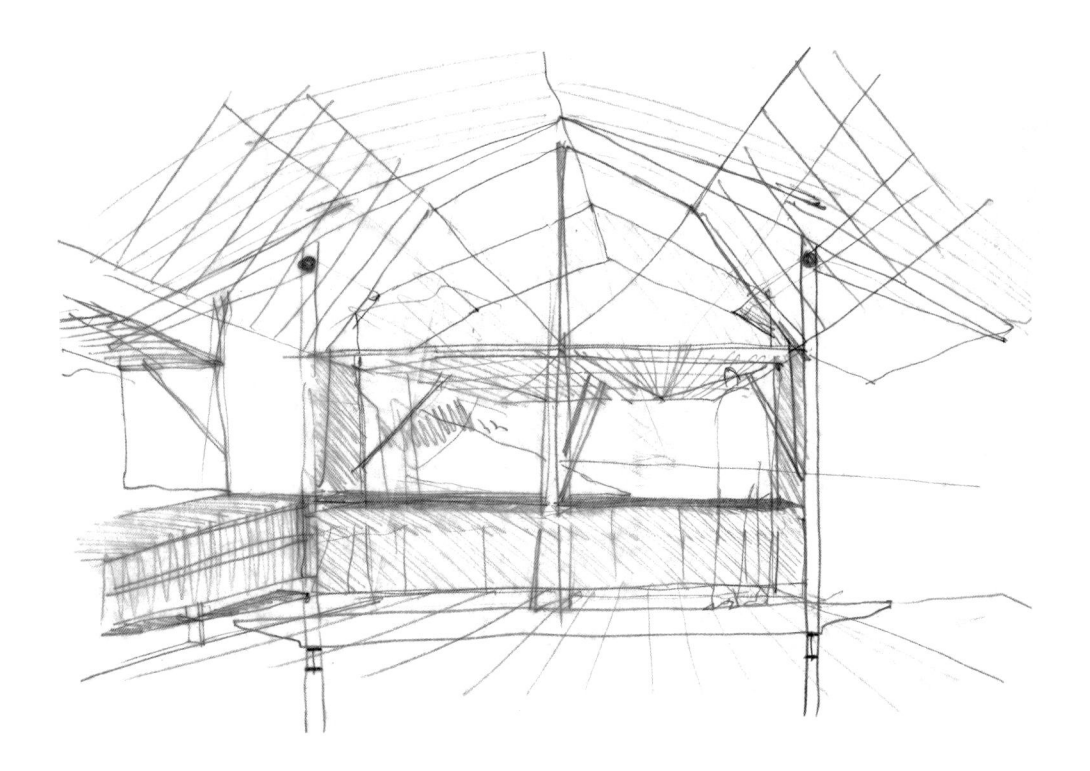

Murcutt Guest Studio

マーカット・ゲストスタジオ

1992 ………… Kempsey, New South Wales

キッチン、バス付きのゲストスタジオは、既存の農家小屋を改築したものである。新しく北につくられた大きなベランダは入口をより明確にし、ガラス戸は建物の外壁を飛び出るように引き分けられる。

This self contained guest accommodation is a precise reconfiguration of an existing rural shed. A new northern veranda formalises the entry and a glazed door slides completely away through the extension of its frame beyond the building envelope.

既存の木の外壁は、バスルームの金属の外壁と対照をなしている。シャワーのコーナー窓は、器具のままあらわされた湯沸かし器などのサービス部分を美的に処理している。

Original weathered wall boards contrast with the metal exterior of the bathing facilities.
The corner window dissolves at the shower and an adjacent exposed hot water system aesthetically foregrounds utility.

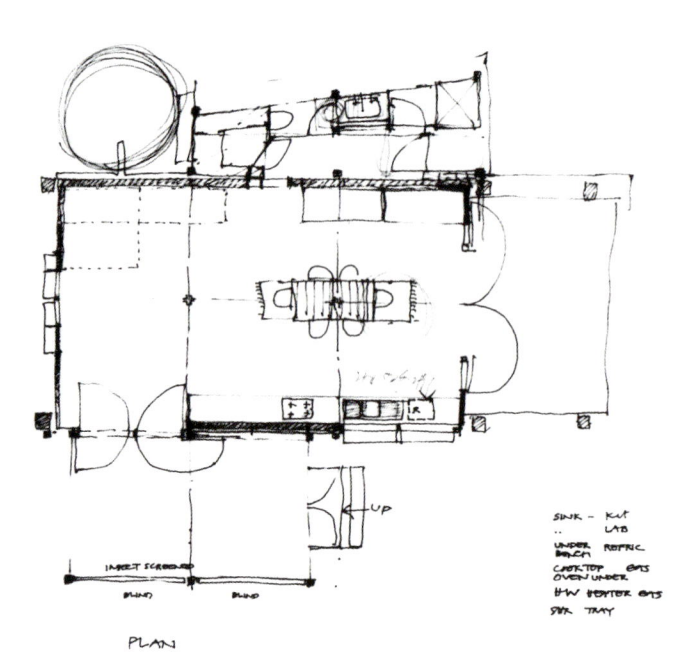

Glenn Murcutt

鋳鉄製の暖炉の両脇に配置され、移動可能な家具のように見せている2つの精美な家具にはキッチンが組み込まれている。無垢材で細かいディテールでつくられ、小屋の荒い木材と対比させている。

Two finely crafted joinery elements accommodate the kitchen facilities, perceived as loose furniture and located either side of a central cast iron fireplace. Made in solid timber and carefully detailed their refinement contrasts with the roughness of the weathered shell.

Glenn Murcutt 169

ケンプシーのマーカットの農場の南側にあった既存の農家小屋は、広大なランドスケープに当てはめるように再構成された。

Located on the southern side of the farm at Kempsey, Murcutt architecturally reworks an existing a rural shed, precisely situating it within the broader landscape.

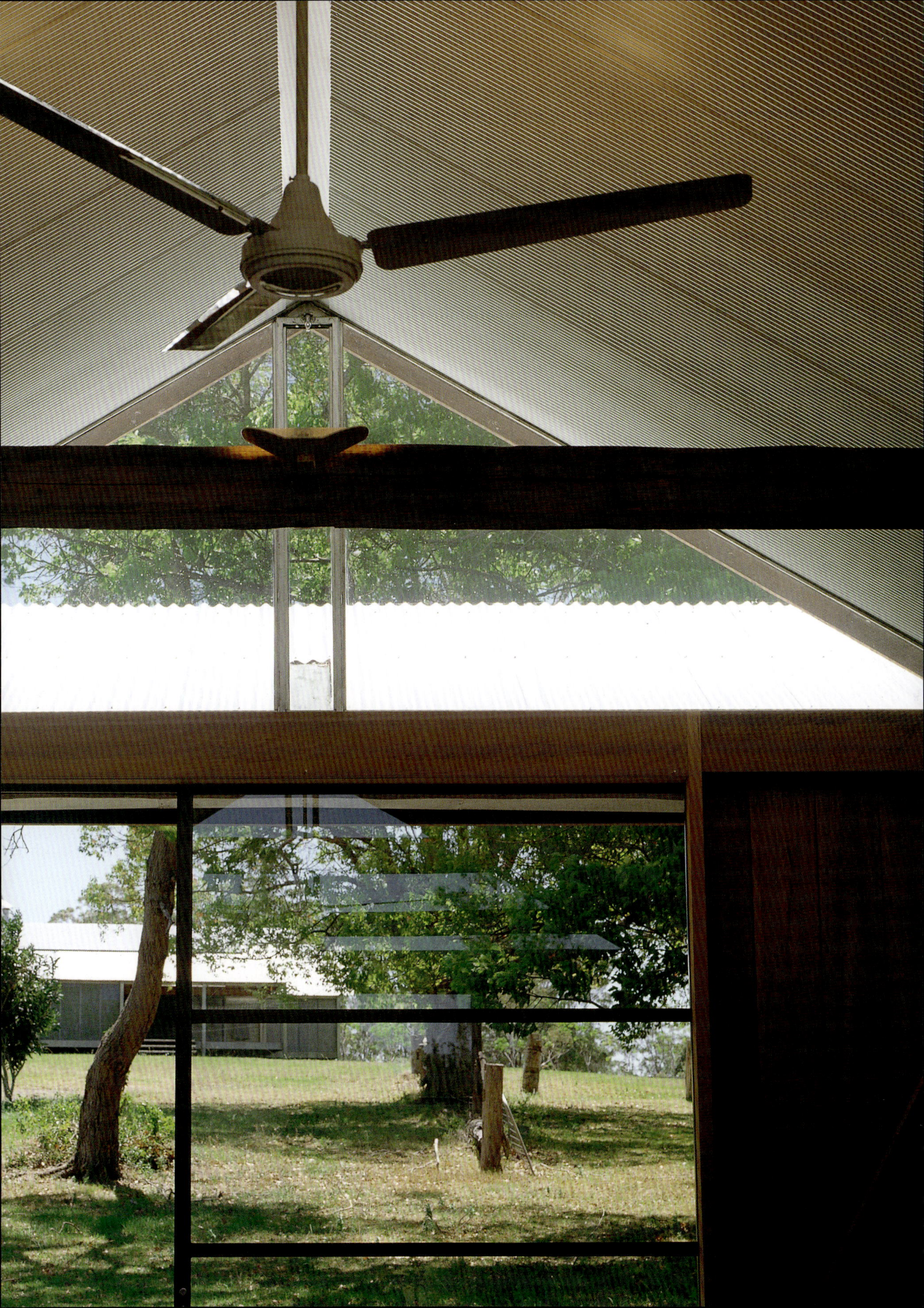

Murcutt Guest Studio

マーカット・ゲストスタジオ

キッチン、バス付きのゲストスタジオは、ケンプシーの農場に建つマリー・ショート／グレン・マーカット邸の南にあった既存の小屋を緻密に改築したものである。以前は、農作業の働き手の住み処や、農具小屋であったりした。風雨にさらされて建っていた小屋の中は、4連に連なる木造トラスがあらわされていた。改築では、この部屋に3つの要素――北の入口を明確にする大きなベランダ、西の小さなバスルーム、東の階段付きのポーチ――が付け加えられた。

マーカットは、既存の小屋に目立たぬように手を入れている。縦羽目の板貼りの外壁は、一旦剥がされて室内側が研磨された。もとに戻す際に、雇い実（ざね）のように鉄錆を入れて互いをつなげて、材の幅を調整するとともに、虫を入れないようにした。幅広の厚い、オイル仕上げのフローリングは、研磨後にワックスがかけられた。ベランダでは、シロアリの被害をとるために、そこにあった柱が短く切られた。そこから先細りの新しい柱と接合して、母屋に差し掛けた新しい屋根を支えている。東と西の新しい開口は既存の左右対称の平面を再構成した。これにより、家具によって強調される斜めの動線ができた。

2つの繊細な家具にはキッチン設備が組み込まれている。中心の鋳鉄製暖炉の両脇に配置され、壁と床から離されていることで家具と見せている。引き出し、棚、飲み物を入れる冷蔵庫、食器棚そしてガステーブルなどの機能を組み込んでいる。無垢材でディテールに気を配ってつくられて、小屋の荒い木材と対比させるとともに、その工作方法では大工仕事を造作に発展させている。

明らかに現代的なのはバスルーム棟で、既存の小屋へ、当意即妙な新しいパビリオンとして加えられた。既存の梁間寸法を利用してシャワーやトイレなどの要素が割り振られた。その3分節された空間は、エントランスポーチから続く主空間のリズムと呼応している。金属の外壁と、器具のままあらわされた湯沸かし器とガスボンベは、ユーティリティと、シャワーのコーナー窓の前景となって立面を調整している。車椅子用としても使われるスロープは細長く、この斜めのアプローチは、その先の広大なランドスケープの中へゲストハウスを位置づけている。

This self contained guest accommodation is a precise reconfiguration of an existing rural shed located on the southern side of the Marie Short/Glenn Murcutt House at the Kempsey farm. It had been variously used as a worker's flat and as storage for farm equipment. Extremely weathered, the original building consists of three symmetrical structural bays with exposed timber roof trusses. Added to this room are three new elements; a generous veranda formalising the entry on the northern side, a compact bathroom on the west wall and a small side porch with steps to the east.

Murcutt subtlety re-works the materials of the original shed. The wall cladding is removed, sanded on the inside and reinstated. A hoop iron tongue inserted between each board allows for movement and prevents insects entering. The thick, oversized and oil stained floor boards are sanded and waxed. And at the veranda, original posts, cut to remove termite damage, are bolted via a tapered connection to new timber supports for a skillion roof. New openings to the east and west reorient the original symmetry of the room. They suggest a diagonal path, supported by the arrangement of loose furniture.

Two finely crafted joinery elements accommodate the kitchen facilities. Deliberately distinct from the wall and floor planes they are perceived as furniture located either side of a central cast iron fireplace. They arrange diverse elements; drawers, open shelves, bar fridge, cupboards and stove with apparent ease. Made in solid timber and carefully detailed their refinement contrasts with the roughness of the weathered shell whilst sympathetically extending its construction.

The most explicit contemporary addition is the bathroom, a new pavilion conceived in playful relation to the shed. Each functional component is individually housed and dimensioned according to the original timber stud spacing. Its organisation echoes the spatial rhythm of the main room where an entry porch leads onto a space with three bays. The exterior metal skin and exposed services (hot water heater and gas cylinders) aesthetically foreground utility and a corner window in the shower dissolves an expected stability. This spatial extension is also registered in the angled ramp providing wheelchair access, an implied diagonal that situates the project within its much broader landscape.

Glenn Murcutt

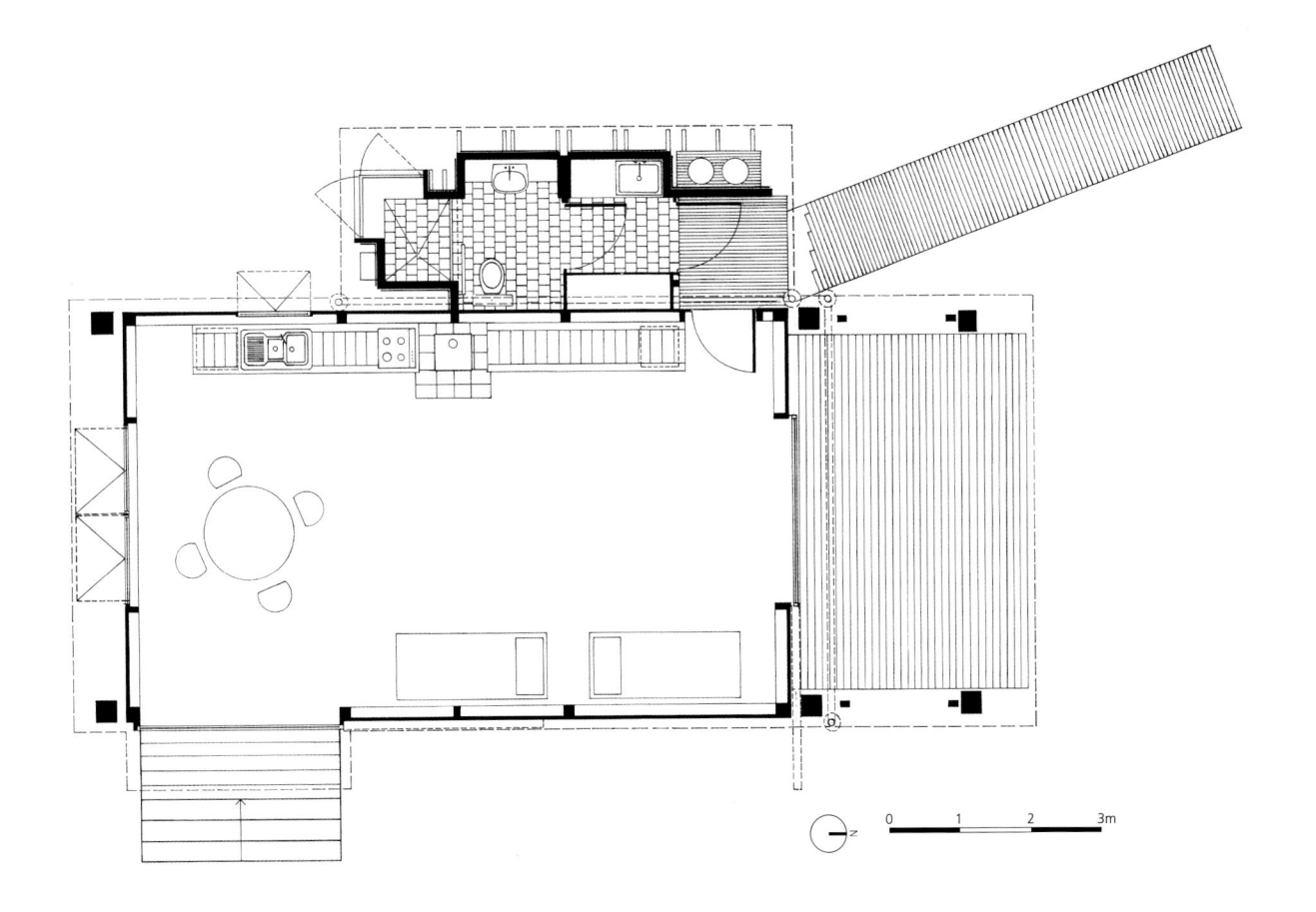

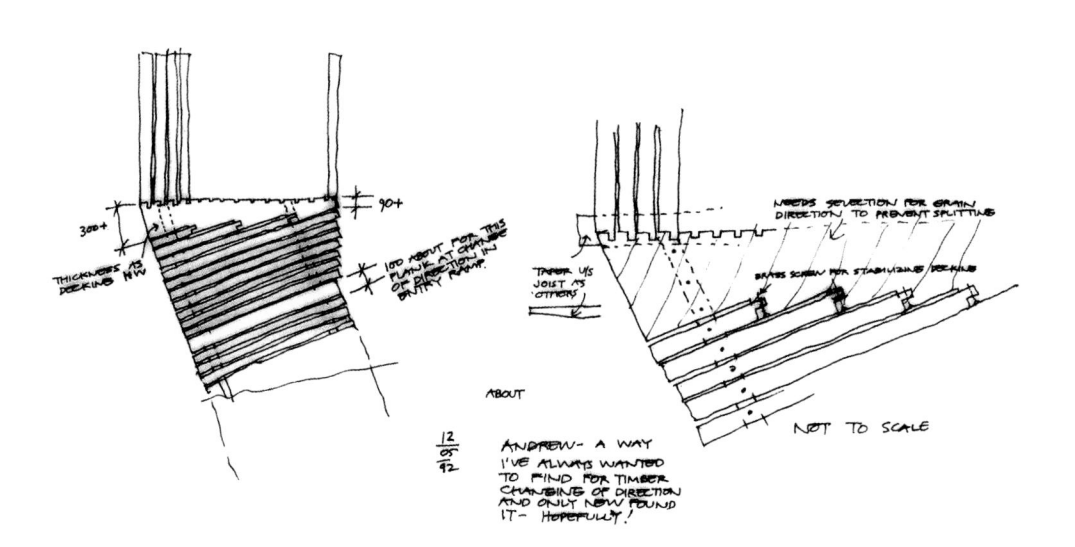

Fletcher-Page House

フレッチャー＝ペイジ邸

1996–98 ·········· Kangaroo Valley, New South Wales

住宅は「シェルター」としての安堵感と、周辺ランドスケープへの開放性を絶妙にあわせもつようにデザインされた。

In the design of this house, Murcutt achieves a complex balance between a sense of enclosure and refuge, and openness to the surrounding landscape.

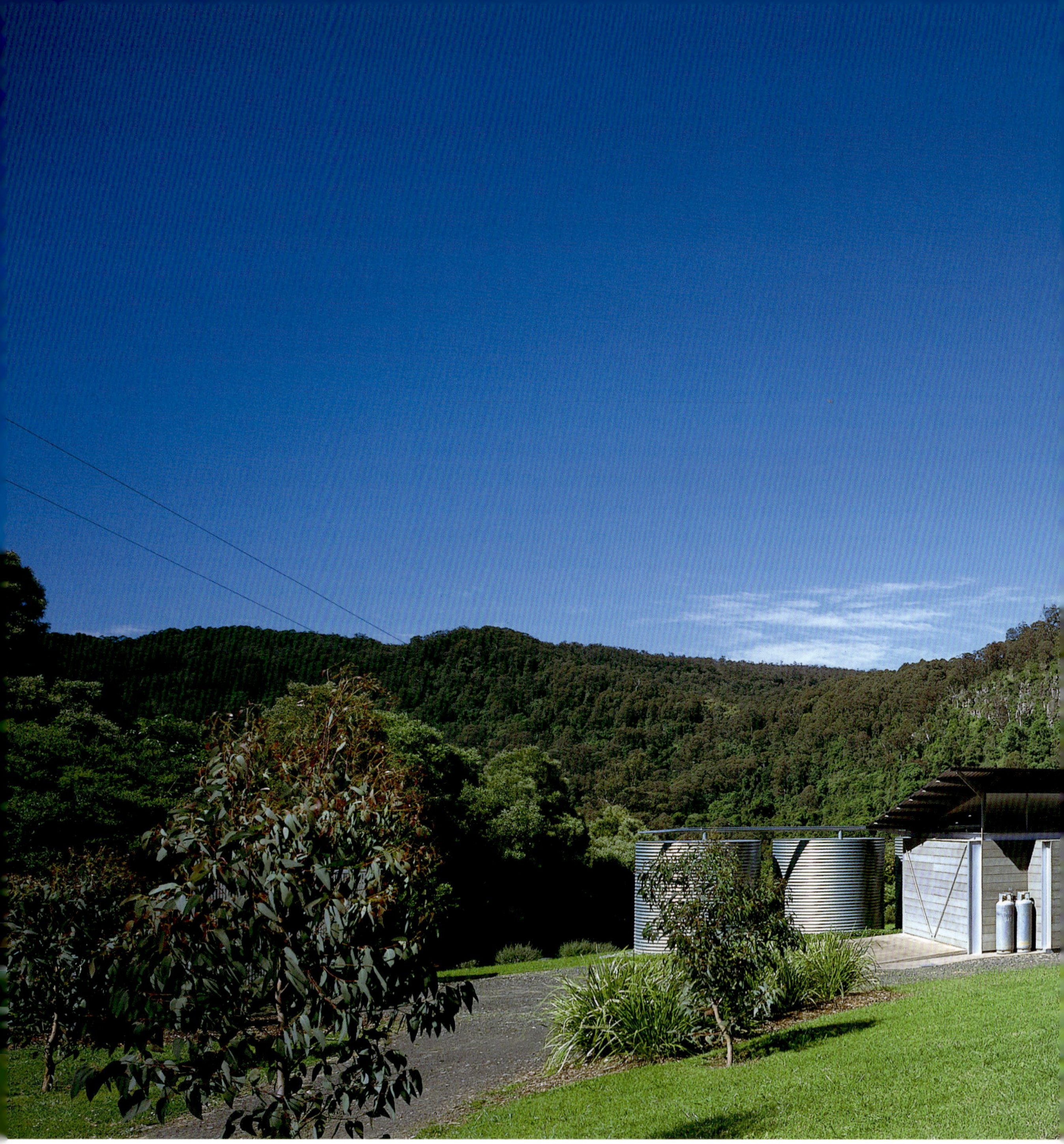

敷地を取り囲むように木々が茂る壮大な峰へと、地面は急速に南へ下る。

The land slopes down steeply to the south, towards the dramatically-scaled, densely-wooded escarpment which encircles the site.

冬に住宅を暖める日射しを入れるため、片流れ屋根の庇は北側が高く、景色へは開かれていない。

To admit winter sunlight, the inclined roof-plane opens to the north, away from the principal landscape scene.

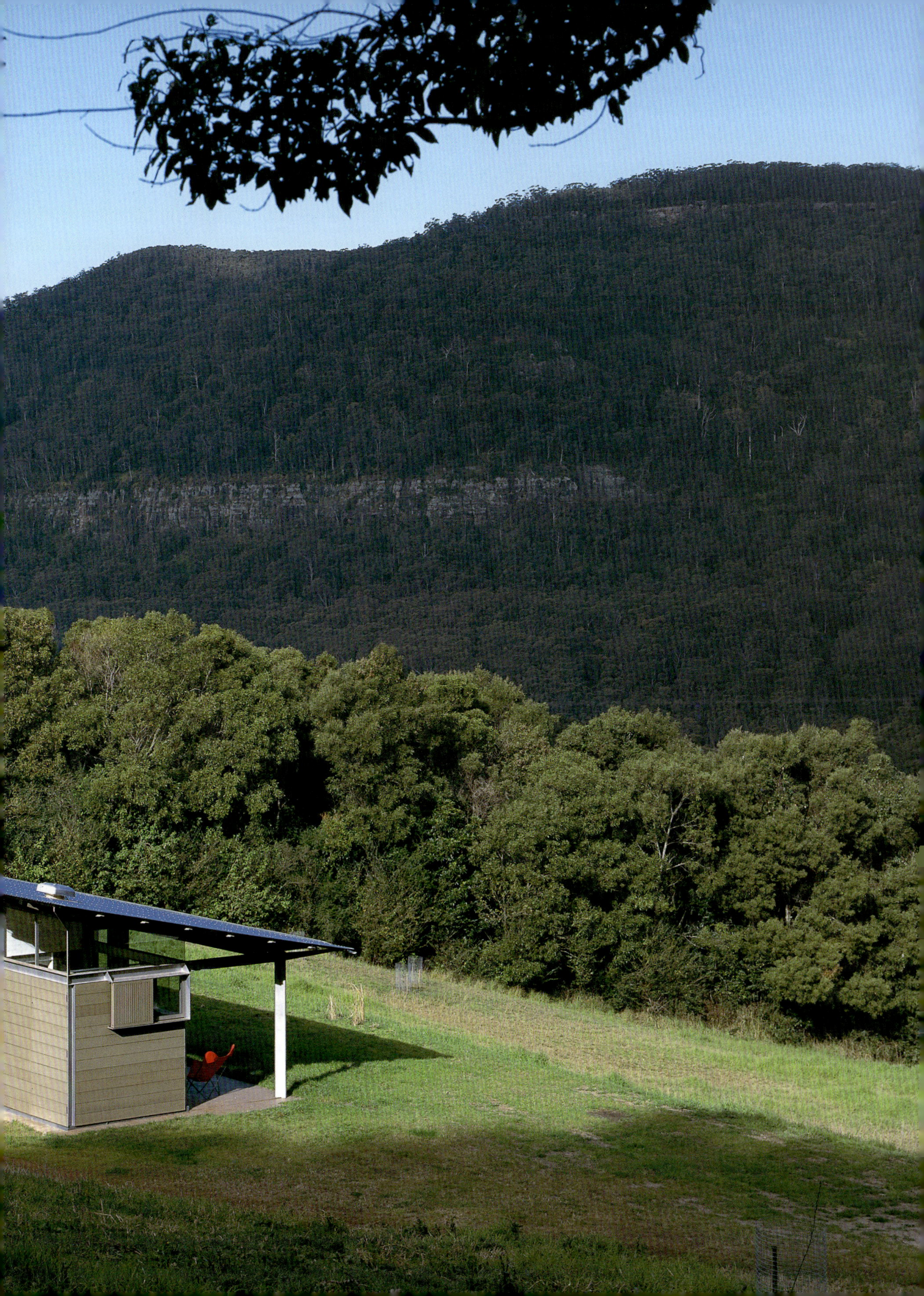

Site Plan

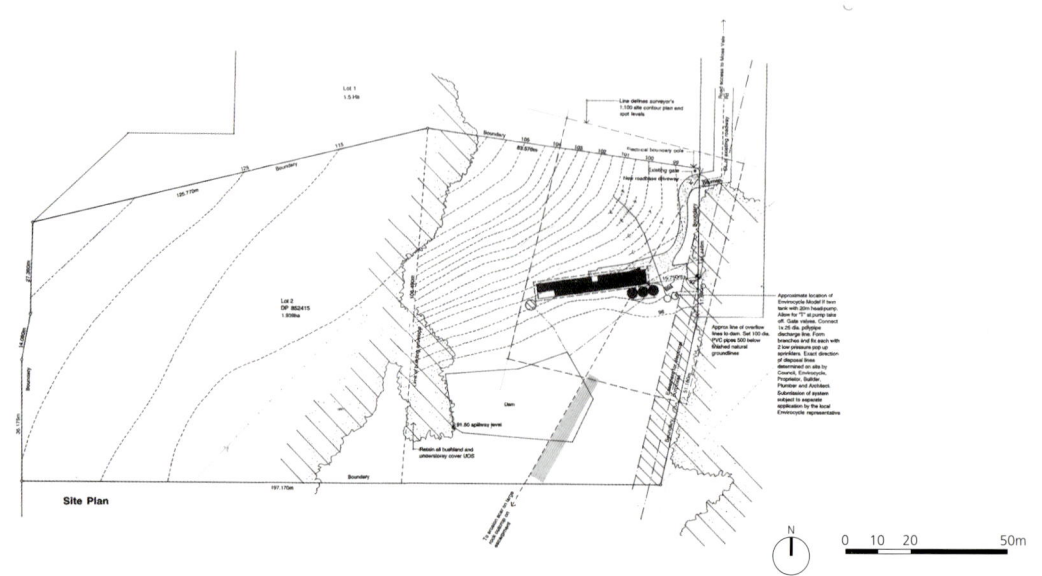

180 | Glenn Murcutt

長く直線的な閉じた空間の上に、片流れの覆い屋根が浮かんでいる。

The house is conceived as a long, thin rectilinear enclosure. Above floats a sheltering inclined roof plane.

Glenn Murcutt | 181

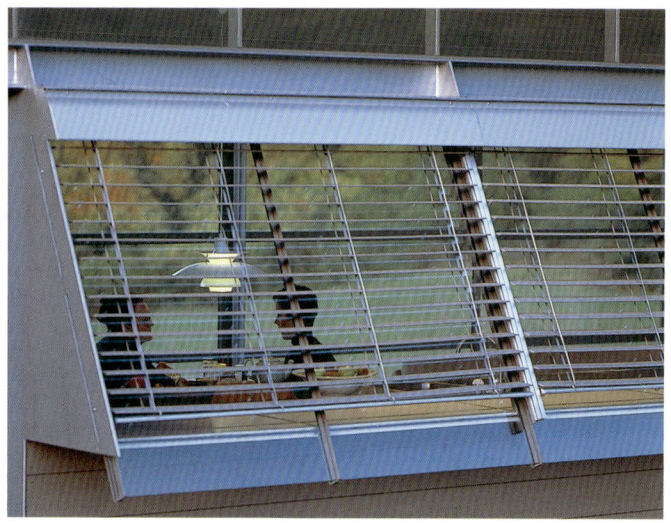

深い庇は、上部窓への夏の高い日射しを除け、冬の日射しはすべての部屋の奥まで採り入れる。下部の出窓では、外部の可動ブラインドが夏の太陽光線を遮る。

The deeply-projecting roof shadows the upper-level windows from the high summer sun, but allows the sun to penetrate deeply into all rooms in winter. The lower windows have external adjustable louver screens to provide summer shading.

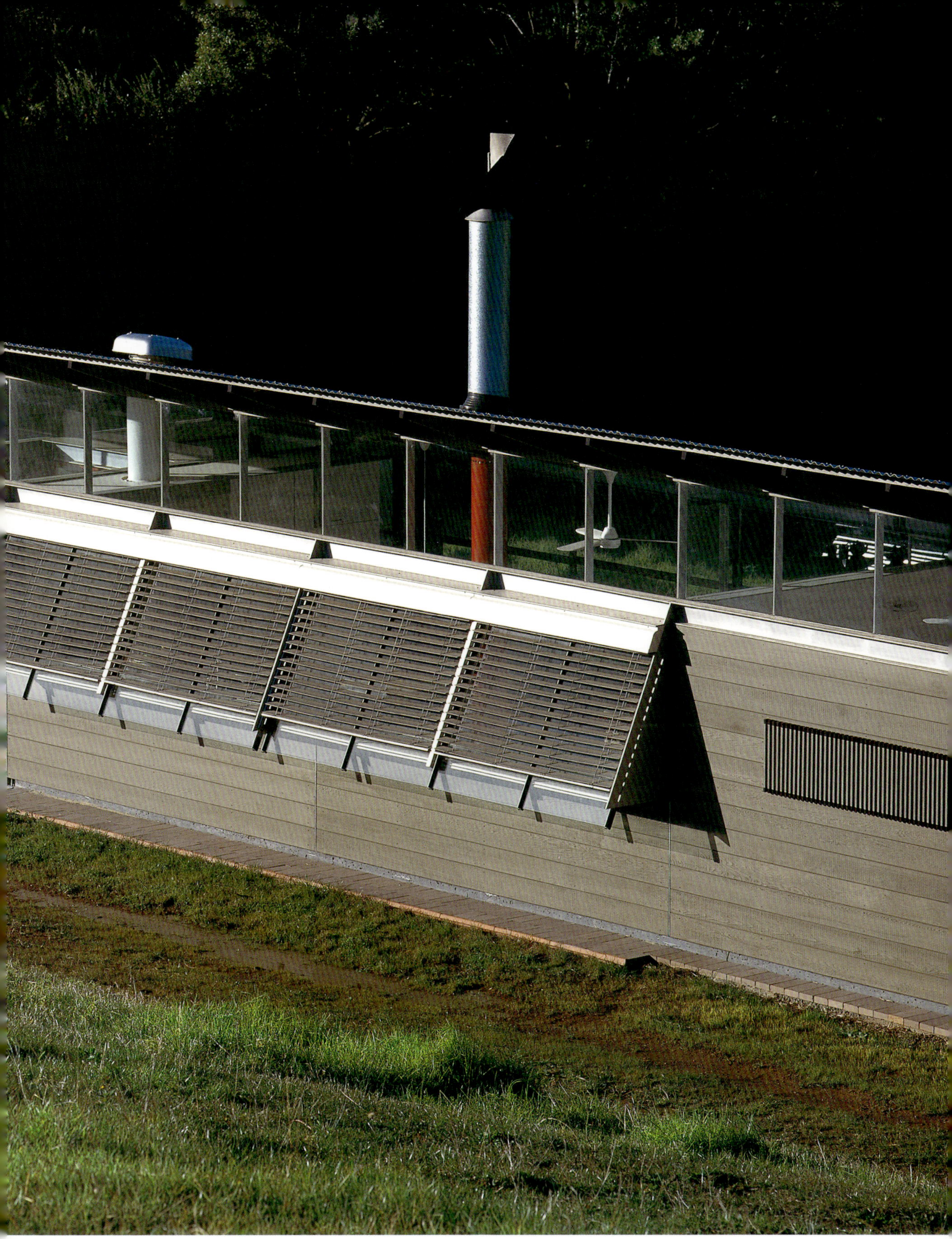

傾斜窓の窓敷居には開閉ハッチが仕込まれていて、
雨天でも自然換気できる。

Openable hatches in the sill of the angled windows
enable cross-ventilation even during rain.

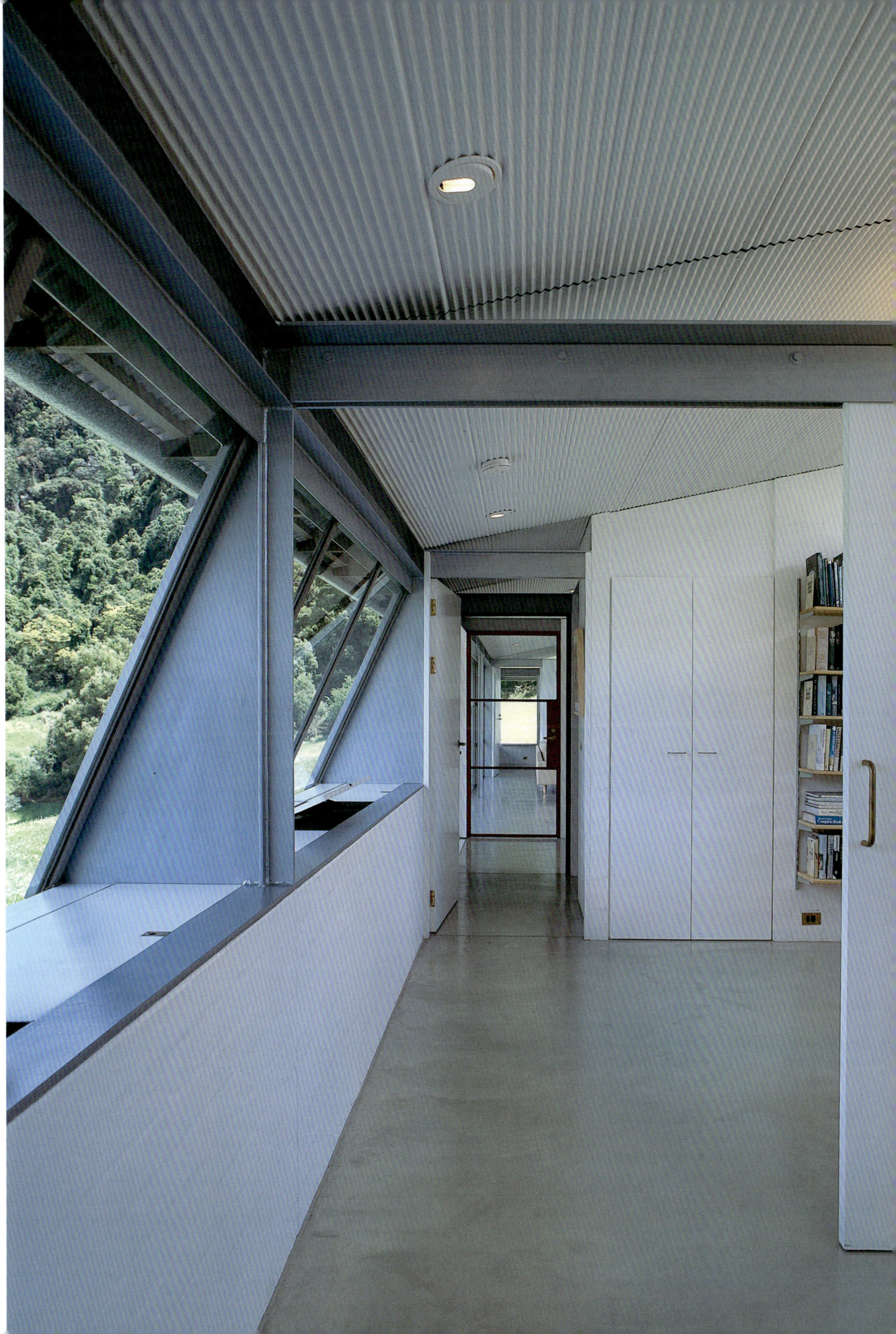

南の窓と鎧戸は、左右に引き込まれると居間と食堂の8m幅にわたる
大きな開口となり、屋外ベランダとして機能する。

The windows and shutters of the southern wall can be entirely slid away to create an 8 meter wide opening—the full width of the sitting/dining room —making this room, effectively, a veranda.

住宅は奥行きが浅く、冬には北の日射しを
景色のよい南側のテラスまで届かせる。

The narrowness of the building allows the low, northern, winter sun to pass through the house and warm the south-side terrace which overlooks the principal landscape view.

SITTING/DINING/COUNTRY KITCHEN

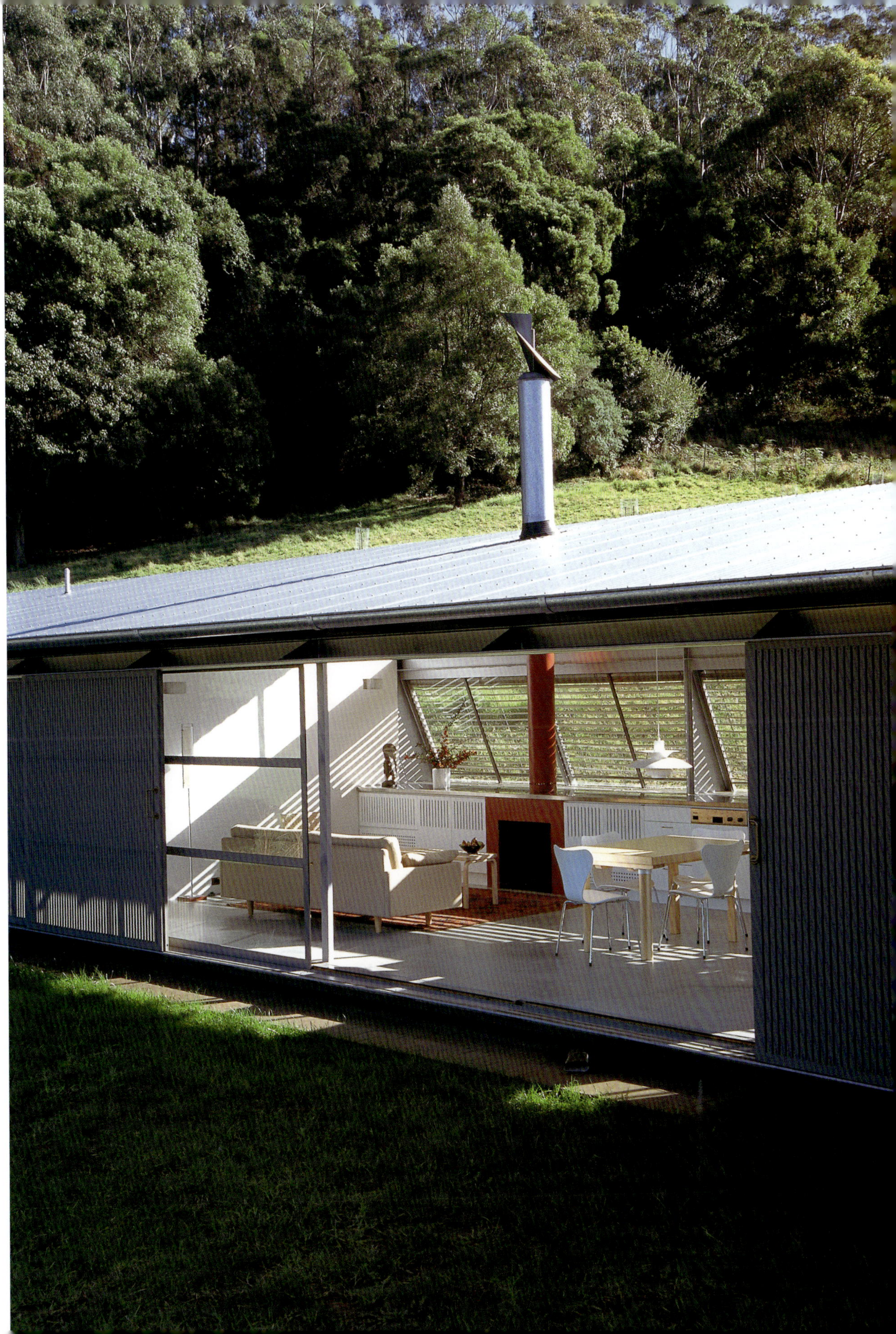

縦列に配置された小さな部屋は、高窓によって広がりが与えらている。

The small size of the house is contradicted by the 'enfilade' linkage of its rooms and their openness to the surroundings through the clerestory windows.

SECTION A

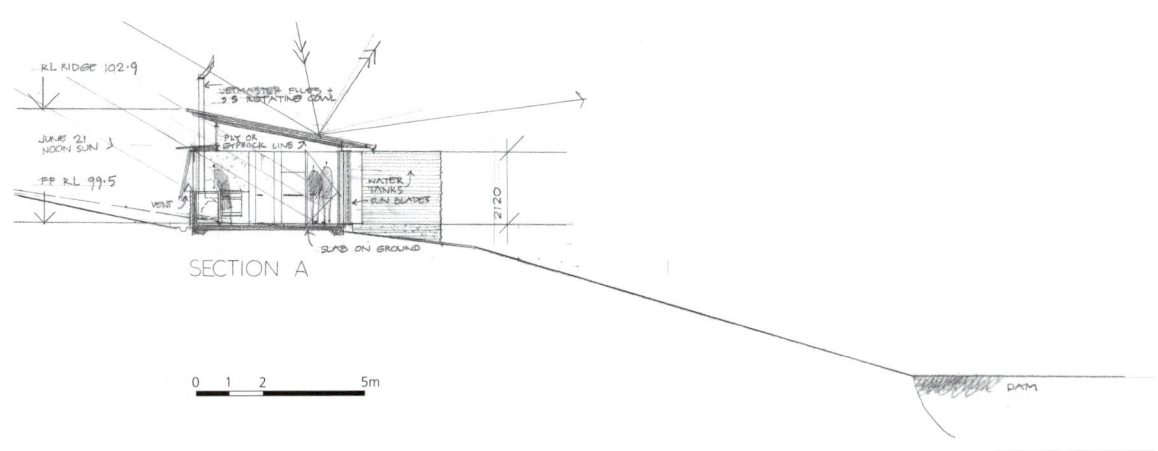

0 1 2   5m

Glenn Murcutt

鉄の構造と杉板の外壁は、素材を実直にあらわすように、飾り気なく立てられている。

The construction of the building is explicit—
the welds of the steel frames and the fixings of the cedar cladding boards are clearly expressed and unembellished.

住宅の窓では、眺望のとり方が多様に考えられている。シャワールームの窓は、小さくしてランドスケープの広がりを感知させ、主寝室の窓枠は、崖への斜めの視線を強調して座をつくるために深いものとなっている。

The windows of the house capture views in very different ways. In the main shower-room the window framing is minimised to give the sense of showering in the open landscape; in the main bedroom the window frame is deepened to emphasize the diagonal view of the escarpment, and to form a window seat.

Glenn Murcutt

マーカットの他の田舎にある建物と同様に、この敷地も上水がない。片持ちの樋は、飲料水、生活用水として集められる雨水の重要性を訴えている。

As with almost all of Murcutt's rural buildings, there is no water supply to the site. Murcutt's cantilevered gutters dramatise the necessity of collecting rain off the roof for use as drinking and washing water.

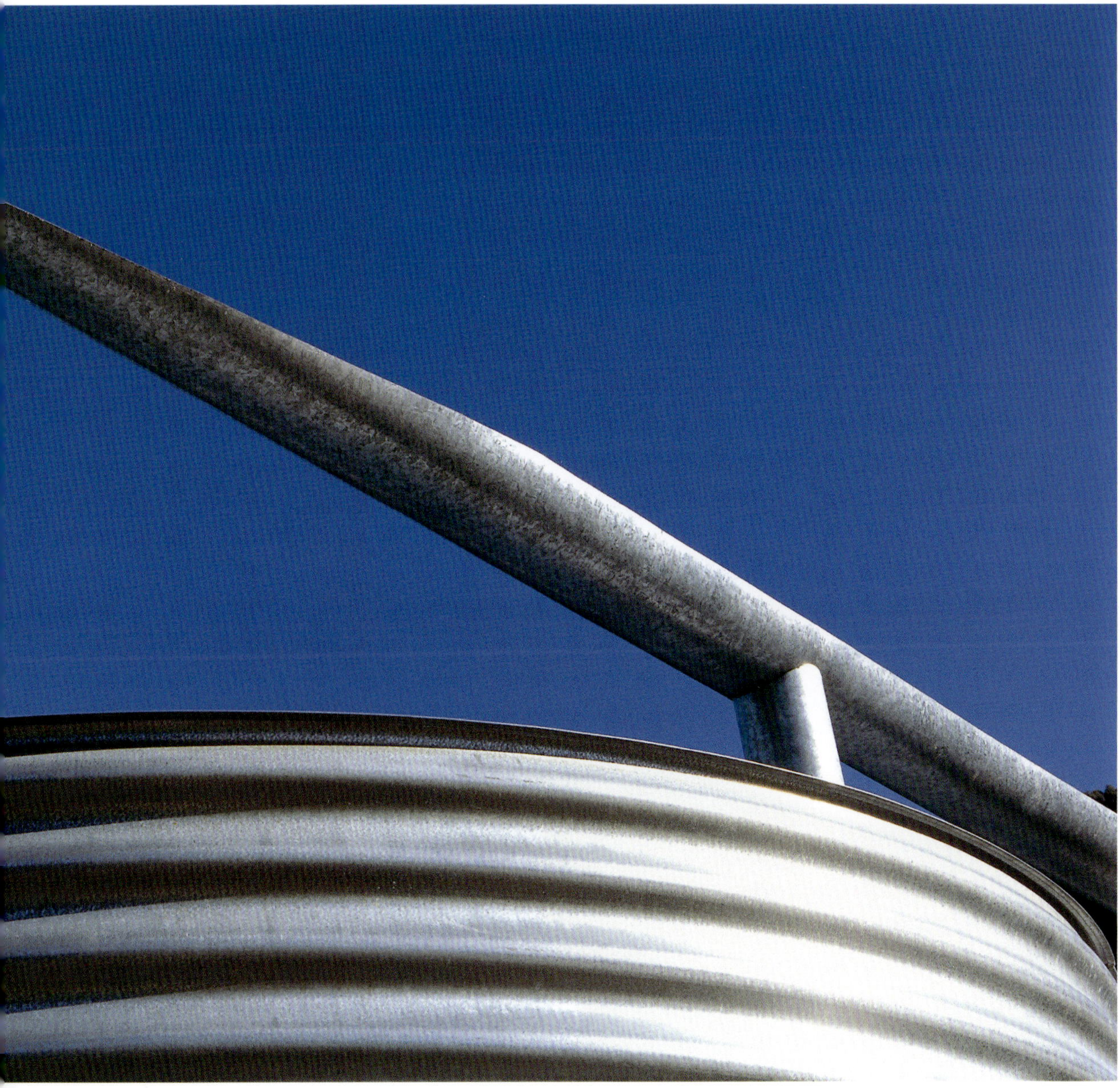

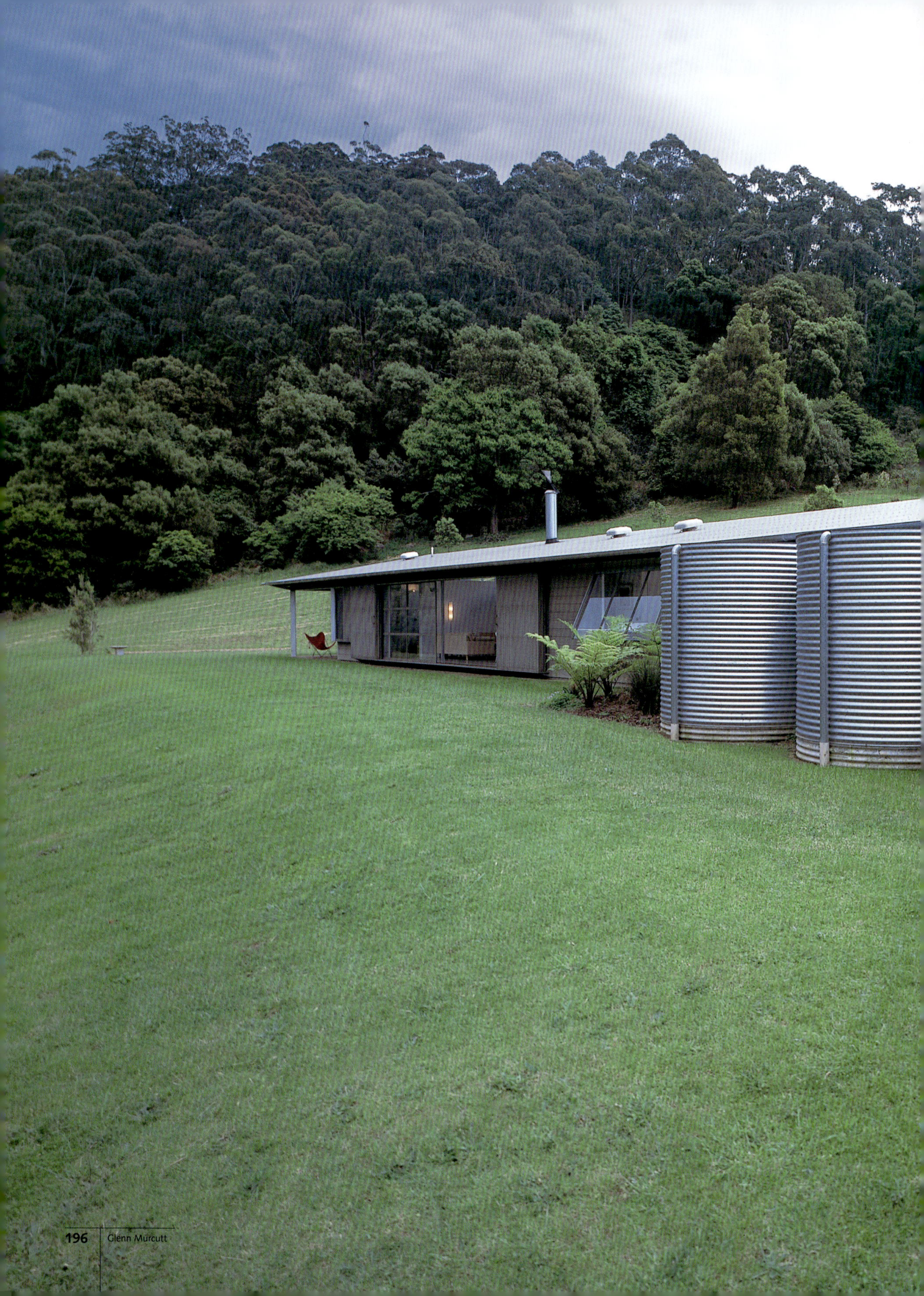

空の光と地面の色を反射させるために、マーカットは
波板鉄板のリブを水平に使う。

Murcutt uses corrugated galvanised steel
horizontally in order that its surfaces reflect both the
light of the sky and the colours of the ground.

マーカットの建築は、その核心的なテーマの検討や進化の継続により成り立っている。多くのプロジェクトに共通して、直線的な細長い住宅が、北の太陽と一番よい景色に向けて開かれる。したがって、フレッチャー＝ペイジ邸はこの型に当てはまらない。この住宅からの一番よい眺めは南方の、敷地を取り囲む木々が茂る峰への景色である。しかし、北からの光を入れるために、景観とは反対の方向へ勾配屋根の庇がもち上げられた。

この矛盾する敷地条件は、平面と断面を豊かなものにした。ここでは正面性は曖昧である。言い換えれば、北面の傾斜するガラス面と格子引戸は、南面とほぼ同じである。しかし南面では、主となる扉は掃き出しの引戸であり、開かれると居間と食堂の8m幅にわたる大きな開口となって、この部屋を屋外ベランダとして機能させる。2m強と背の低い扉と下がり天井は、遠くの丘への眺めを強調し、枠組みしている。

ここでマーカットは、住宅をランドスケープの形状に嵌め込んでいる。敷地の門からは、屋根を超えた先にある崖の、浸食によって樹木がない部分が見える。視線の軸は、屋根の最初の高いコーナーを通ることでさらに理由づけられている。内部からも同様にこの傷跡への視線は意識され、キッチンから南の開口を通る視線、主寝室のコーナー・ウィンドウを通る斜めの視線が計画された。

この住宅は、簡素で経済的につくられている。小さな部屋は、縦列に配置されたことと、高窓によって広がりが与えられた。また、予算の制約にもかかわらず、よい素材とディテールを使うことで、ゆったりとしたスケール感を出している。ここでの工法はまったく率直である。鉄の梁と柱の溶接、杉板張りの外壁は実直で飾り気がない。知的な厳格性と物理的な精密性を兼ね備えた建物であるのにかかわらず、気が置けない週末住宅となっている。

Fletcher-Page House

フレッチャー＝ペイジ邸

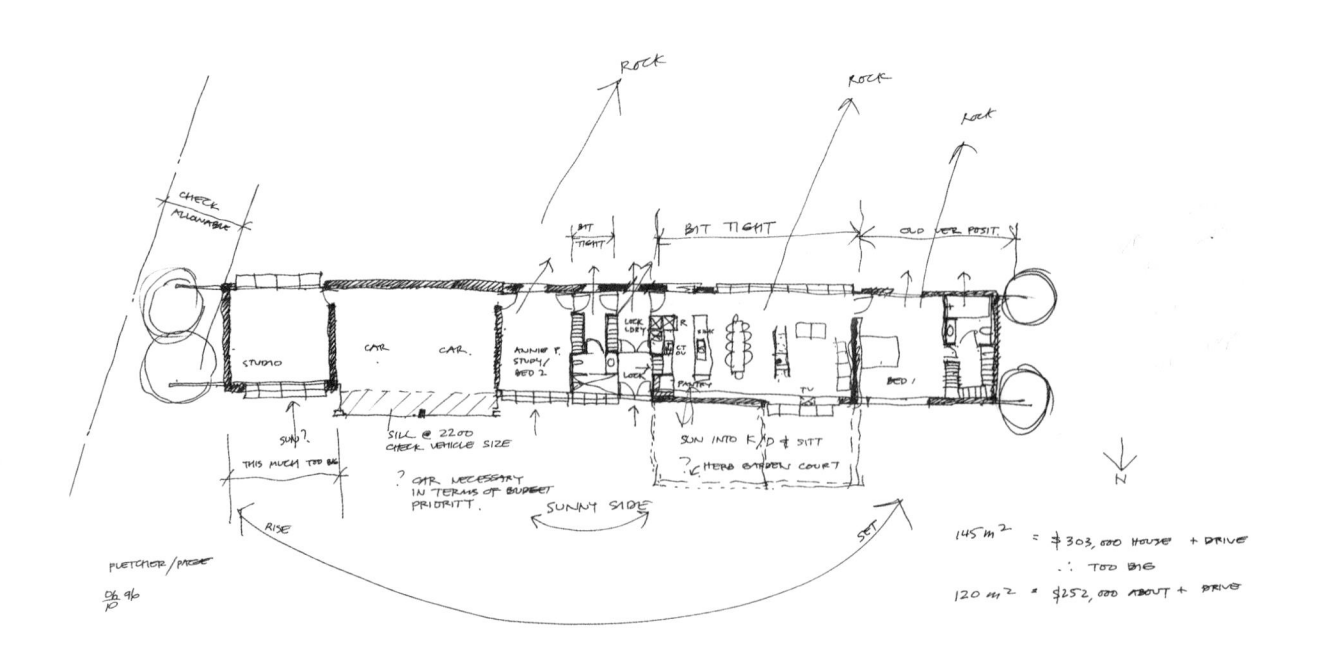

初期平面スケッチ（下が北）。崖の岩への視線を意識した窓の配置。
Early sketch plan with south facing windows oriented toward views of a distant rock face.

Murcutt's architecture is founded in the constant re-investigation and refinement of core themes. Typically, his houses are designed as slender rectangular volumes with one long side opening towards the northern sun and the most significant view. Fletcher-Page House, therefore, is untypical. Its primary view is to the south—the ridge of densely-wooded cliffs which encircles the site. Consequently, the inclined roof-plane, on this occasion, opens away from the view in order to admit controlled sunlight from the north.

This contradictory orientation creates a rich complexity in the plan and section. There is ambiguity as to which is the 'front,' and which the 'rear' side of the house. Indeed, the main elements of the northern wall—the angled glazing and sliding slat-shuttered windows—have approximately identical counterparts in the southern wall. To the south, though, the principal windows are full-height, and can be slid away to create an 8 meter wide opening—the full width of the sitting/dining room—making this room, effectively, a veranda. The low height of this opening—just over 2 meters—and the descending angle of the ceiling on this side of the house, sets up an intense view of the distant hillside, which it frames.

Murcutt has locked the building into the geometry of the landscape. From the gate that leads into the property a distinctive erosion scar is seen on the rock of the distant escarpment, and the axis of this view-line is reinforced by its coincidence with the corner high-point of the house roof, seen in the foreground. Internally, the kitchen is placed precisely on a view-line to the scar that is framed by the southern window opening, and the master bedroom views the same natural feature along a diagonal view-axis through its corner windows.

This is a very simply and economically-planned building. Its small size is contradicted by the 'enfilade' linkage of its rooms and their openness to the surroundings through the clerestory windows. Fine materials and detailing are achieved despite the modesty of the budget. The method of its making is absolutely explicit—the welds of its steel sections and plates, and the fixings of its cedar cladding boards are honestly expressed and unembellished—giving a sense of casual ease appropriate to its use as a weekend house, despite it being a work of intellectual rigour and physical precision.

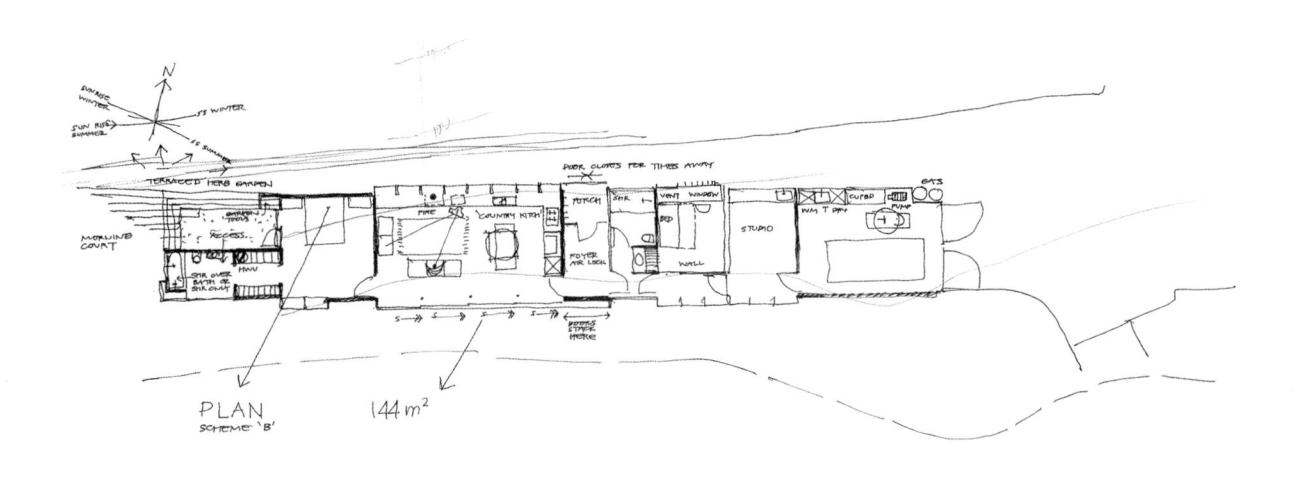

初期平面スケッチ（上が北）。ほぼ最終形の平面図だが、西端に午前中の太陽光があたる「朝庭」がある。
Sketch plan showing roughly the final arrangement but with a 'morning court' at the north west corner of the building.

Arthur and Yvonne Boyd Art Centre

アーサー&イヴォンヌ・ボイド・アートセンター

1996–99 ········· Riversdale, West Cambewarra, New South Wales
Collaborating architects: Reg Lark and Wendy Lewin

玄関庇は、ショールヘブン川への雄大な眺めを枠組みしている。
The entrance portico frames spectacular views of the Shoalhaven River.

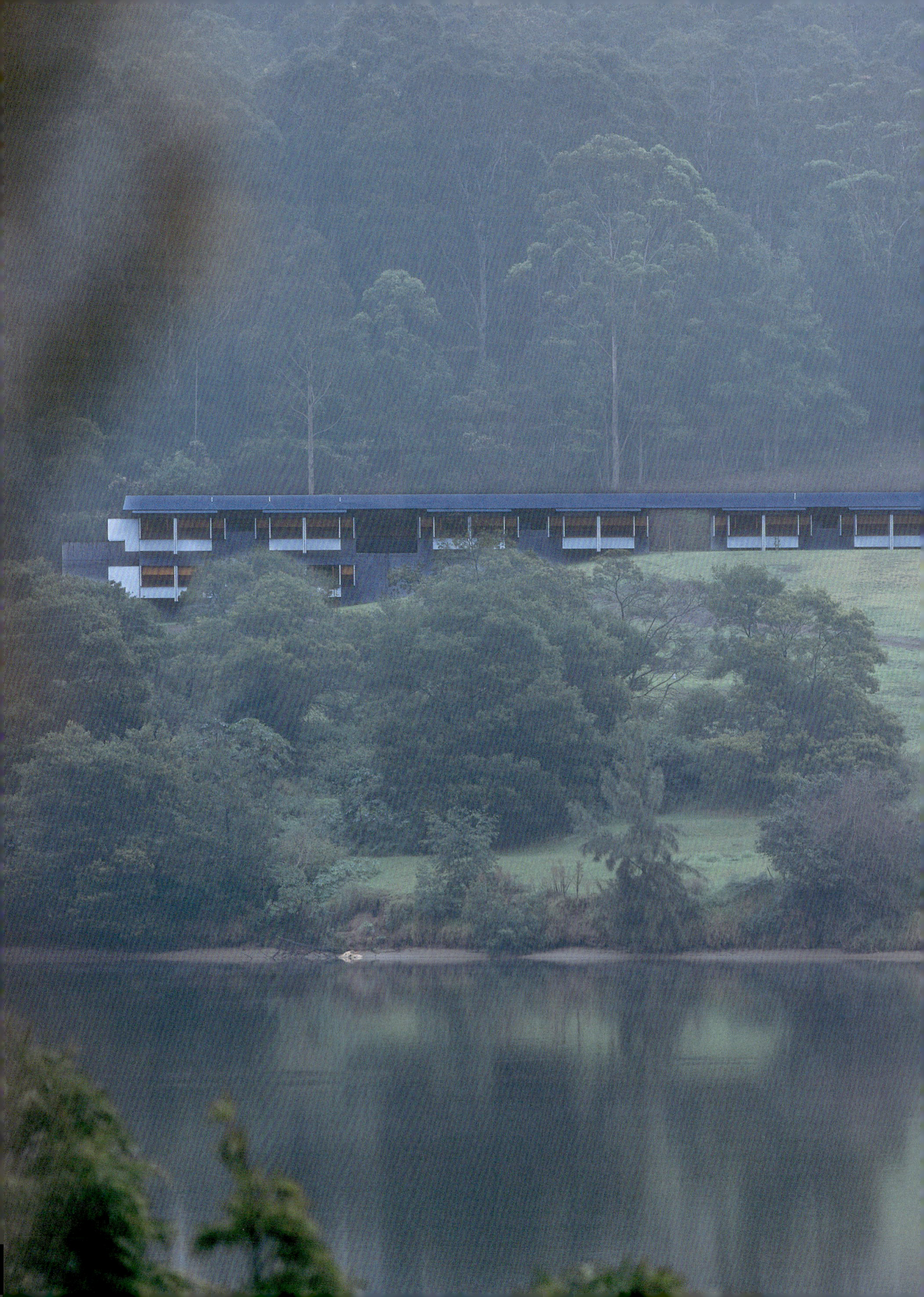

32人の生徒を収容する宿泊棟をもつ芸術家ための教育施設は、
絵画のような環境の中にある。

A picturesque landscape forms the setting of an educational facility for artists and up to thirty two students in dormitory accommodation.

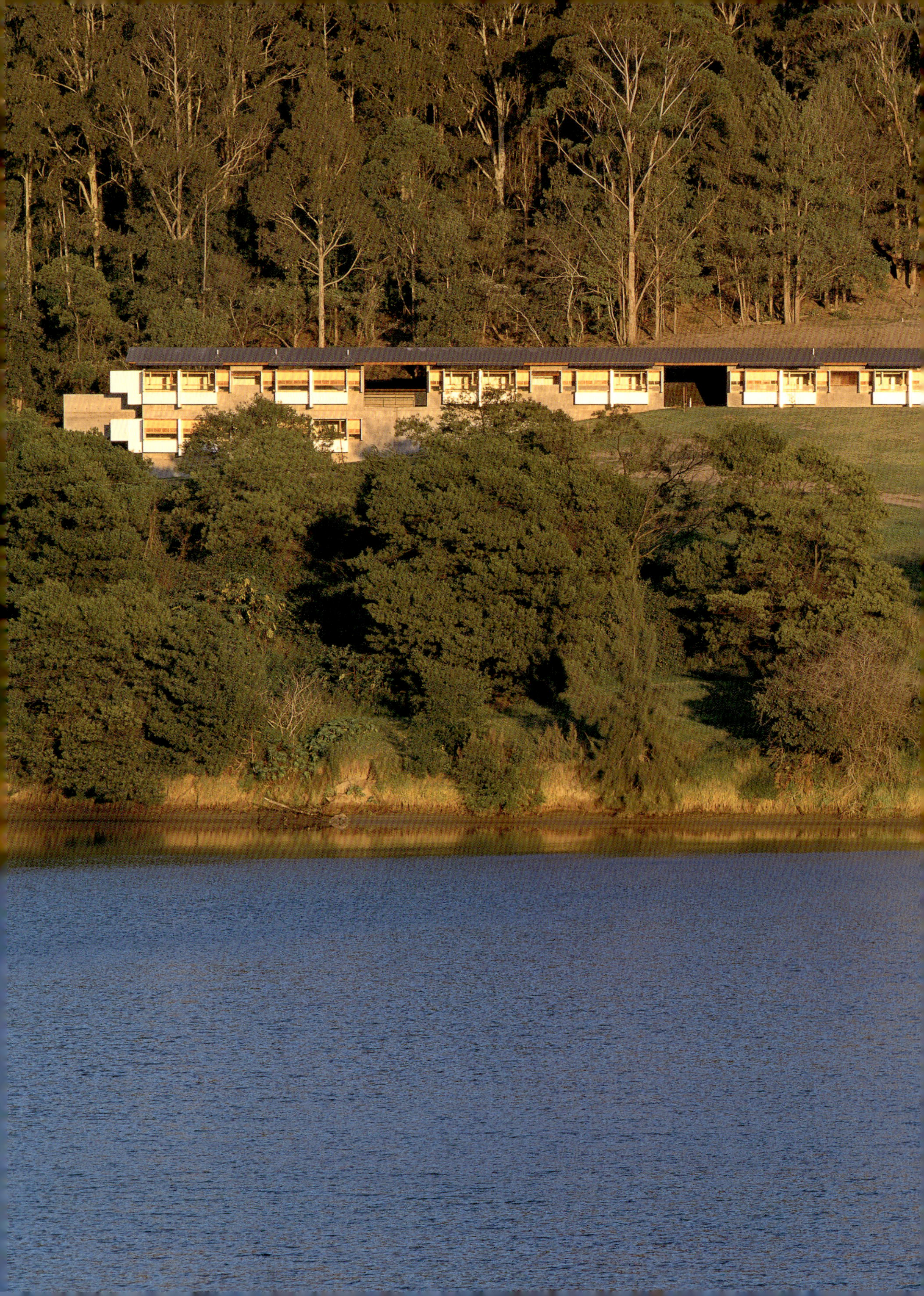

手入れされた農地と原生林の間にある建物からは、
前後へのランドスケープへの眺めがある。

Situated between cultivated farmland and natural bush,
the building frames views to both landscapes.

施設は、長いアプローチを形づくる既存の木造家屋に関連づけて配置された。
The project is situated in relation to three existing timber cottages which define and prolong the entry sequence.

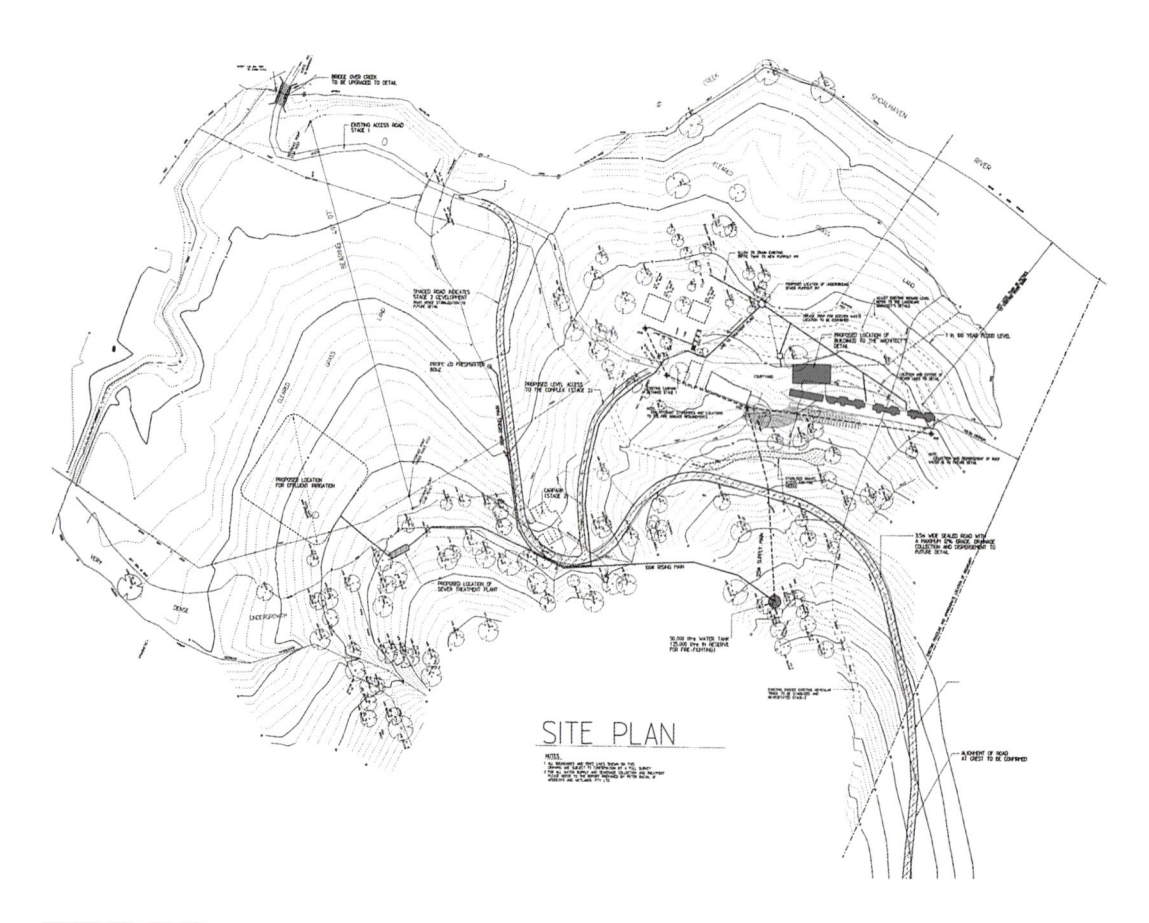

SITE PLAN

寝室と浴室の並列配置は、集会室の大きなスケールで
収束される。

The publicly scaled meeting hall anchors a linear
arrangement of sleeping and bathing spaces.

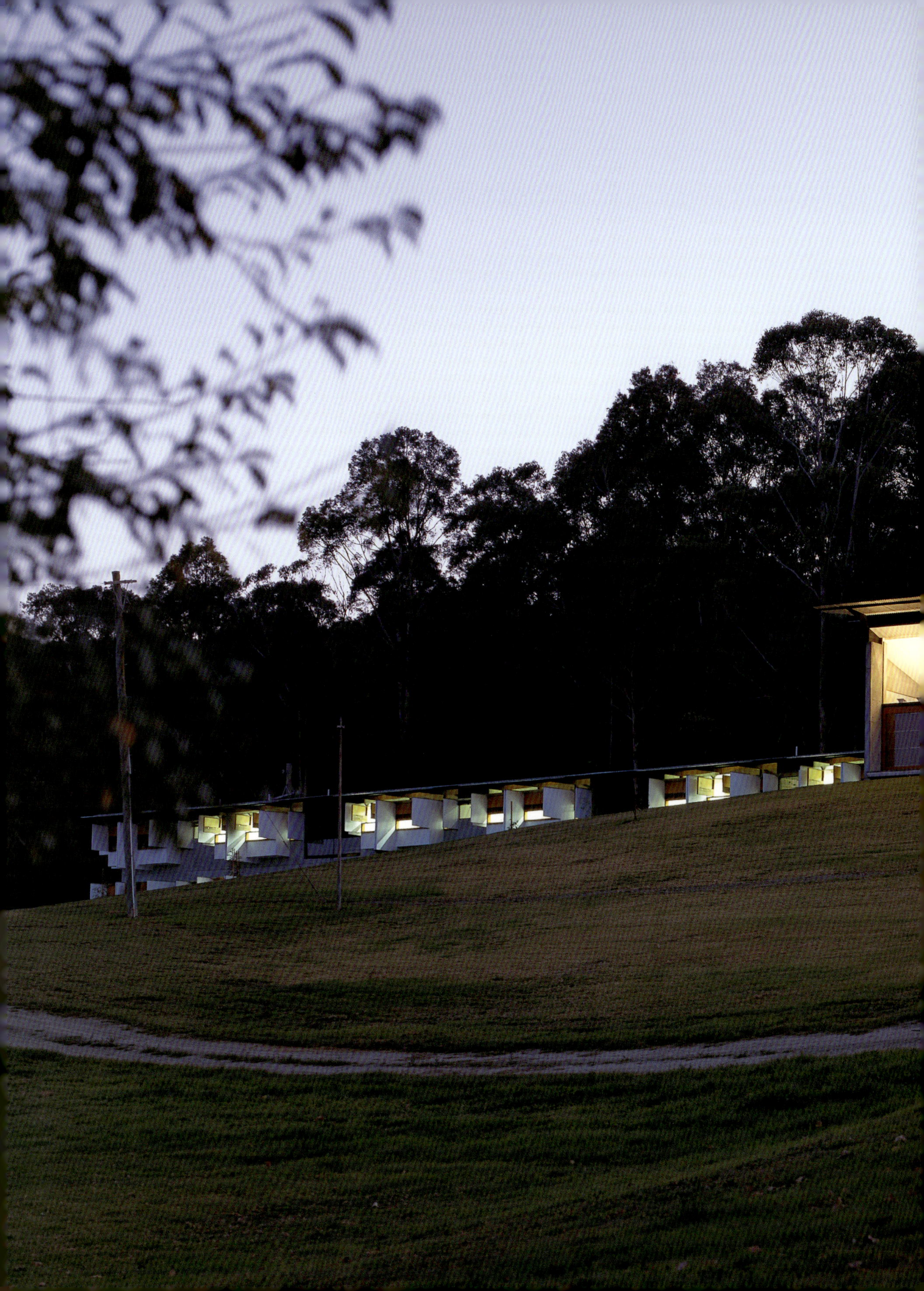

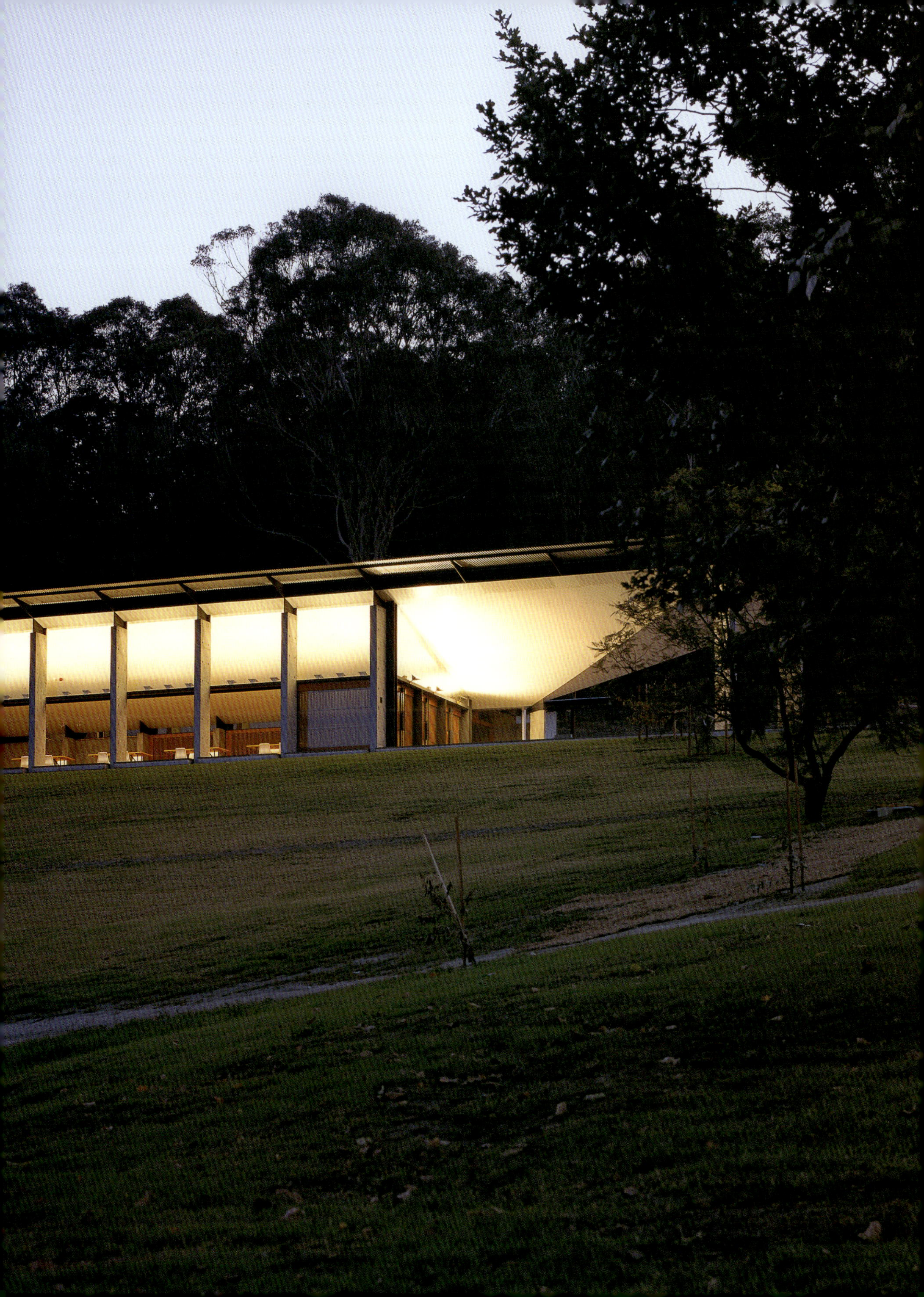

エントランスコートは屋外ステージであり、多目的集会室の大庇で覆われる。その威風堂々とした象徴的なかたちはサービス棟と対照的である。

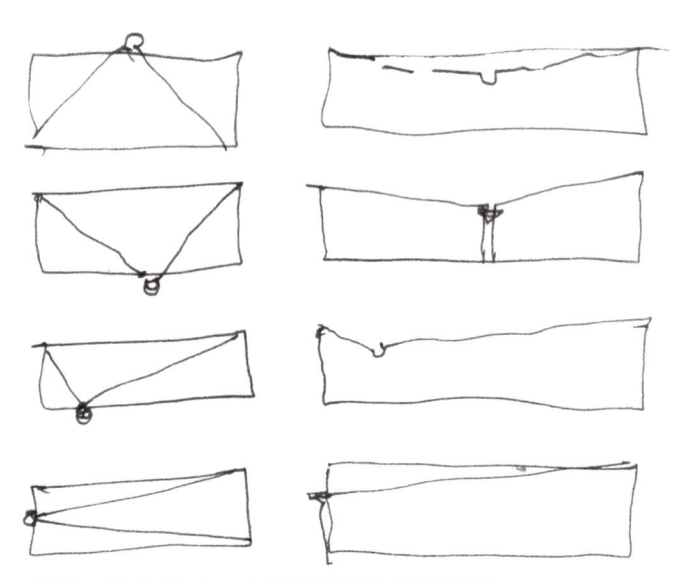

屋根面の折り曲げ方によってきまる谷樋と縦樋の位置のスタディ。
Sketches study the location of the gutter and downpipe in relation to folded roof forms.

The entrance court serves as a stage for a proposed amphitheater and is dominated by the large portico of the multi purpose hall. This elevated symbolic expression is in contrast with the scale of the service building.

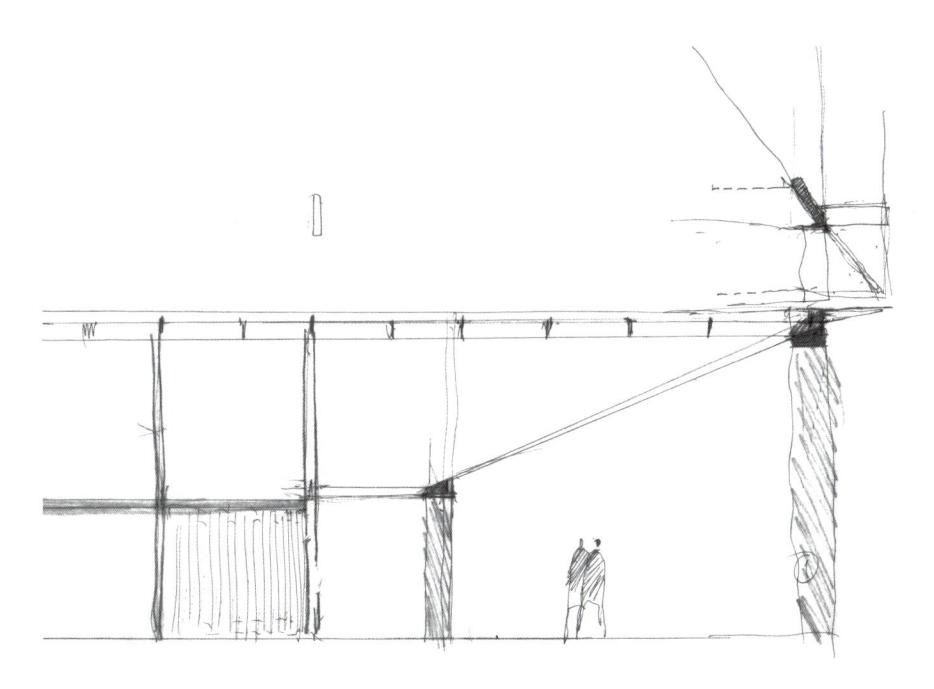

Glenn Murcutt

広い集会室は、ダイニングルームとして使われるとともに、
多人数の授業や、絵画の教室となる。

The large hall offers both a communal dining area and
a collective classroom/painting studio.

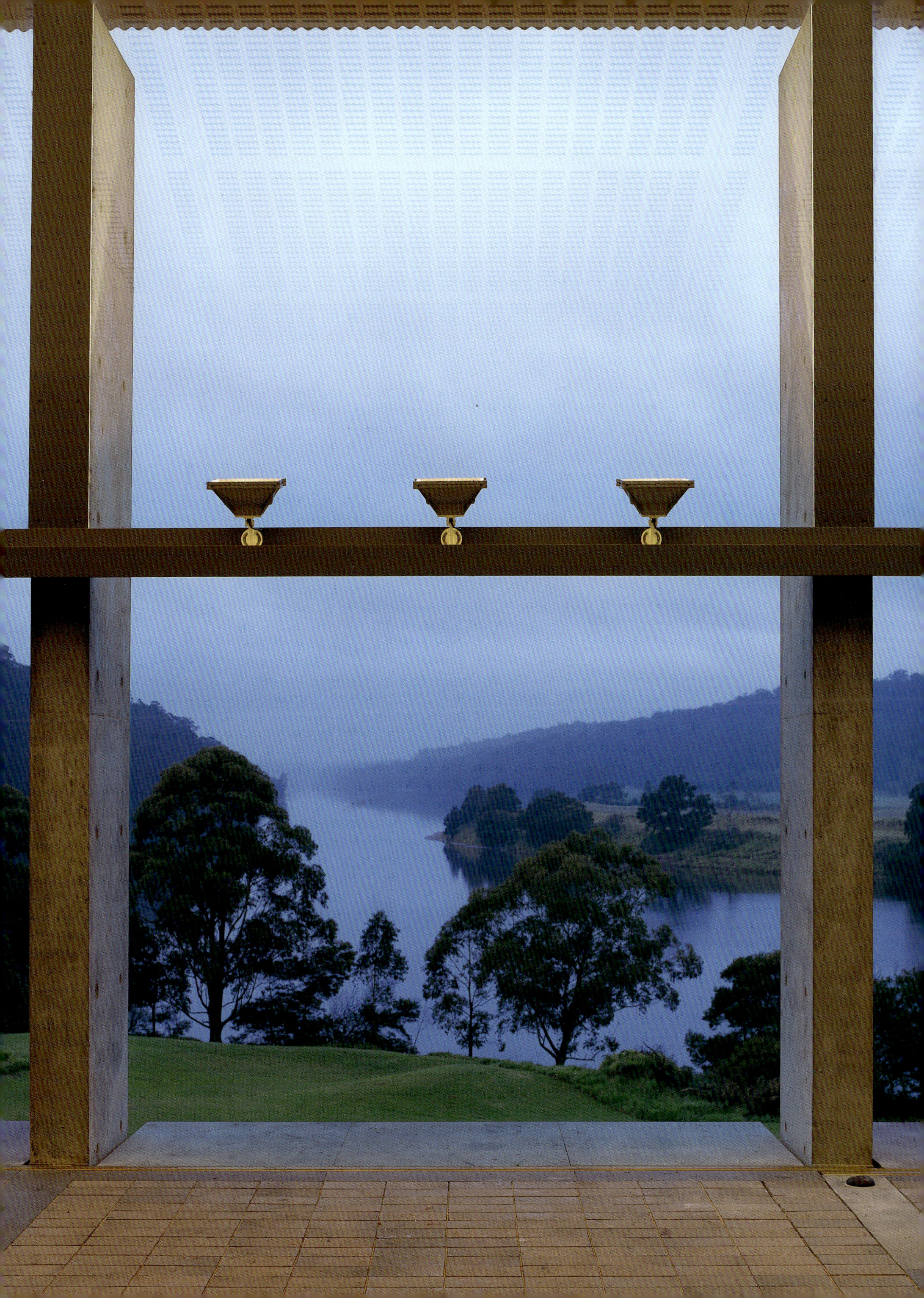

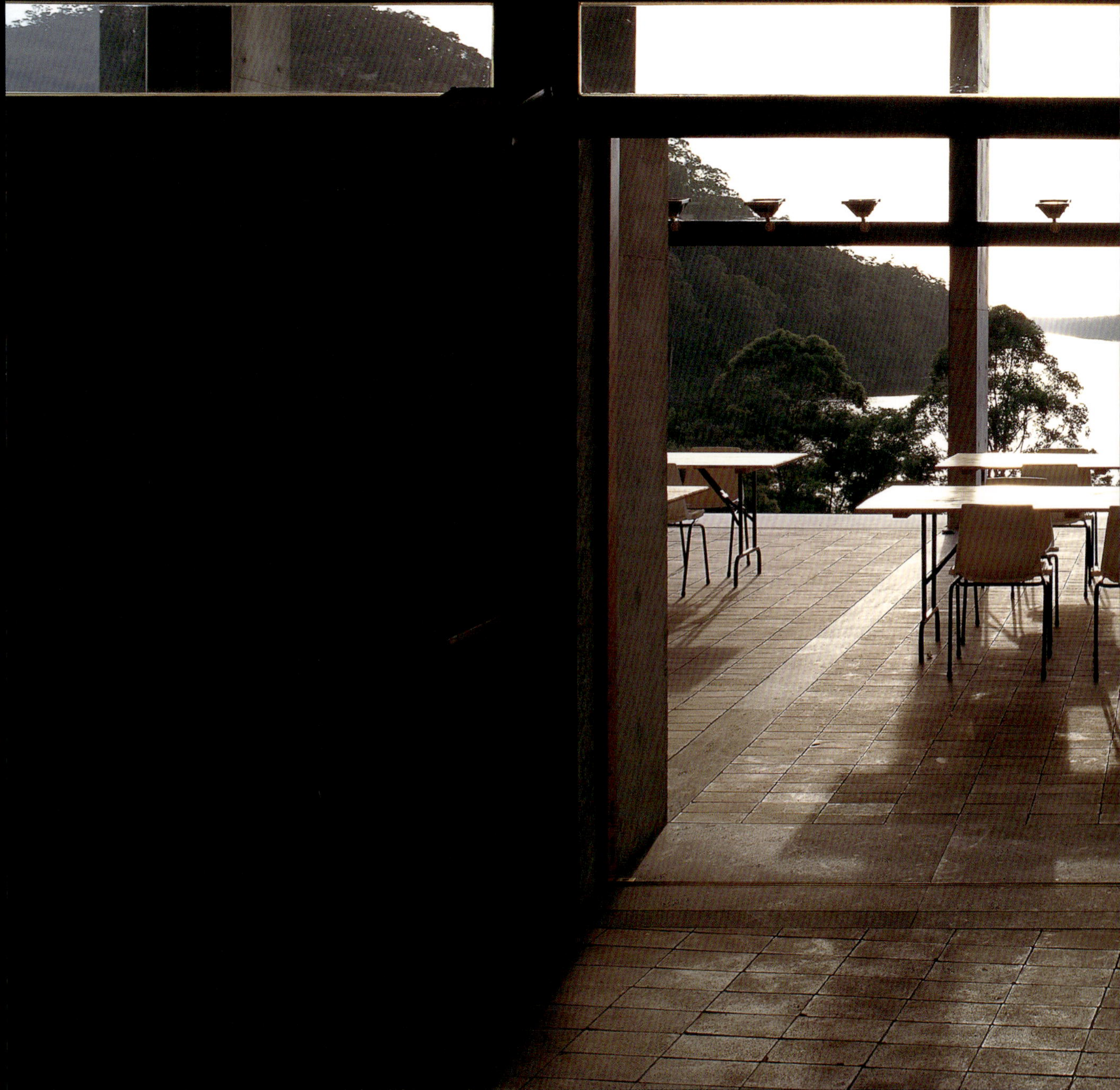

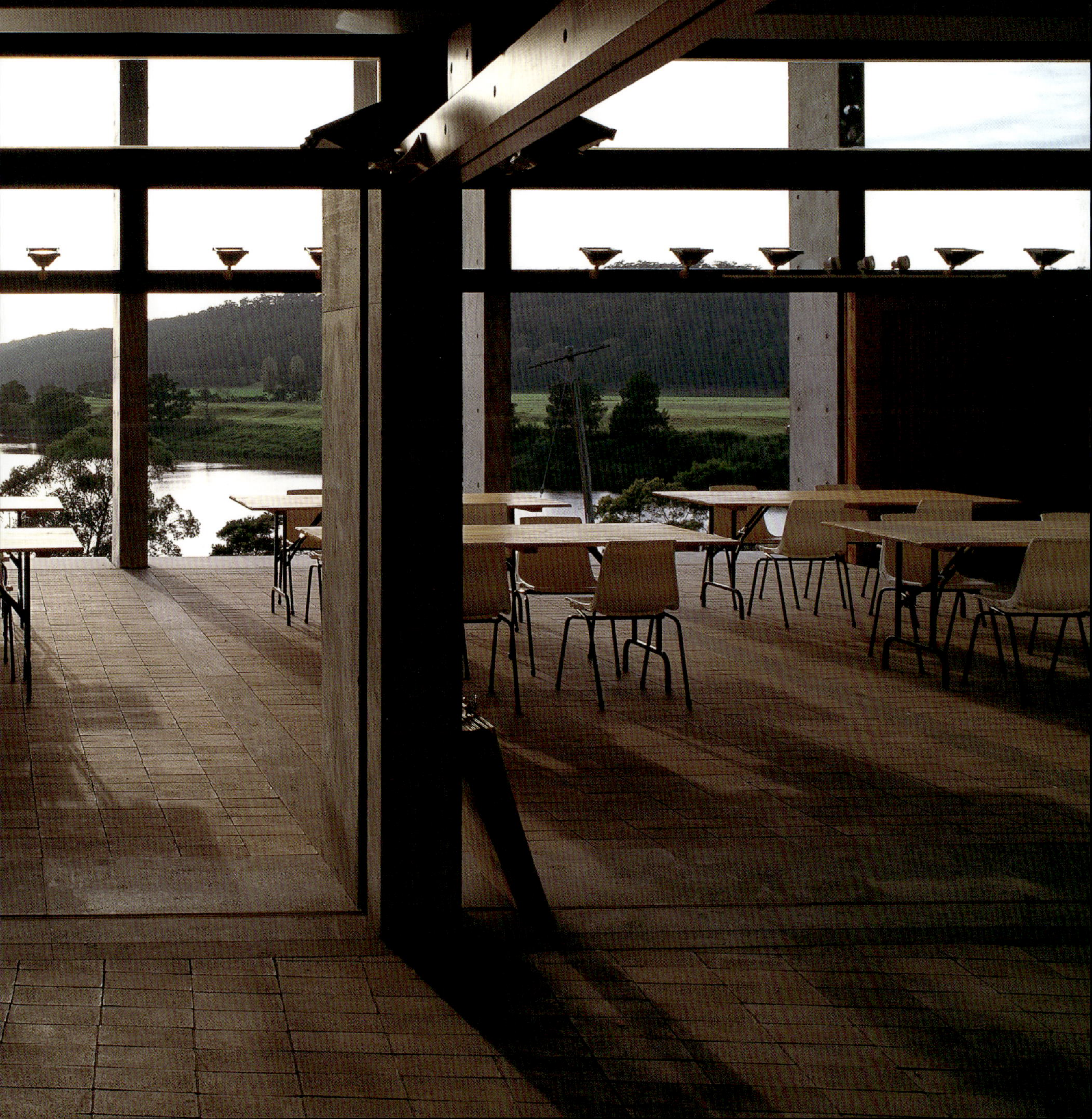

打ち放しコンクリート、合板、再利用の地元産ハードウッド、波板鉄板を使用して、注意深いディテールで、納まりよく組み立てられた。

The entire facility is carefully detailed and finely crafted using a palette of exposed concrete, plywood, recycled local hardwoods and corrugated metal.

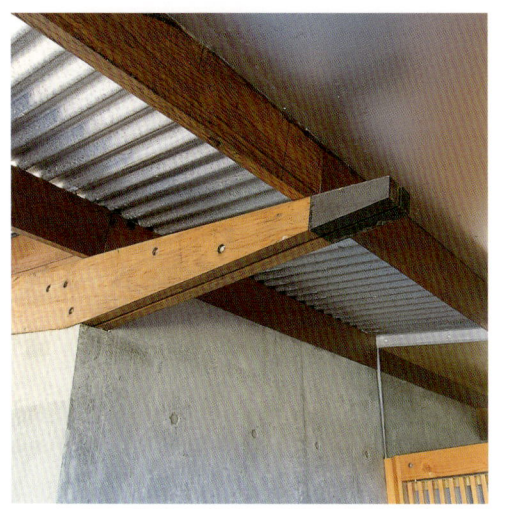

Glenn Murcutt | 217

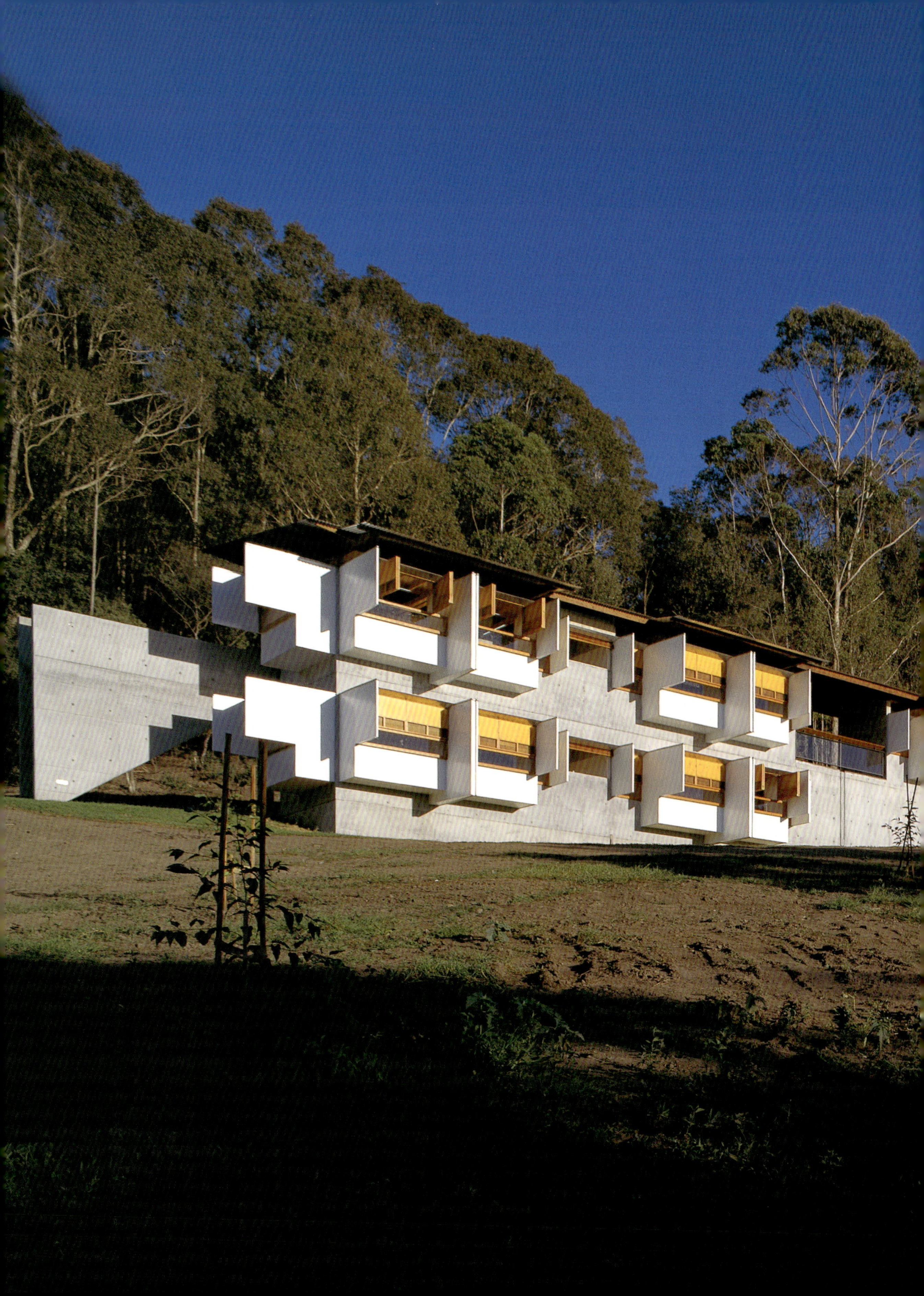

外部に付けられた合板の仕切り壁は、マリカ=アルダートン邸で最初に試みられたファサードが発展している。繰り返しにより、小さな建物の手法を公共のスケールへ変化させている。

External plywood blades develop the façade strategy first employed in the Marika-Alderton House. Clustering and repeating the bays gives a public scale to this previously domestic device.

塗装された合板の壁は、壁から飛び出た寝床を形づくり、独立性を与えてプライバシーを確保する。大きい仕切り壁は、部屋分割のための引戸を収納する。

Painted plywood blades externally frame each bed, and provide privacy. The larger blades completely accommodate a sliding door which can divide each room into two.

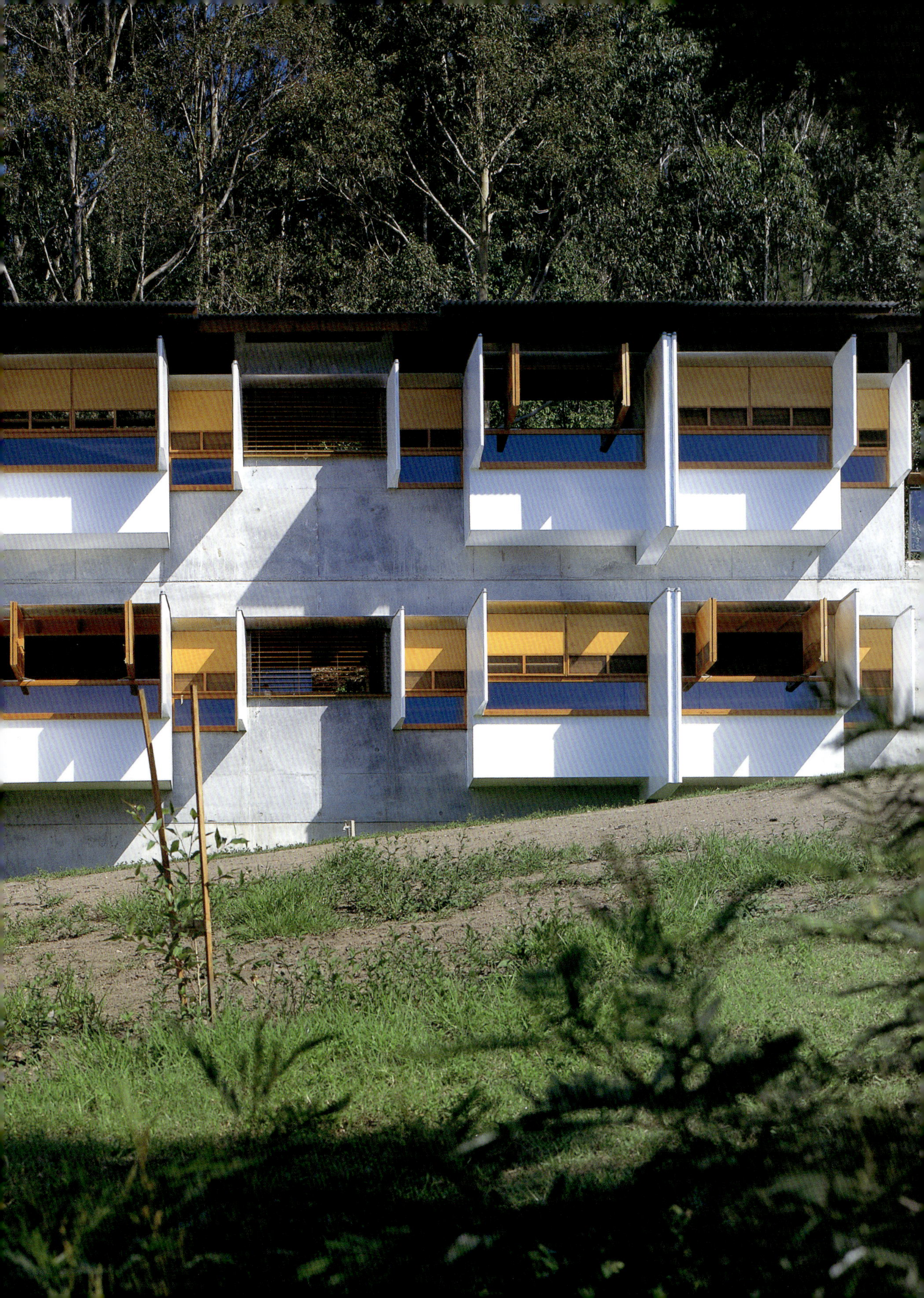

222 Glenn Murcutt

宿泊棟は、4人部屋が細長く並んだ構成である。外廊下でつなげられた共有バスルームを中心にしたユニットは、屋外ベランダを介して独立している。

The sleeping areas are treated as a linear arrangement of rooms, each accommodating four people. Situated along an open walkway and grouped around shared bathrooms, each cluster of rooms is separated from the next by a breezeway.

各寝床には、それぞれ独立した眺めの窓がある。ガラスが嵌められた上には木のパネル窓があり、軸回転して大きく開けるか、部分的に網戸の付いた窓で換気する。

Each bed has a personal view of the landscape. Fixed glazing is positioned below timber panels which pivot open or can be adjusted for screened ventilation.

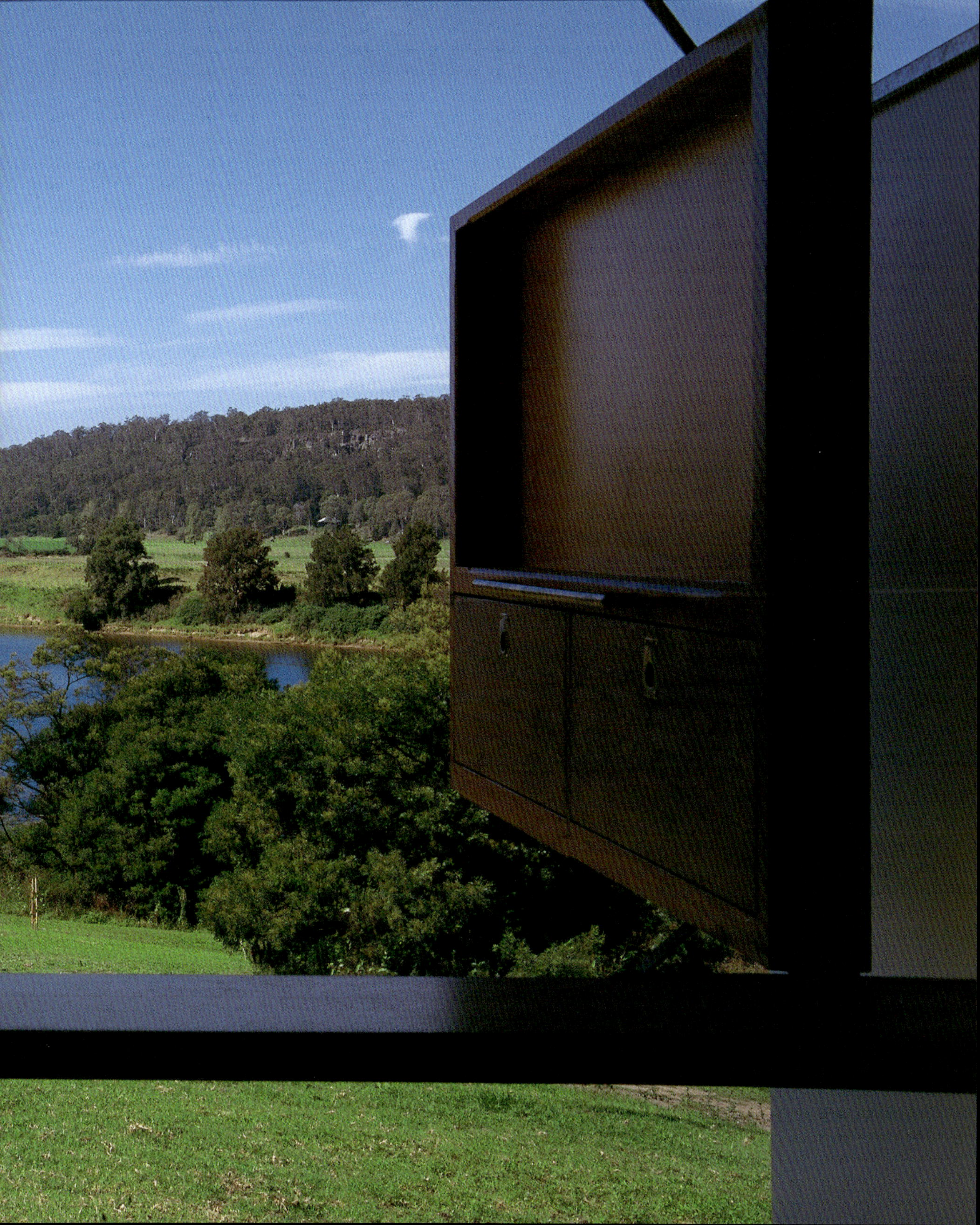

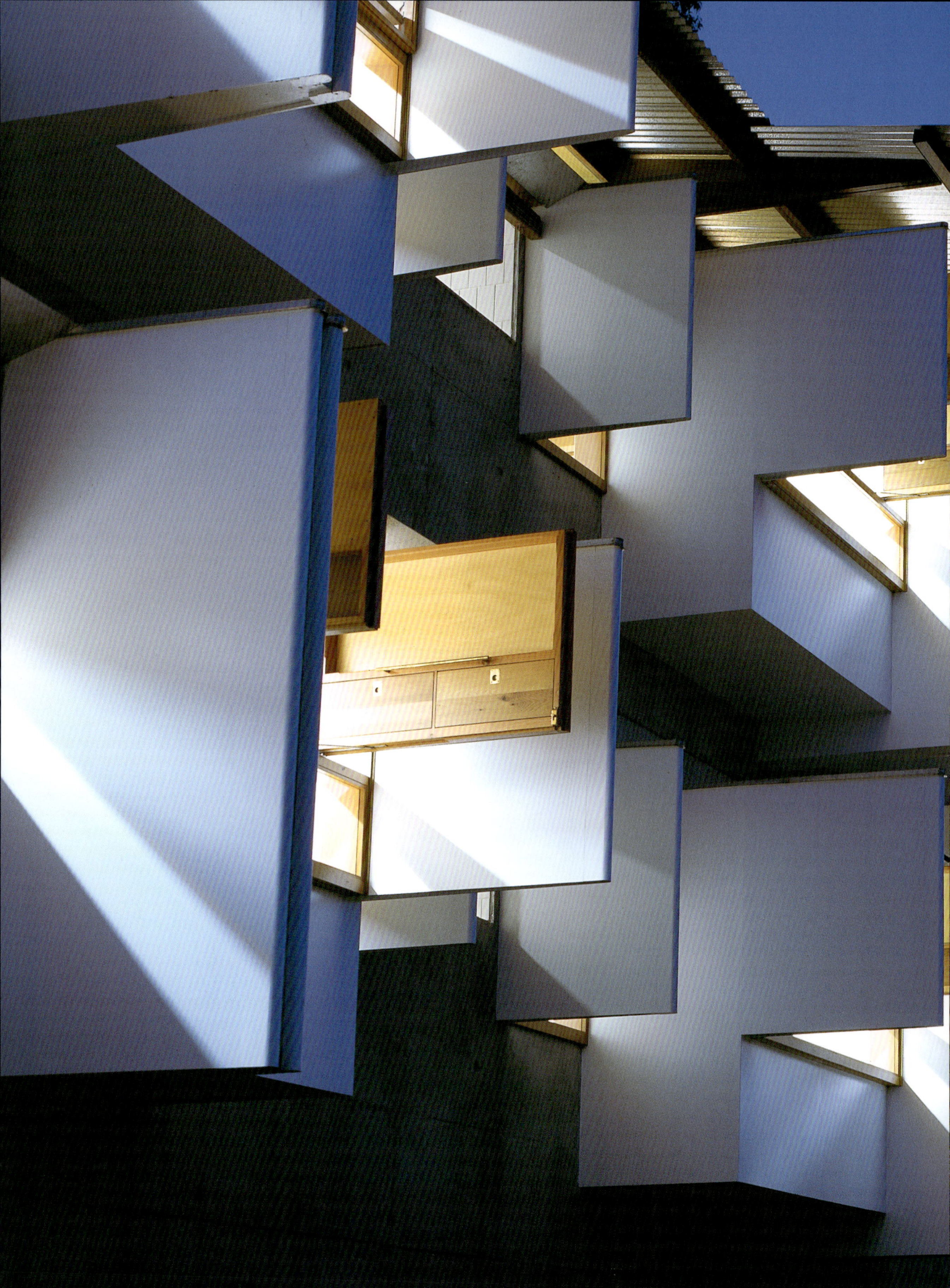

ベッドの広さがそのままヴォリュームとして壁から飛び出した寝床は、
滞在者を表す独立窓となり、東立面を形作る。

Precisely scaled according to the specific dimensions of a bed,
the external sleeping bays form individual window, which register
each occupant on the eastern façade.

Arthur and Yvonne Boyd Art Centre

アーサー＆イヴォンヌ・ボイド・アートセンター

オーストラリアの有名な画家アーサー・ボイドとその妻イヴォンヌにより、ショールヘブン川の渓谷にある土地が、彼らが興した美術財団へ遺された。その美しい自然環境の中へ、アーティストと美術学生のための研修施設をつくることが建築家に求められた。建物は農地と原生林の間にあり、建物のいくつかのバルコニーによって枠組みされた両側の景色の違いが強調されている。大きな集会室とキッチン、32人の生徒を収容できる宿泊室とシャワー室が建物を構成している。

既存の3棟の木造施設は長いアプローチを形づくり、駐車場、これらのコテージ、そして古いベランダを抜けると、大きく開けた広場へ辿り着く。川への素晴らしい眺めのあるエントランスコートは、斜面を利用して提案された屋外演技場(アンフィシアター)のステージでもあり、多目的に使われる集会室の大庇によって覆われている。その威風堂々とした象徴的なかたちは、並んで建つサービス棟の、ドアや手洗い場の低いカウンターとは明らかに対照的である。

この中心施設では、住宅の先例のように、空間を機能分けする断面が採用され、雄大な景色に面する大きな集会室が、動線によって裏のサービスと分割されている。ここで要素の大きさは建物の公共性に比例している。

宿泊棟は、4人部屋が並んだ細長い構成である。外廊下でつなげられた共有バスルームを挟んだ各部屋は、ベランダを介して独立している。ベッドの広さがそのままヴォリュームとなった寝床は、それぞれの眺めをつくる窓をもつ。ガラスが嵌められた上には木のパネル窓があり、軸回転して大きく開けるか、網戸の付いた窓を開けて風を入れる。塗装された合板の仕切り壁は、寝床を形づくり視線を遮る。大きい仕切り壁は、部屋分割のための引戸を収納する。このファサードは、マリカ＝アルダートン邸で最初に試みられた出窓の発展形であると言える。東立面では出窓を繰り返すことにより、当初は小さな建物の手法だったものを、ベッド（とそこに寝る子ども）に象徴性を与えつつ、公共的なスケールへと発展させている。

The distinguished Australian artist Arthur Boyd and his partner Yvonne donated this land in the Shoalhaven River valley for use by their Education foundation. The architects were commissioned to propose an arrangement of facilities in this spectacular landscape, a retreat for artists and students. Located between cultivated farmland and natural bush, the building emphasises the differences of each condition, framing views to both. It provides a large meeting hall with kitchen, bathing facilities and shared accommodation for up to thirty two students.

Three existing timber cottages prolong an entry sequence where one moves from a car-park between the dwellings and finally arrives at a large open platform via an old veranda. This entrance court with striking river views serves as a stage for a proposed landscaped amphitheater and is dominated by the large portico of the multi purpose hall. The elevated ambition of this arrangement contrasts with the scale of the entry door and utility of the low bench with washbasin.

The bipartite section employed in previous houses informs the organisation of the main pavilion where a large hall oriented toward the significant view is separated from its rear service facilities by a circulation zone. Here the greater scale acknowledges a more public situation.

The sleeping areas are treated as a linear arrangement of rooms, each accommodating four people. Located along an open walkway and grouped around shared bathrooms, each cluster is separated from the next by a breezeway. Precisely scaled according to the specific dimensions of the beds, each sleeping bay forms a window framing a personal view of the landscape. Fixed glazing is positioned below timber panels which pivot open or can be adjusted for screened ventilation. Painted plywood blades externally bracket each bed, and provide privacy. The larger blades accommodate a sliding door which can divide each room into two. The system is a development of the façade strategy employed in the Marika-Alderton House. Clustering and repeating the bedroom bays on the eastern façade gives a public scale to this previously domestic device whereby each bed (and implied child) is given symbolic presence.

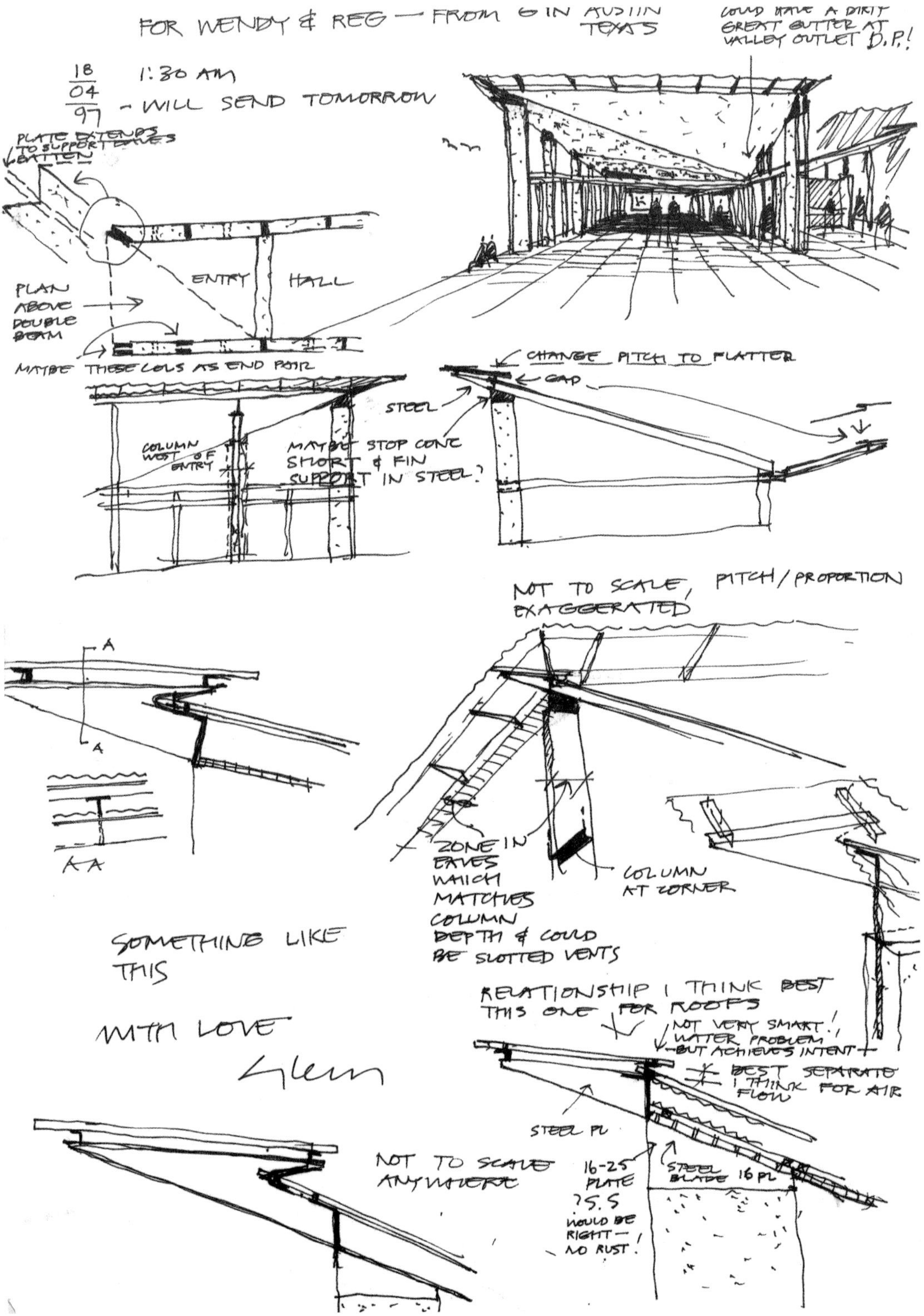

FOR WENDY & REG — FROM G IN AUSTIN TEXAS
COULD HAVE A DIRTY GREAT GUTTER AT VALLEY OUTLET D.P.!
18/04/97
1:30 AM
- WILL SEND TOMORROW
PLATE EXTENDS TO SUPPORT EAVES BATTEN
ENTRY HALL
PLAN ABOVE DOUBLE BEAM
MAYBE THESE COLS AS END PAIR
CHANGE PITCH TO FLATTER
GAP
STEEL
COLUMN WEST OF ENTRY
MAYBE STOP CONC SHORT & FIN SUPPORT IN STEEL?
NOT TO SCALE, PITCH/PROPORTION EXAGGERATED
A
A
AA
ZONE IN EAVES WHICH MATCHES COLUMN DEPTH & COULD BE SLOTTED VENTS
COLUMN AT CORNER
SOMETHING LIKE THIS
WITH LOVE
Glenn
RELATIONSHIP I THINK BEST THIS ONE FOR ROOFS
NOT VERY SMART! WATER PROBLEM BUT ACHIEVES INTENT
BEST SEPARATE I THINK FOR AIR FLOW
STEEL PL
NOT TO SCALE ANYWHERE
16-25 PLATE ?5.5 WOULD BE RIGHT — NO RUST!
STEEL BLADE 16 PL

House in the Southern Highlands

サザンハイランドの住宅

1997−2001··········Kangaloon, New South Wales

住宅への南のアプローチ道路からは、長さ80mの彎曲した金属板が重なり合って見える。空の光が反射して、前面に新たにつくられた池の波紋に呼応する。

From the southern approach-road, the house appears as an eighty-meter long layering of curved metallic forms, reflecting the light of the sky and echoing the shining surface of the newly-created lake in the foreground.

長い彎曲した波板鉄板の覆いが、冬期の寒さの厳しい南西の
卓越風から家を守る。

A long, curved, corrugated steel shield protects the house from the prevailing south-westerly winds which are often severe, and harshly cold in winter.

重さを感じさせない光輝く抽象的なカーブをもつ南面とは
対照的な北面。日除けのシャッターによりメリハリがつけら
れ、スレート貼りの礎石が地面の上に重厚に立つ。

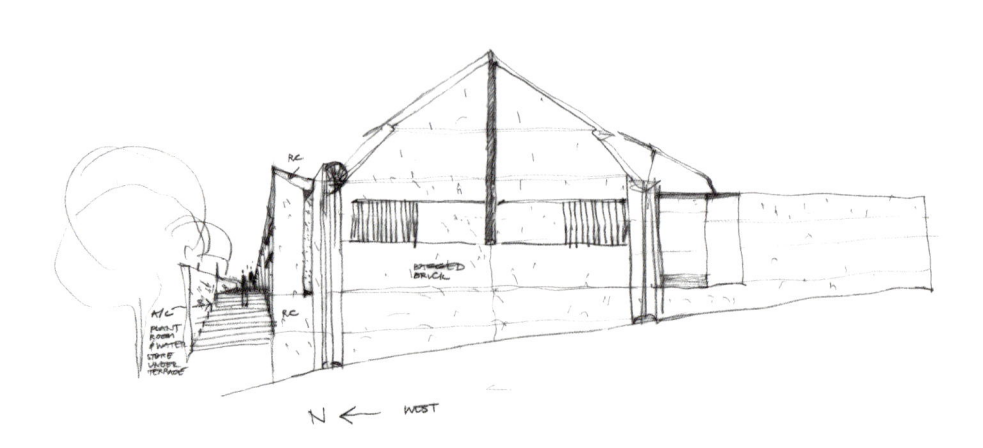

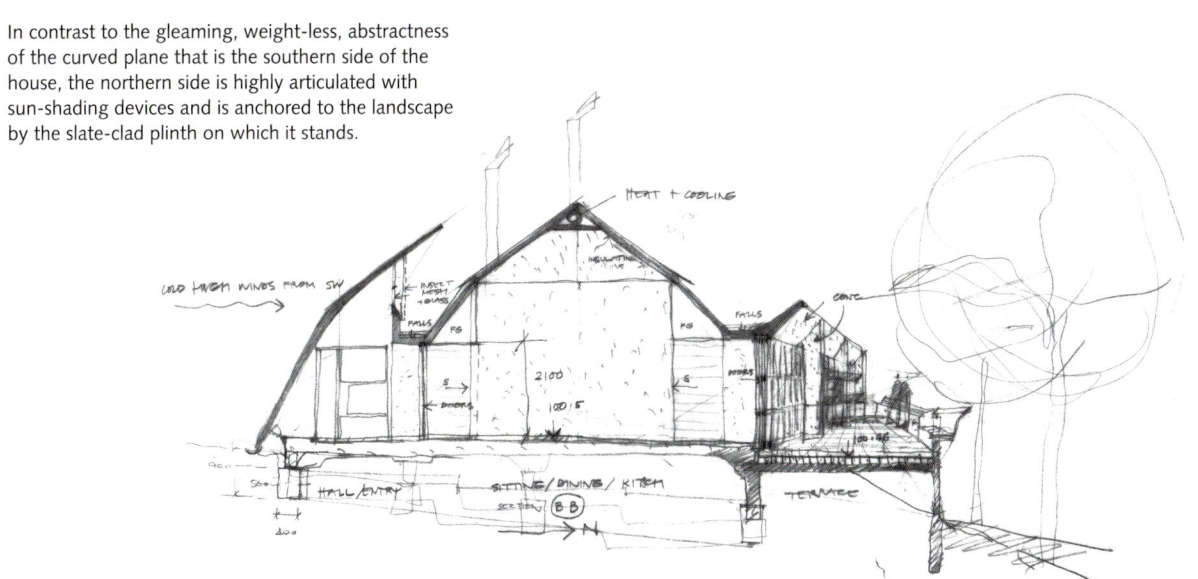

In contrast to the gleaming, weight-less, abstractness of the curved plane that is the southern side of the house, the northern side is highly articulated with sun-shading devices and is anchored to the landscape by the slate-clad plinth on which it stands.

植えられた広葉樹は将来、テラスを覆って日陰をつくる。
冬には深い庇がテラスを冷たい南西の風から守る。

The young deciduous trees will grow to enclose and
shade the living room terrace, which is protected from cold
south-west winds by the deeply-projecting canopy.

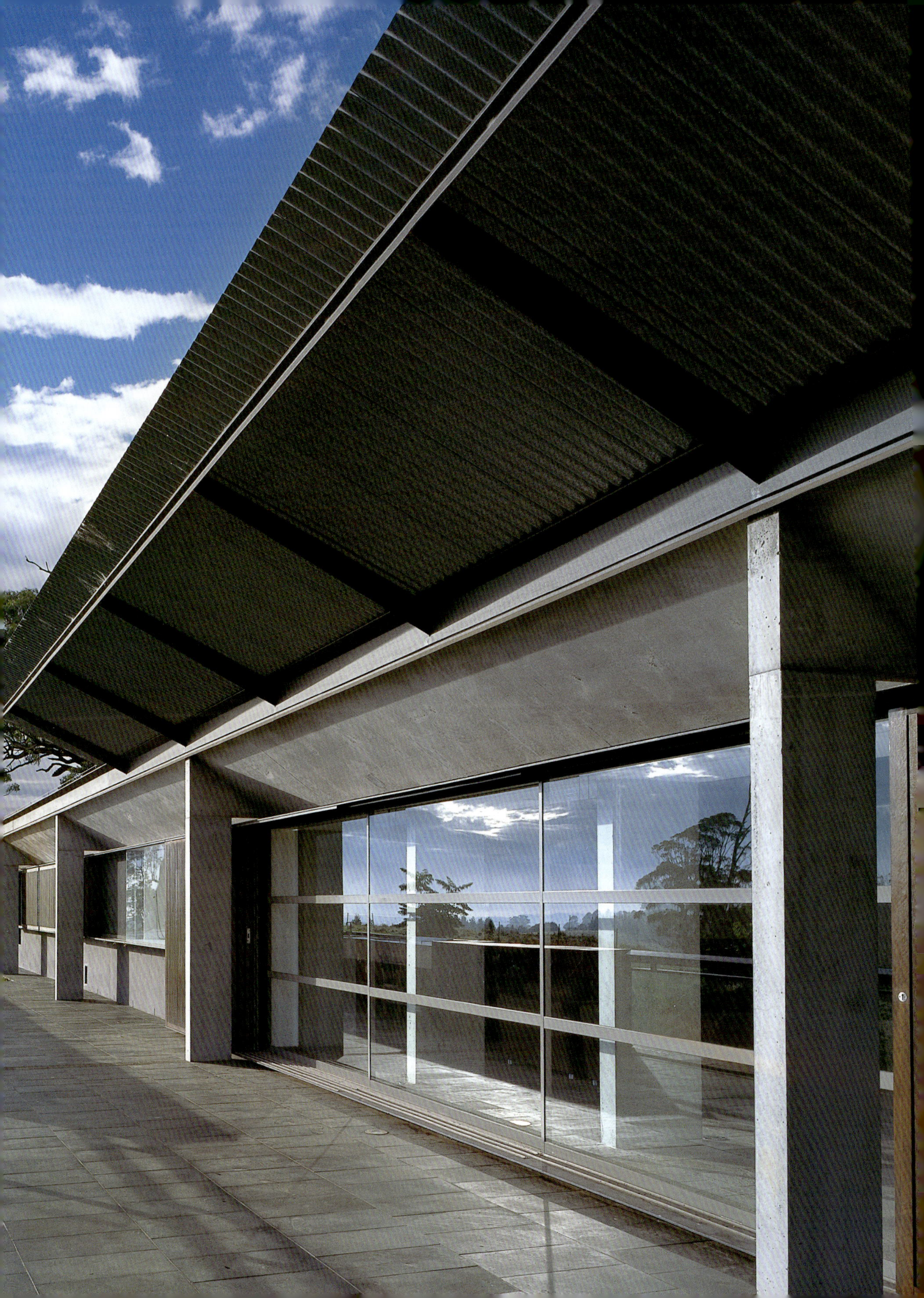

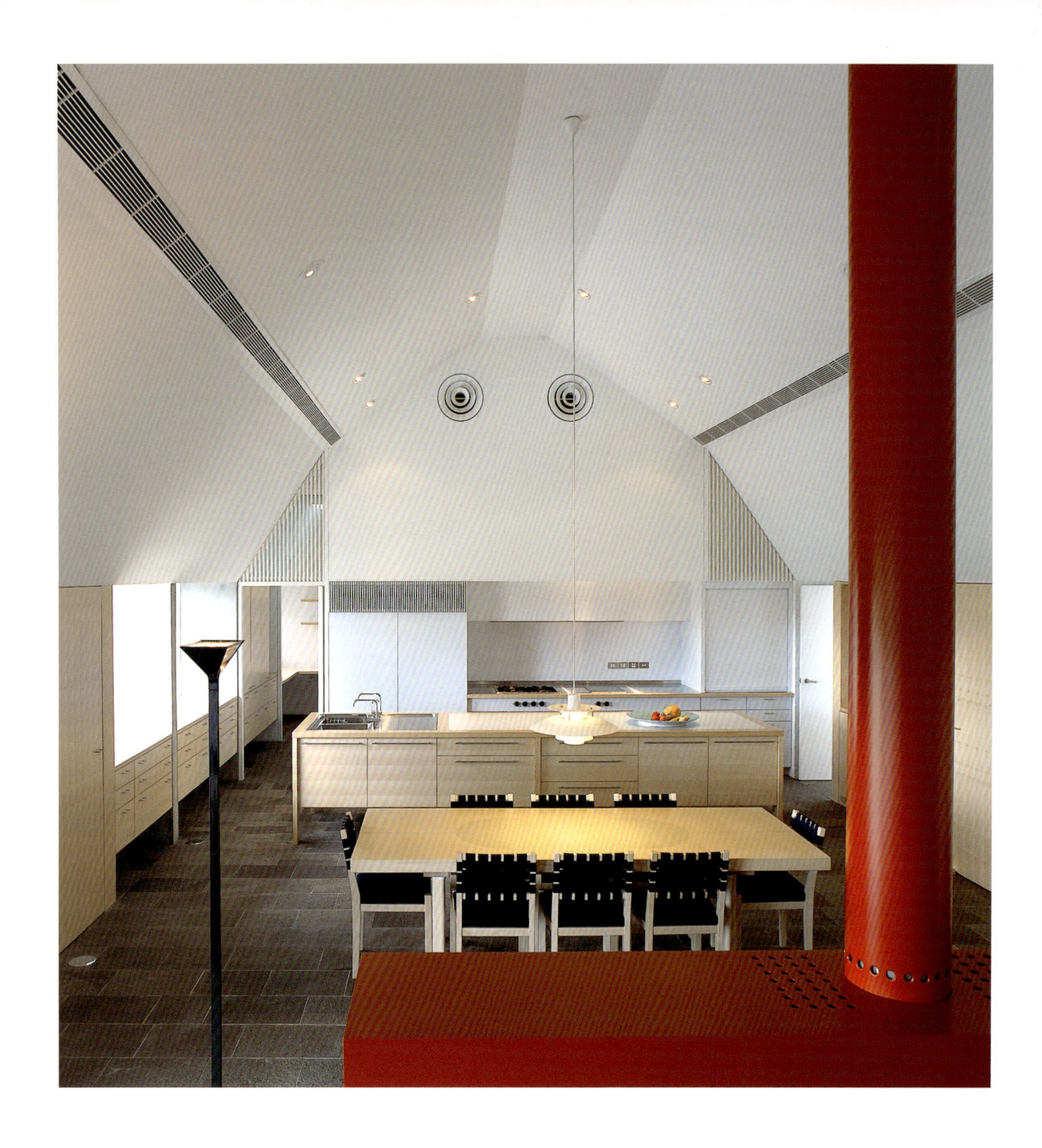

背の高い納屋のような室内は、閉じた空間であることと、冬の風からの防護であることを強調する。暖かい日には、ガラス戸を完全に引き、居間とテラスを、屋外と室内が1つになった大きな場所として機能させる。

The tall interior spaces give a strong sense of enclosure and protection from the winter winds. On temperate days the glass doors can be fully opened to unite the sitting room with the terrace, making a single large inside/outside space.

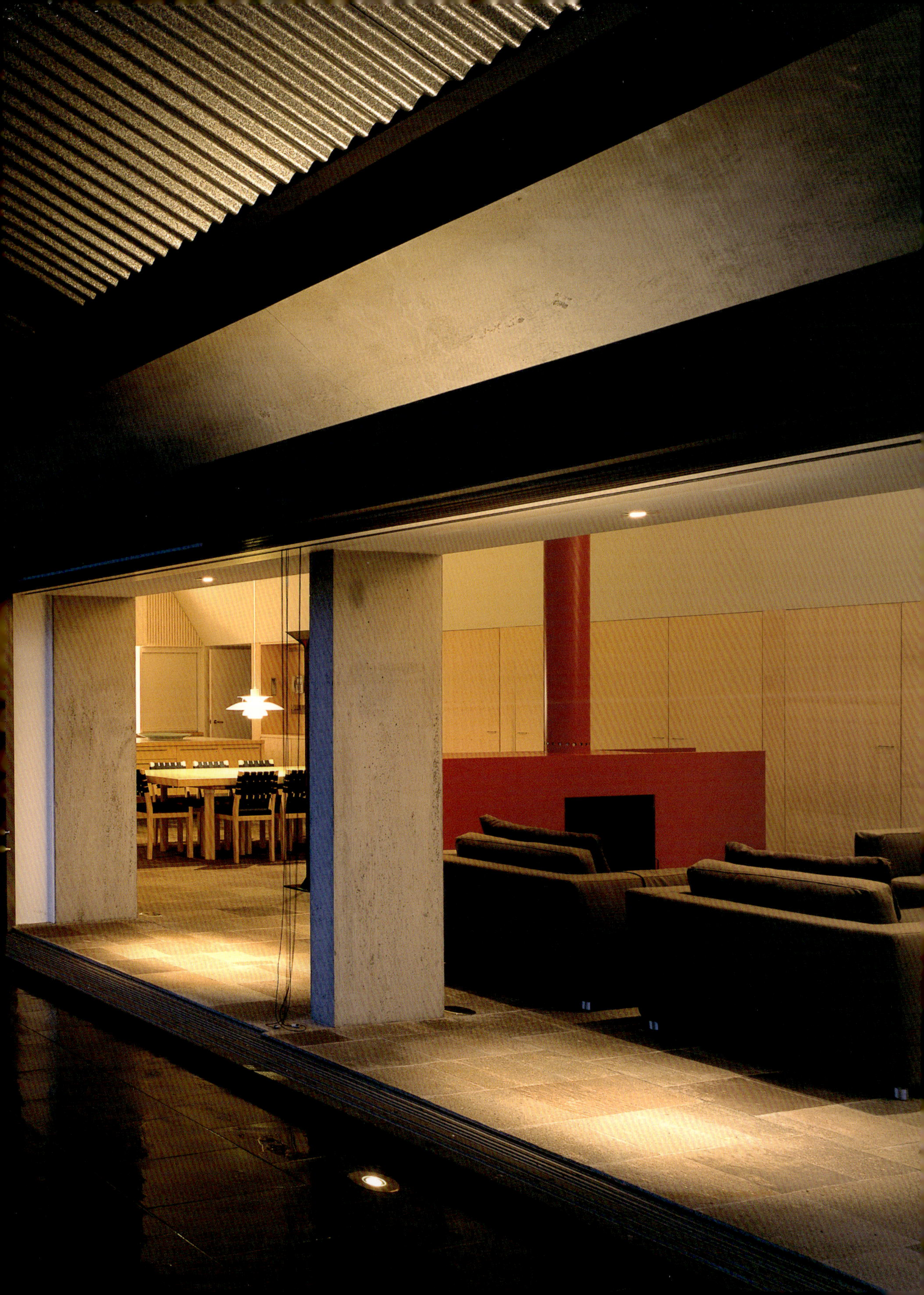

前庭を通り、風除け覆いの内側である廊下へと続く。
ガラリアは、その長さだけ続く北向きのハイサイドライトからの
光で明るく照らされている。

The entrance court leads to an internal galleria, formed
by the inside-face of the wind-shield. The space is side-
lit along its length by high level, north-facing windows.

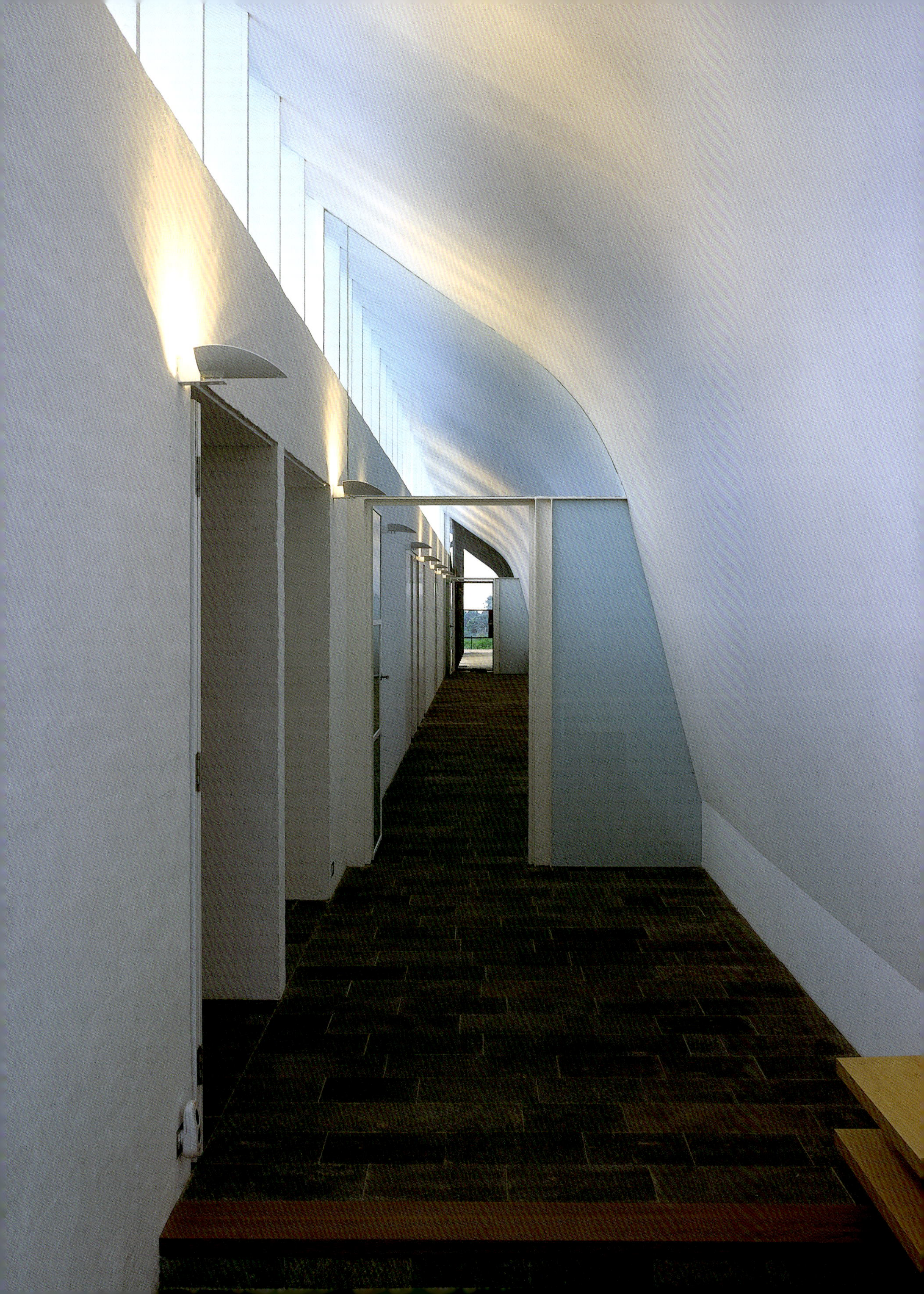

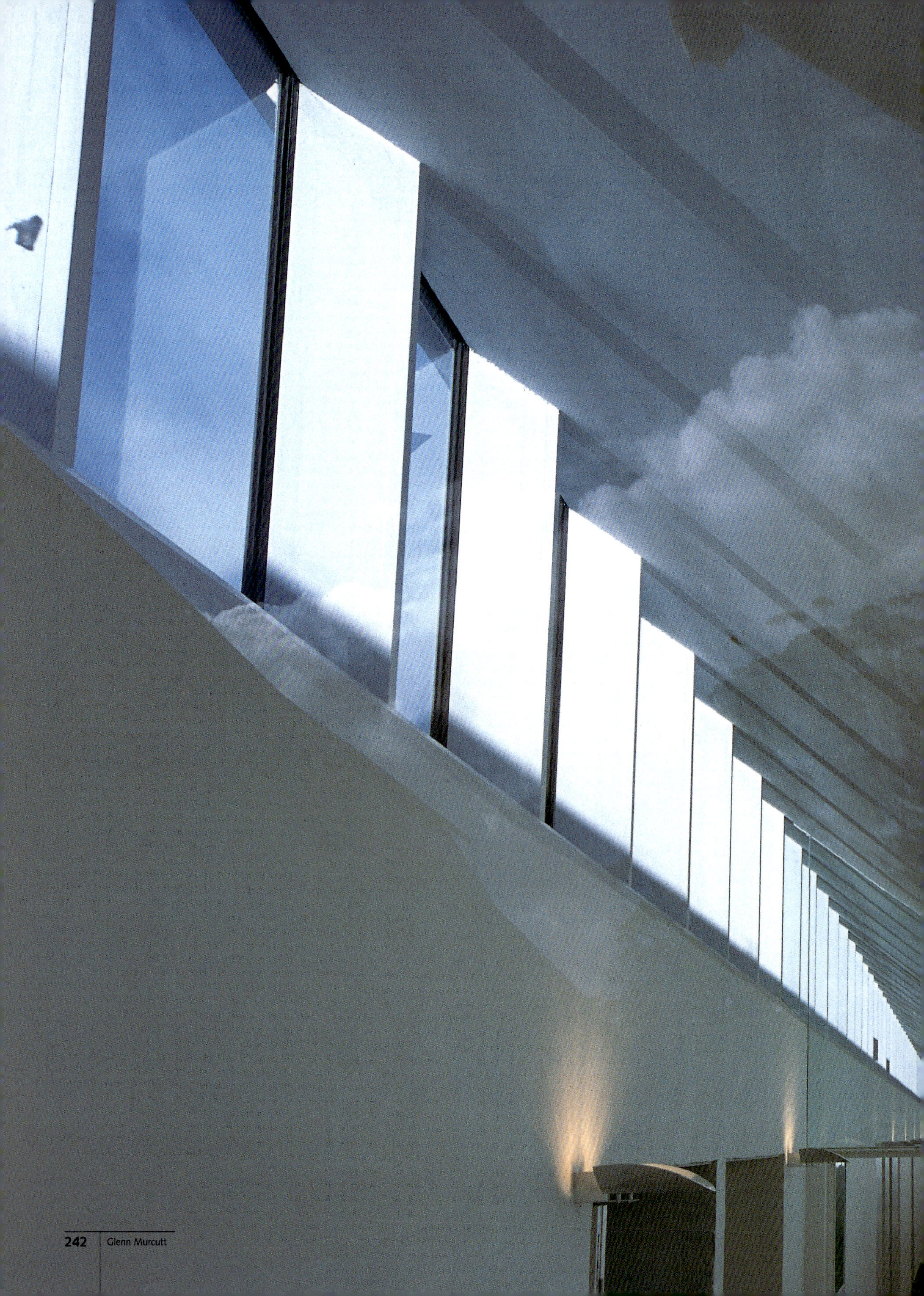

ハイサイドライトは、夏は風除け覆いの突端が庇となって
日射しが入らないが、冬には廊下を日光で満たす。

In summer, the high-level windows are shaded by
the projecting edge of the wind-shield. In winter,
the galleria is warmed by entering sunlight.

人里離れた場所に建つ住宅の供給水として使われる雨水の収集は、
象徴的な意味を与えられている。

The collection of rain, to be used as the water-supply of this
remote house, is given symbolic significance.

Glenn Murcutt | 245

敷地が北西へ下ることから地面からもち上げられたテラスからは、周辺の田園風景へ広がる眺望を臨むことができる。

The terrace, raised above the ground as the land falls to the north-east, gives panoramic views over the surrounding countryside.

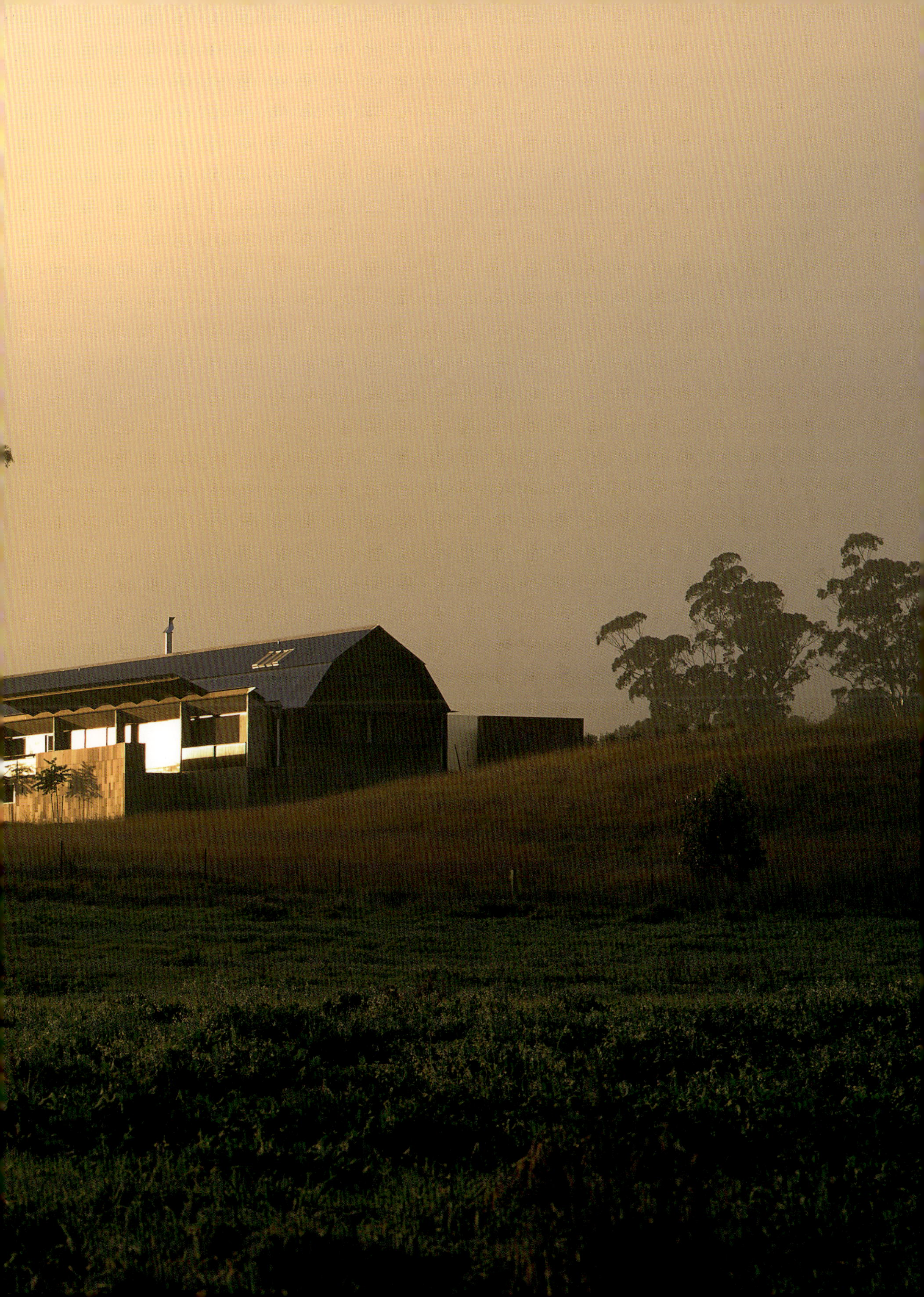

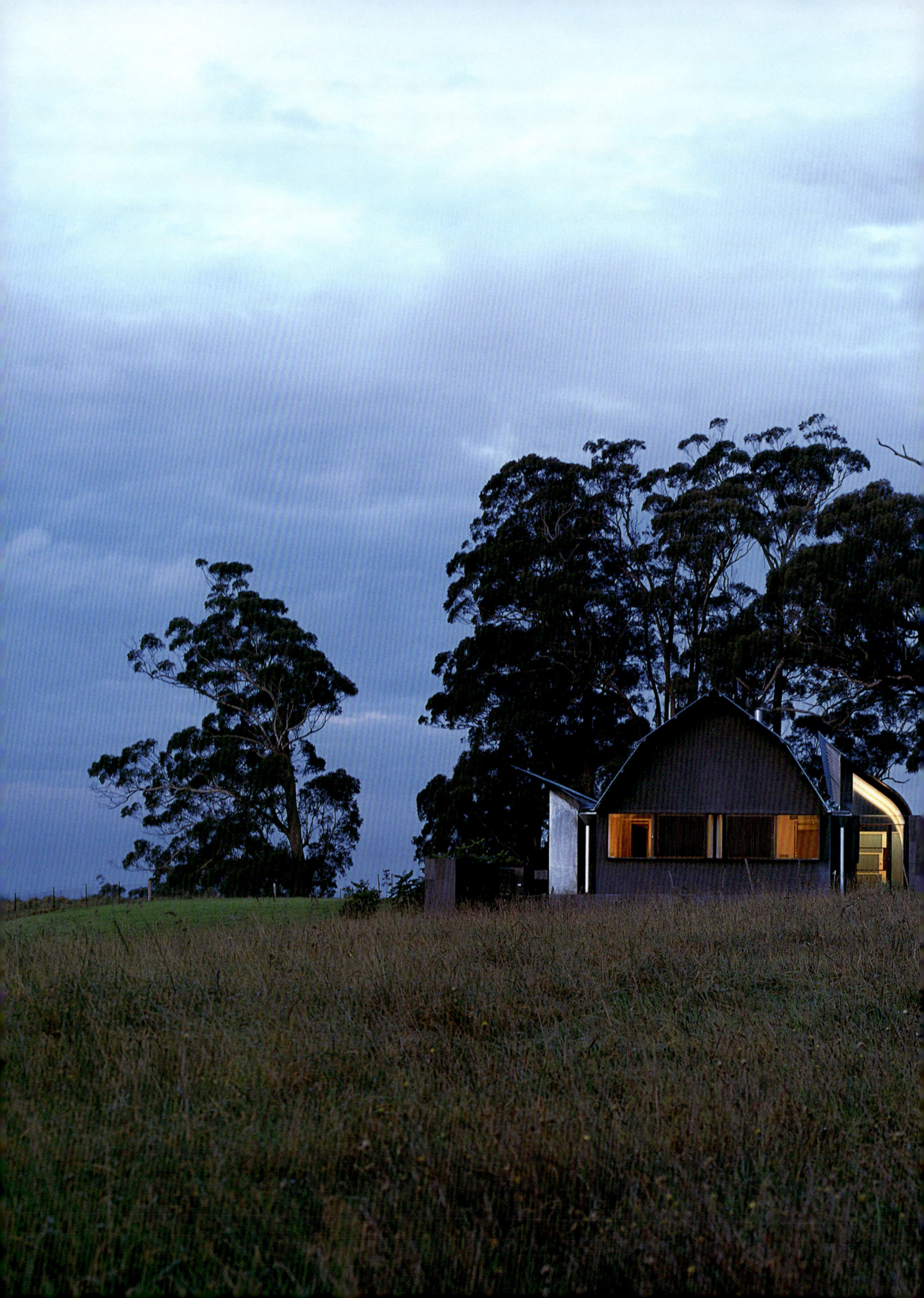

広く開けた平らなランドスケープにおいて、マーカットは、住宅をユーカリの木々の間に配置した。ユーカリは、住宅にスケール感を与え、それを冬の寒い風や夏の日射しから守る役割も果たしている。

In this flat, broad, open landscape, Murcutt has located the house between clusters of eucalyptus trees, giving it scale, protection from cold winds and shading from the northern, summer sun.

この住宅はサザンハイランドの農場が広がる田園地帯にある。夏の間の気温はかなり高くなる時もあり、冬は厳しい寒さをもたらす南西の卓越風が吹きつける。住宅は最適な方角の北を向き、南面は幾重にもなった垣根やユーカリの木々や、高さ4mで長さ80mの窓のない彎曲した波板鉄板によって卓越風から守られる。この壮大なスケールの金属の覆いは、日の光や夜の空を反映し、その光はアプローチにある池の水の波紋に呼応する。

施主と関係のある日本の美学を認識し、住宅へは間接的にアプローチされる。小さな前庭は、風覆いの内側である白く抽象的な廊下(ガラリア)に続く。この劇的な空間は、全部屋をつなぐため住宅の長さだけ続き、その上部にあるハイサイドライトからの光で照らされている。夏は風覆いの突端が庇となって日射しが入らないが、冬には暖かい日光で満たされる。

彎曲した南立面の、光り輝き、重さを感じさせない抽象性とは対照的に、北面はスレート貼りの礎石によって地面に重厚に結びつけられている。そのファサードは、日射量と眺望を調節するさまざまな種類のハードウッドの鎧戸によって表情づけられた。

平面計画は、親は東、子は西と分けられ、中心にある共有スペースと北向きのテラスによってつながっている。暖かい日には、居間のガラス戸を完全に引くことで、内外が一体化した大きなスペースとなる。冬には上部の深い庇が冷たい南西の風から守る。テラスに沿って植えられた広葉樹は、やがて北の太陽を防ぐ木陰をつくりだすだろう。

この住宅は床面積600m^2、部屋の幅12m、天井高4.6mで、マーカットが設計した作品の最も大きいものの1つである。しかしその大きさは、立面の対照的な性質と素材、樹齢が長く背の高いユーカリの木々の間に住宅を置いたマーカットの注意深い配置計画によって和らげられている。このユーカリの林は、住宅にスケール感を与えるとともに、それを寒風や夏の北の太陽から守る役割を果たしている。

House in the Southern Highlands

サザンハイランドの住宅

The house is located in the farming country of the Southern Highlands, where summer temperatures can be very high, and the prevailing winds from the south-west are often severe, and harshly cold in winter. The house faces north for optimum orientation, and is screened from the winds by layers of hedge and eucalyptus trees, and by a 4 meters high, 80 meters long, windowless, corrugated-steel curved plane which wraps the southern side of the house. This imposingly-scaled metallic sheath reflects the light of the day or night sky, and echoes the shining, rippled surface of the lake in its foreground.

In acknowledgement of traditional Japanese aesthetics with which the owners have an affinity, the house is entered indirectly. A small court leads to the purified, white, abstract space of the long internal galleria that is enclosed by the inner-face of the wind-shield. This dramatic space runs the full length of the house, linking all rooms, illuminated by high level windows which in summer are shaded by the deeply-projecting edge of the wind-shield, but in winter flood the galleria with warming sunshine.

In contrast to the gleaming, weight-less, abstractness of the curved southern façade, the northern side of the house is unified with the ground by the heavy, slate-clad plinth on which it stands, and the façade is highly articulated with adjustable hardwood window shutters and screens which modify sun-penetration and views.

The parents' quarters occupy the eastern end of the house, with the childrens' quarters to the west, both linked by the central communal spaces and by the north-facing terrace onto which the sitting room can be opened on temperate days—making a single large inside/outside space. The terrace is protected from cold south-western winds by the deeply projecting canopy, and will eventually be shaded from the northern sun by deciduous trees, newly-planted along its length.

This is one of the largest houses that Murcutt has designed, being of almost 600 square meters in area, with rooms of 12 meters width and 4.6 meters high ceilings.

Its expansive size is tempered, however, by the contrasting characteristics and materials of its façades, and by the manner in which Murcutt has embedded it between clusters of tall, mature eucalyptus trees, giving it scale, protection from cold winds and shading from the northern, summer sun.

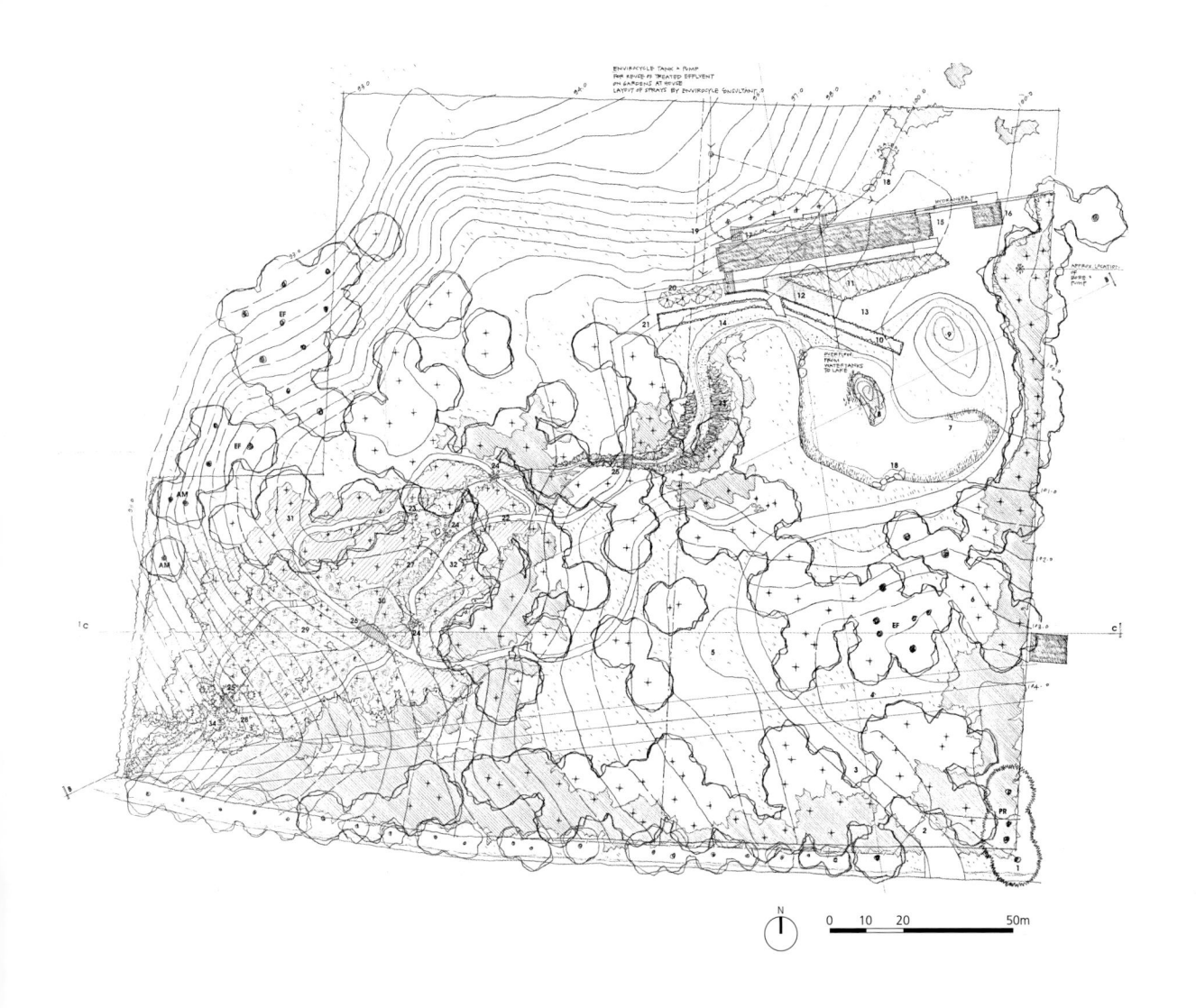

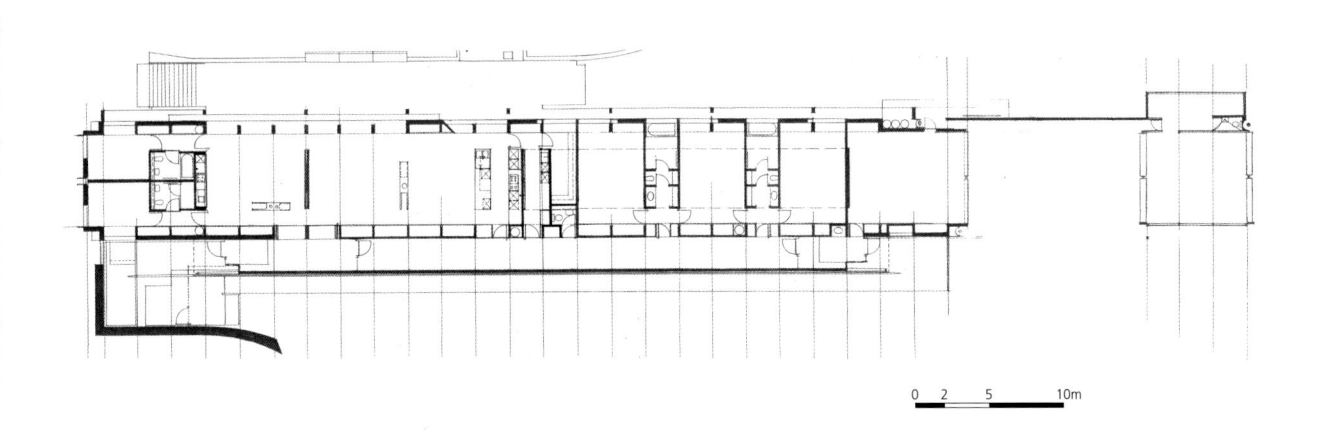

Glenn Murcutt

Murcutt-Lewin House and Studio

マーカット＝ルーウィン邸＆スタジオ

2000−03..........Mosman, Sydney, New South Wales
Collaborating architect: Wendy Lewin

この革新的な住宅では、伝統的、革新的な素材工法の両方において、繊細ですぐれたクラフトマンシップが発揮された。

The house is a work invention, and of meticulous craftsmanship in both conventional and unconventional building materials and methods.

プロポーションのよい2層の高さのある鉄とガラスのスクリーンが、上階のリビングと階下のスタジオを枠組みしている。スクリーンには、外部にあわせて内部を調節する窓とルーバーが設置された。

The upper living floor and lower studio are framed by a finely-proportioned two-storey steel and glass screen in which adjustable windows and louvers enable the fine-tuning of the relationship between interior and exterior.

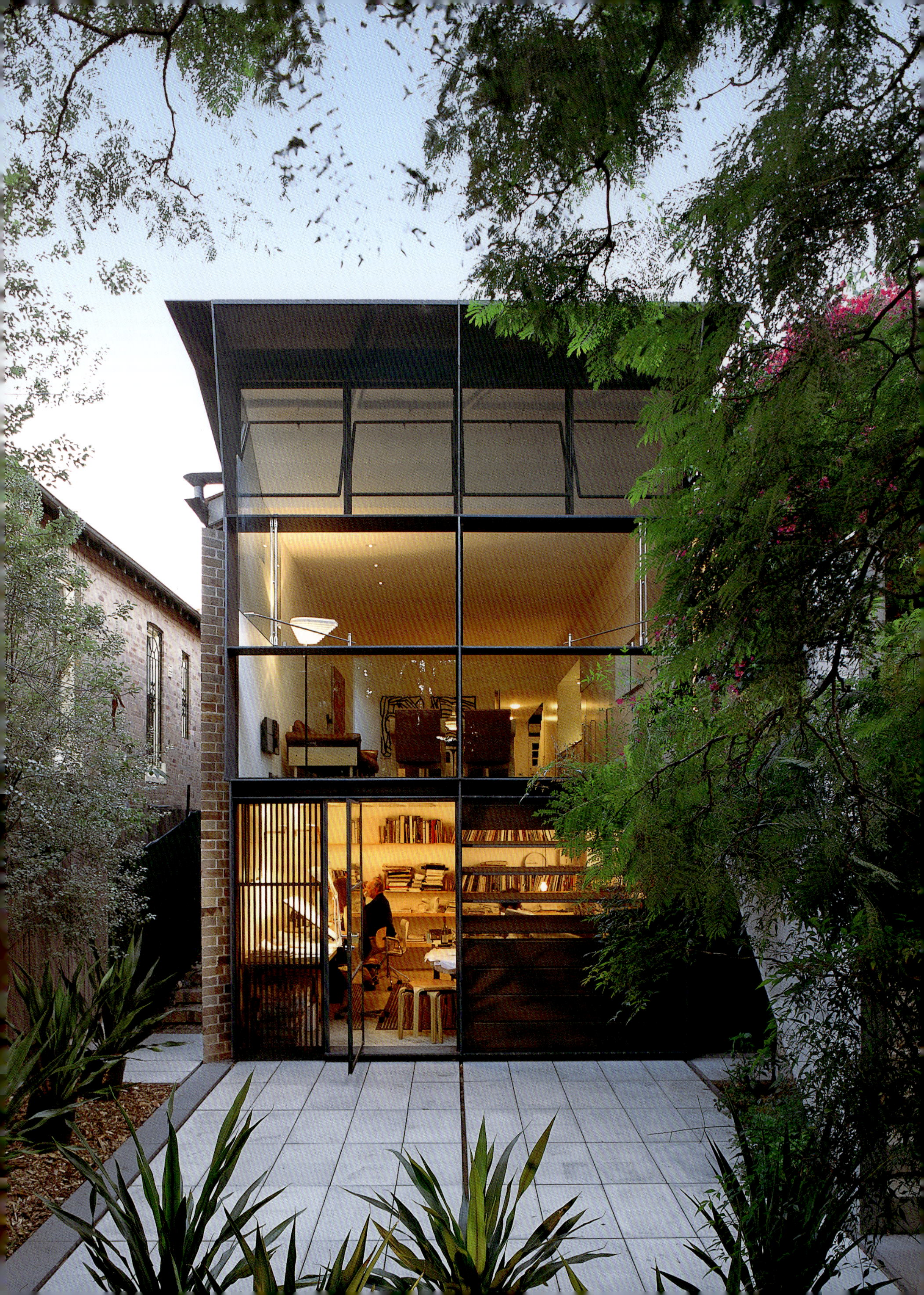

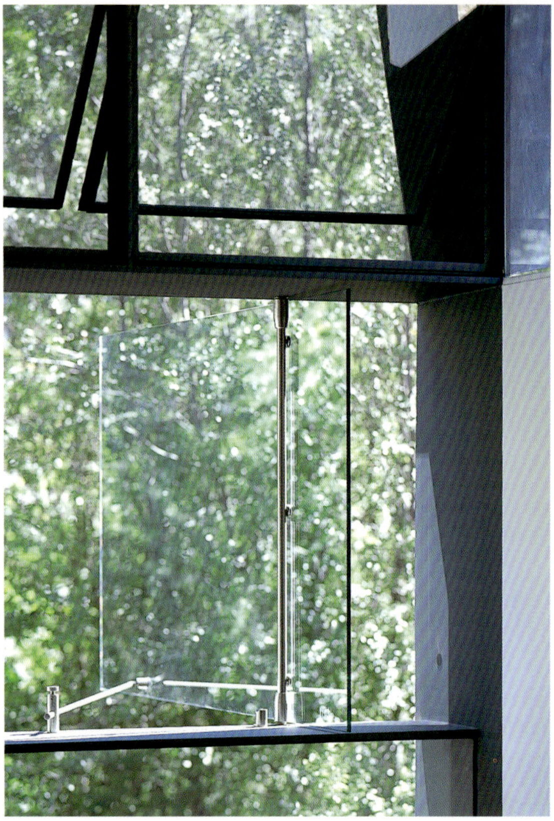

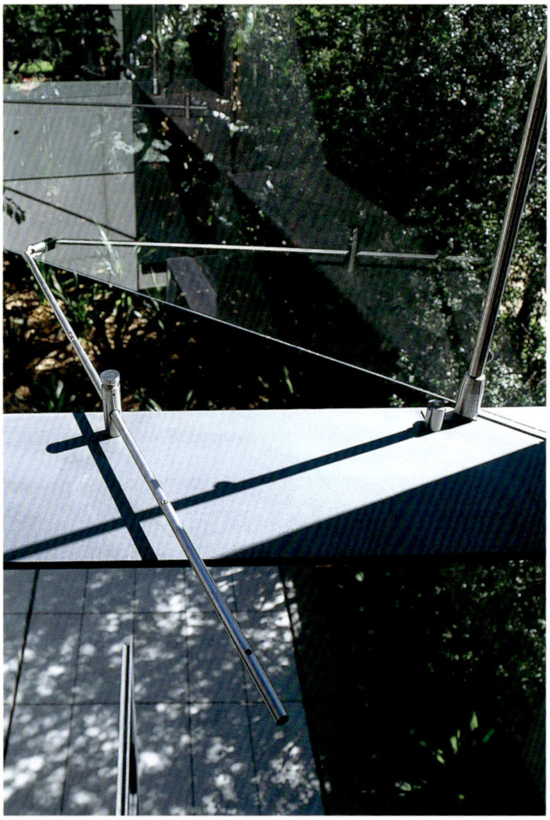

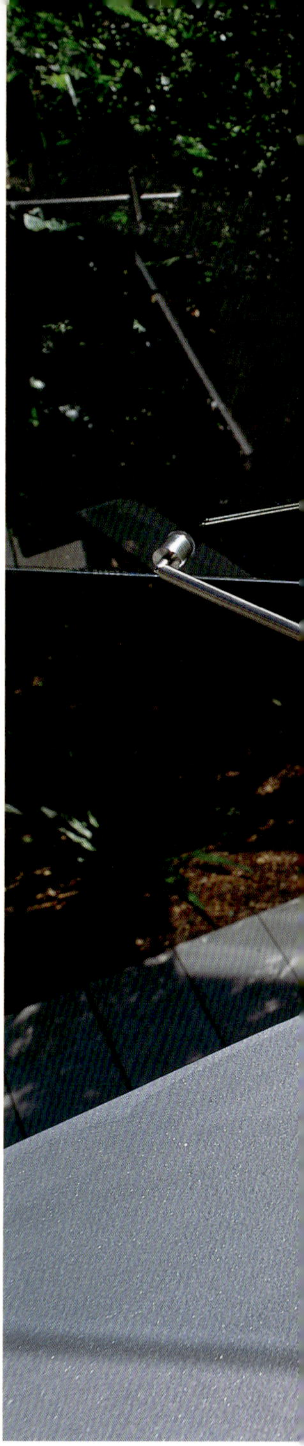

枠のない大きな回転ガラス窓は、その複雑な機構を解決した、カスタムメイドの
スチール製シャフトと、驚くほど繊細な水平材でサポートされる。

The complex opening geometries of the very large, frameless, rotating
glass panes are resolved by custom-designed stainless steel spindles
and stays of surprising delicacy.

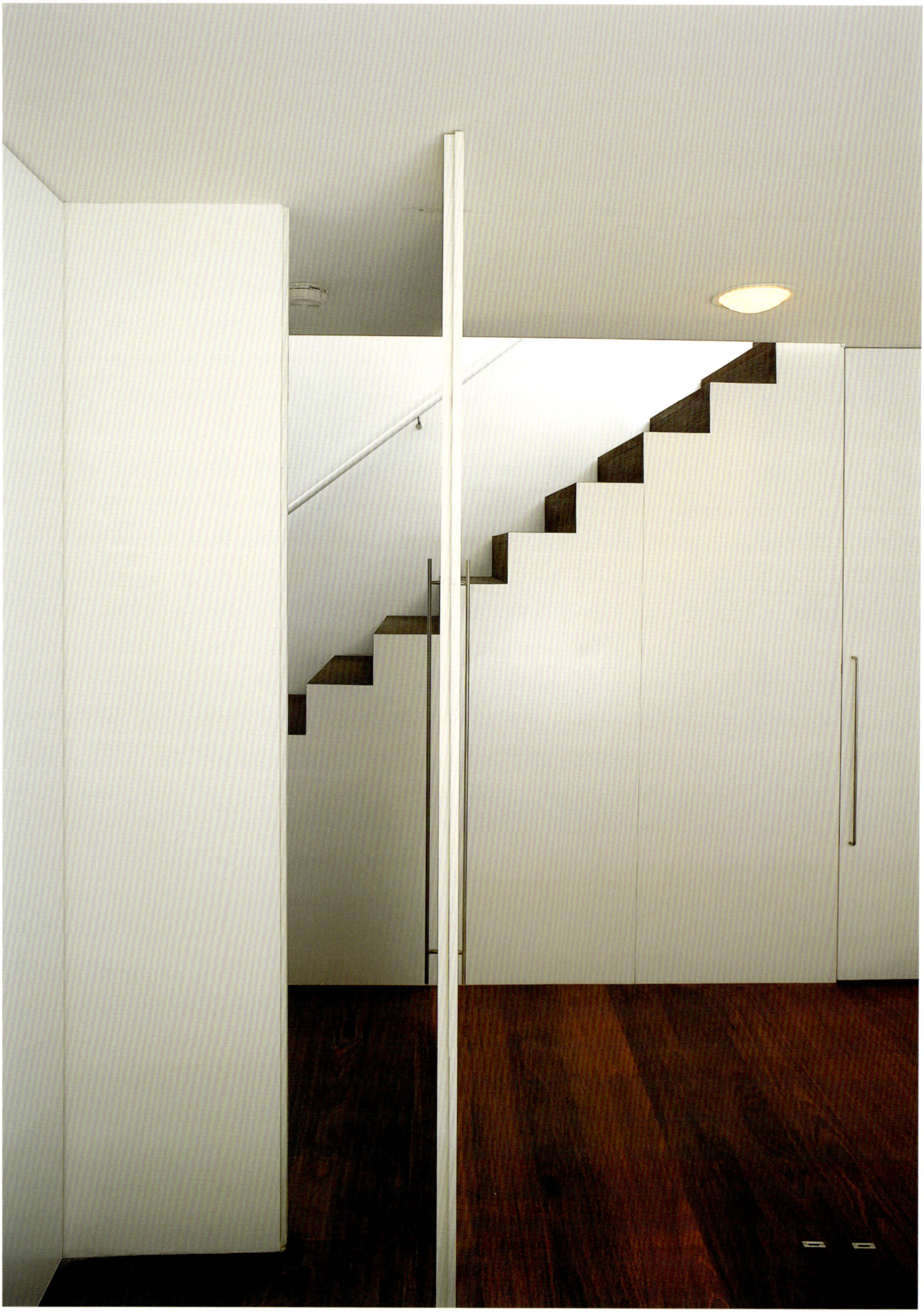

切れ目のないジャラのフローリングは、住宅内の床に統一感を与え、部屋を流れるようにつないでいる。

An unbroken surface of Jarrah-wood flooring unites all levels of the house, giving the interior a flowing continuity.

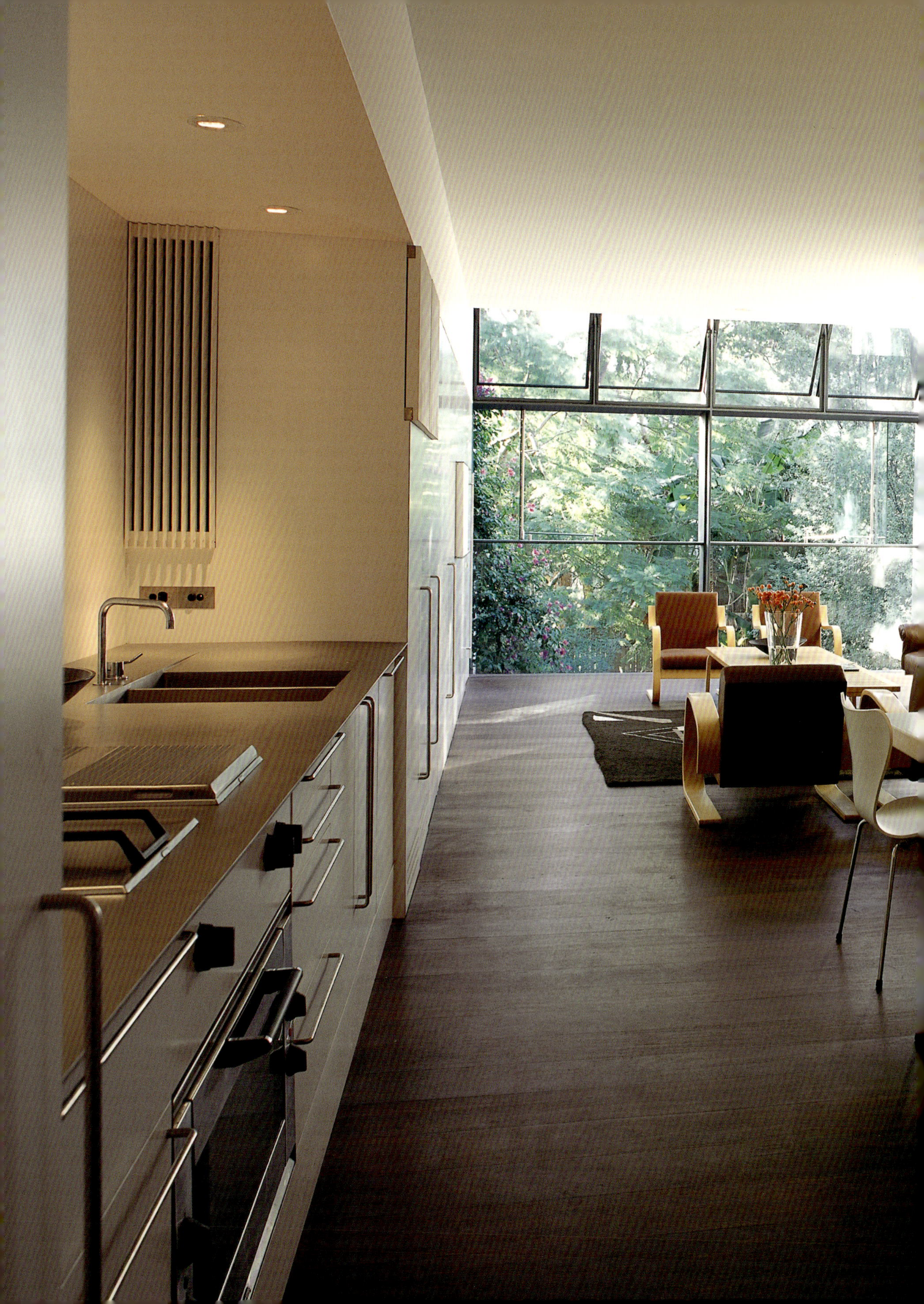

室内空間と家具の優美な簡潔さは、庭の梢への眺めと、
著名なアボリジニ画家であった故エミリー・カーメ・ウングワレーの
絵画を際立たせている。

The refined simplicity of the interior space and its furnishings gives emphasis to views of the garden foliage and the artworks of the late, eminent Aboriginal artist Emily Kame Kngwarreye.

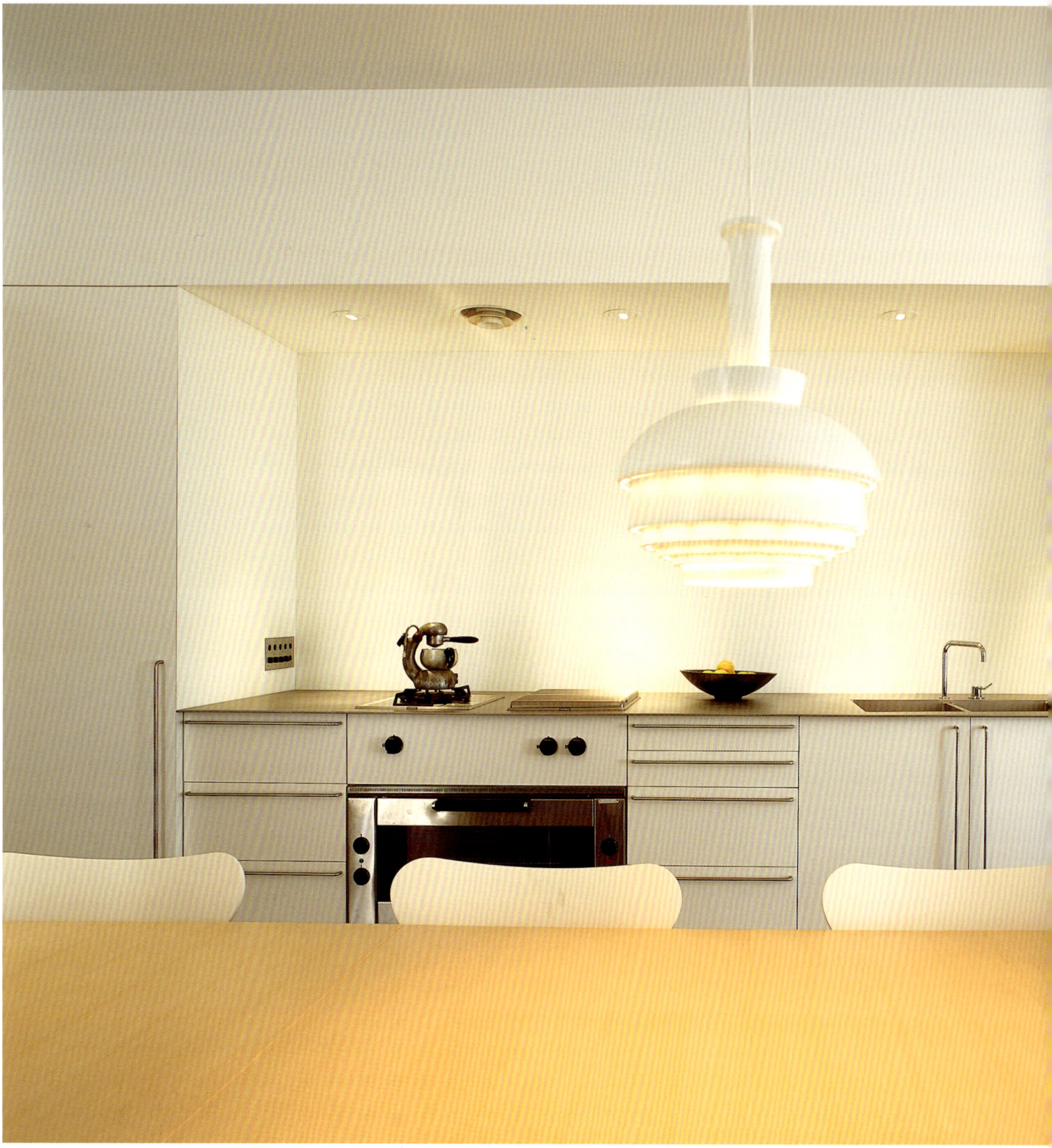

キッチンは、ミニマルな、美しいディテールの家具である。
The kitchen is a minimal, finely-detailed piece of furniture.

縦に細長く、角度のついた側壁のスリット窓から、長いリビングの中心へ光を入れる。
階段は玄関扉を見せるように形づくられている。扉の青いガラスからの光は、玄関
ホールの暗い箇所を明るい色で照らして、活気ある場所としている。

A thin, vertical slit-window let into the side wall at an oblique angle admits sunlight into the deepest part of the long living room. The intense blue glass panels of the front door—revealed by the cut of the stair—activate the darker space of the entrance hall with luminous colour.

寝室の窓は、朝の光を受け、空への景色をもたらし、北東からの通風を行う。
外部の可動ルーバーは、太陽熱と日射しを制御する。

The bedroom windows scoop in the morning light, sky-views, and breezes from the north-east. Adjustable external louvers control light and solar heat gain.

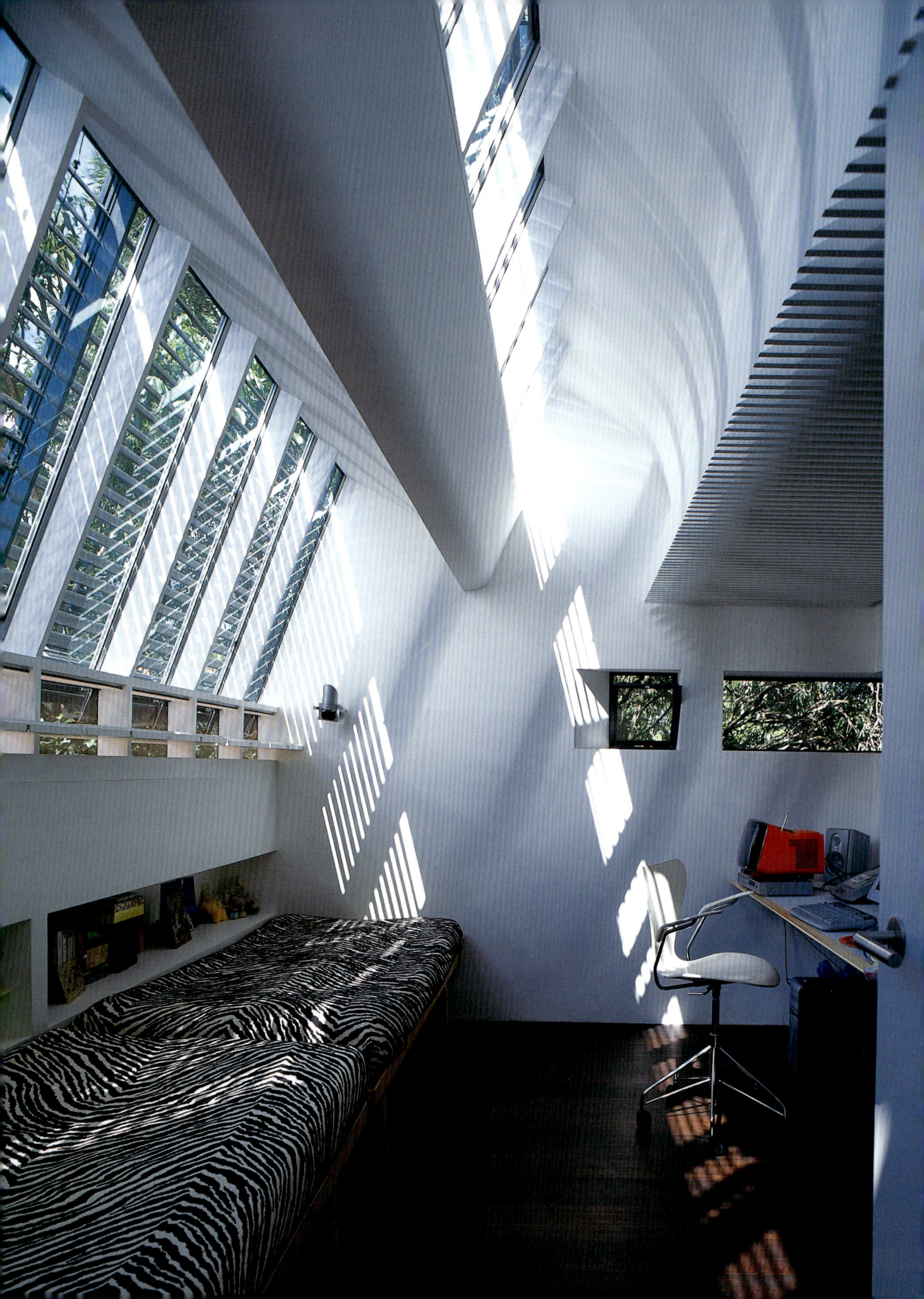

3つの小さな部屋が細い屋根裏に組み込まれたが、波打つ
形状の天窓によって、屋根裏と認識できないほど、
空間に広がりが生まれた。

Three compact rooms were inserted into the narrow
roof-space, their small size being contradicted by the
spatiousness of their undulating section.

この住宅の複雑な空間は、この小さな市街地住宅の右半分の中で展開されている。通りからは、冬至の低い太陽光線も採り入れるように配置された天窓が、内部を予感させるのみである。

The complex interior has been created inside only the right-hand half of this small suburban house. From the street, the only hints of the new interior are partial views of the new skylights, which are positioned to take in the sun, even at its lowest in winter.

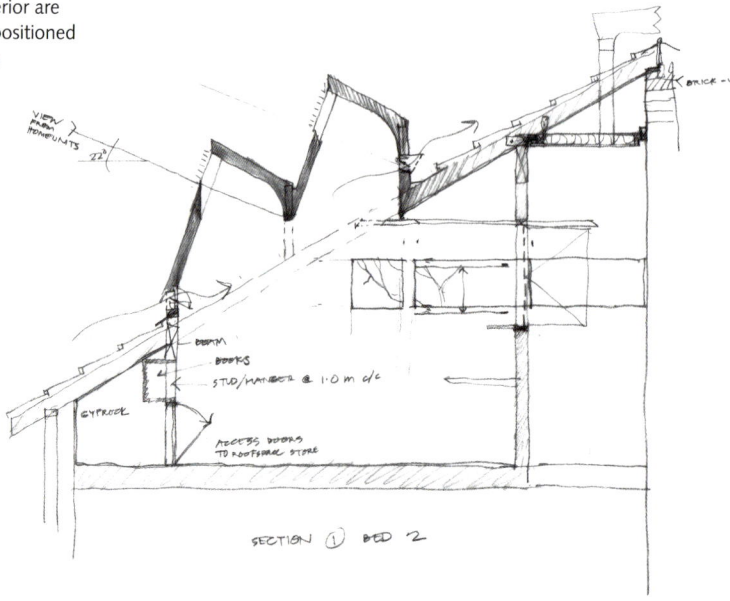

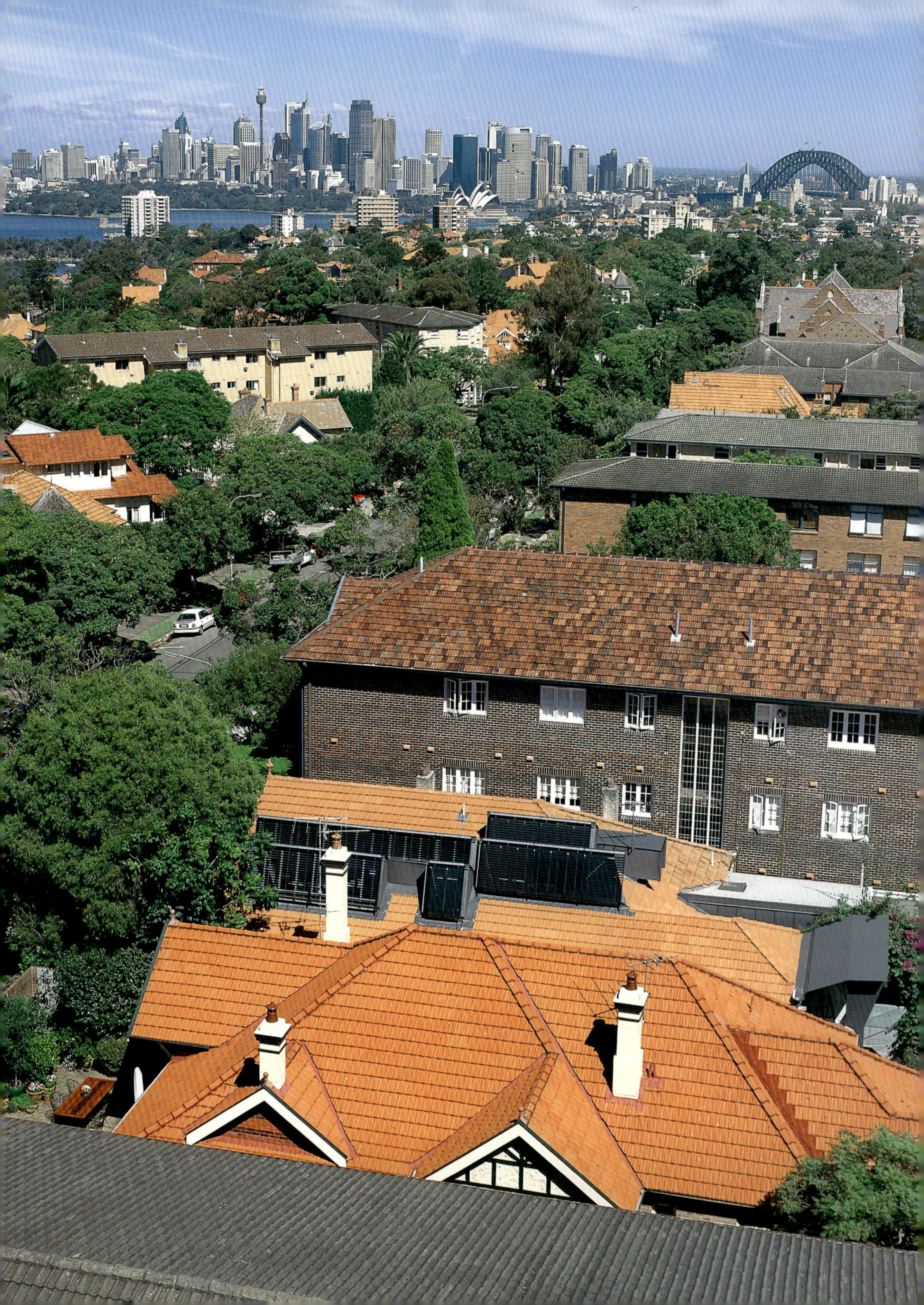

Murcutt-Lewin House and Studio

マーカット＝ルーウィン邸＆スタジオ

グレン・マーカットとウェンディ・ルーウィン、2人の建築家により設計された自邸兼事務所である。密集したシドニー市内にある典型的な1900年代の2戸1棟式家屋(セミ・デタッチド)の内部を大規模に改築した。正面から一見すると、側屋根へ光を採り入れる天窓が窺える以外は、周辺の住宅と見分けがつかない。しかし内部は、既存の平屋が全面的に再構成されている。

リビングルームの床は、階下スタジオの天井高を確保するために1段もち上げられ、既存の屋根裏空間には、床レベルの違う2つの寝室とバスルームがつくられた。これらの部屋は、その溢れんばかりの形態の闊達さによって空間の狭さを打ち消す波のような天窓によって照らされ、北東の朝の光を受け取り、空を眺め、風がそよいで入ってくる。住宅の、5つの違う床レベルをもつ空間は、切れ目なくジャラ材のフローリングが敷かれて、インテリアスペースが流れるようにつなげられた。

住宅の庭側は、プロポーションのよい2層高さの鉄とガラスのスクリーンがリビングとスタジオをまとめ、外部の気候にあわせて調節できる建具が嵌め込まれている。住宅の向きと、日陰をつくる庭の樹木への近さにより、マーカット独特の3層スクリーンは必要とされず、ここでは技術が縦方向に集約されている。固定されたガラス、水平回転窓、縦回転窓、木製ルーバー、木製格子が、その日の天気と時間によって内部の気候を調節するために使用される。そして内と外との区別を最少にするため、鉄の部材寸法は最小限に、ガラス窓には枠を付けていない。そのため、ガラス荷重を支えている細いスチール製シャフトを回転させると、大きなガラスのエッジに太陽光が屈折して虹の模様がメインルームに射し込む。

複雑に絡み合った空間を、小さくて平凡な建物の外殻の中につくりだしたことは、3次元空間への操作の卓越した巧さを表している。この住宅は想像と創意、機智によってできている。

This is the work of two architects—Glenn Murcutt and Wendy Lewin—and is their family home and workplace. The design involved comprehensive alterations to the interior of a typical 1900's semi-detached bungalow in a tight inner-suburban Sydney street. From the front, the house remains indistinguishable from the neighbouring dwellings, aside from partial views of the new skylights let into the side roof. However, internally the originally single-storey house has been entirely re-configured.

The floor of the living room was raised by a single step to give sufficient headroom for use of the basement as studio, and a bathroom and two bedrooms were inserted at slightly different levels into the roof space of the former attic. These are illuminated by wave-like roof-windows which deny the small scale of the rooms by their effusive ebullience, and scoop in morning light from the north-east, sky-views, and breezes. The resulting five different floor-levels are united by an unbroken surface of Jarrah-wood flooring which gives the interior a flowing continuity.

At the rear of the house, the living room and studio are united by a finely-proportioned two-storey-high steel and glass screen in which adjustable devices enable the fine-tuning of the relationship between interior and exterior. Given the orientation of the house and the proximity of shading trees in the garden, Murcutt's customary tripartite layering of window screens is unnecessary, and is replaced by a compendium of different techniques: fixed glazing, windows which open horizontally, windows which open vertically, wooden louvers and wooden slats, all of which can be adjusted in response to the weather and the time of day. The structural steel members are of minimal dimensions, and the glazing is frameless in order to minimise the sense of separation between exterior and interior, and so that the edges of the large glass sheets refract rainbow patterns of sunlight into the main room as the panes rotate on the slender, custom-made steel spindles which bear them.

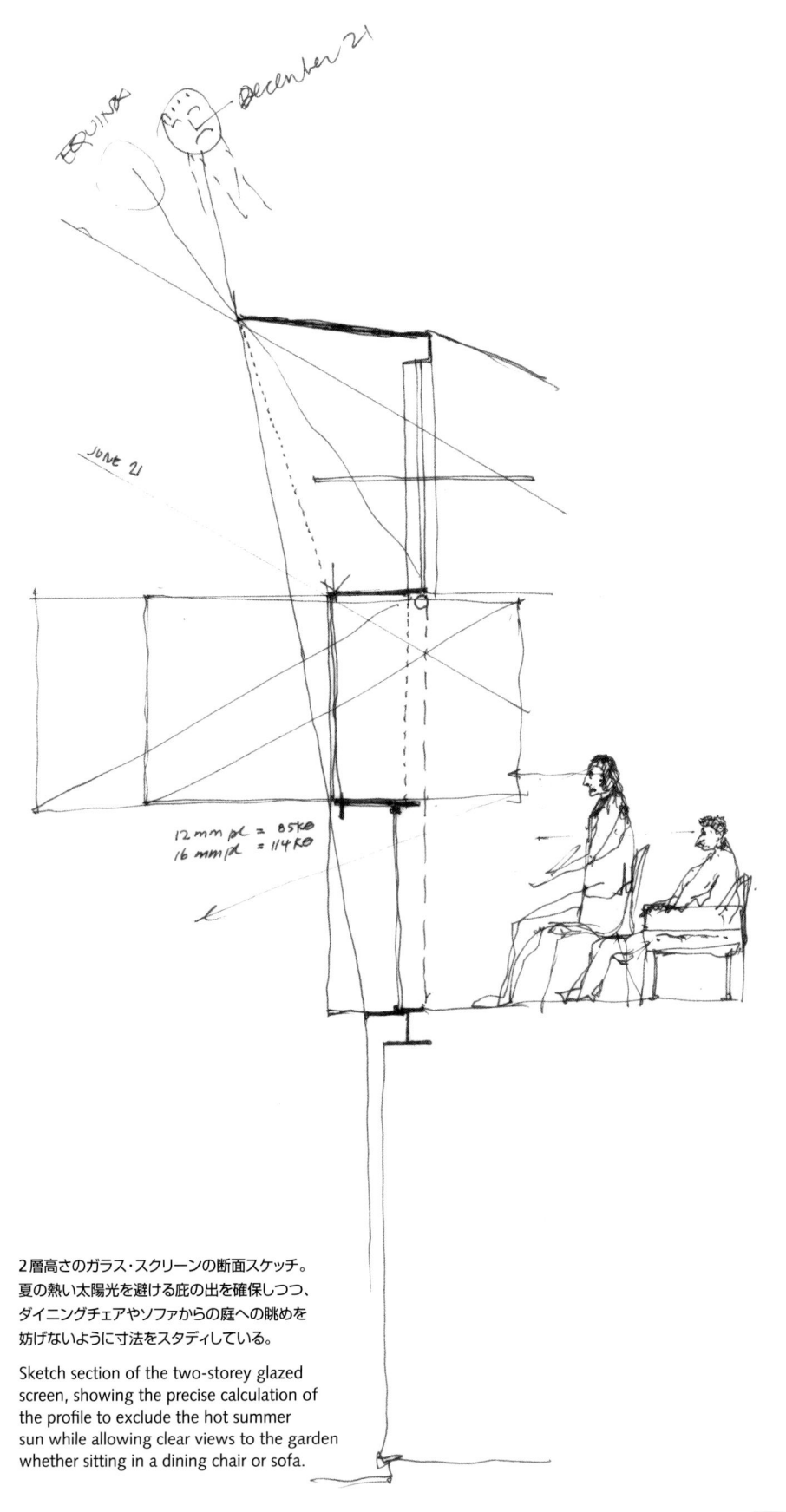

2層高さのガラス・スクリーンの断面スケッチ。
夏の熱い太陽光を避ける庇の出を確保しつつ、
ダイニングチェアやソファからの庭への眺めを
妨げないように寸法をスタディしている。

Sketch section of the two-storey glazed
screen, showing the precise calculation of
the profile to exclude the hot summer
sun while allowing clear views to the garden
whether sitting in a dining chair or sofa.

Glenn Murcutt

Walsh House

ウォルシュ邸

2001-05 ·········· Kangaroo Valley, New South Wales

住宅は開けた草原に建ち、北の国立公園の鬱蒼とした丘陵にその正面を向ける。

The house stands on open grassland, with its principal façade addressing the forested hills of a National Park, to its north.

住宅の長手の軸は、東の遠方に見える隆起した岩を指している。
The long axis of the house is directed precisely towards
a large knoll of rock, in the distance to its east.

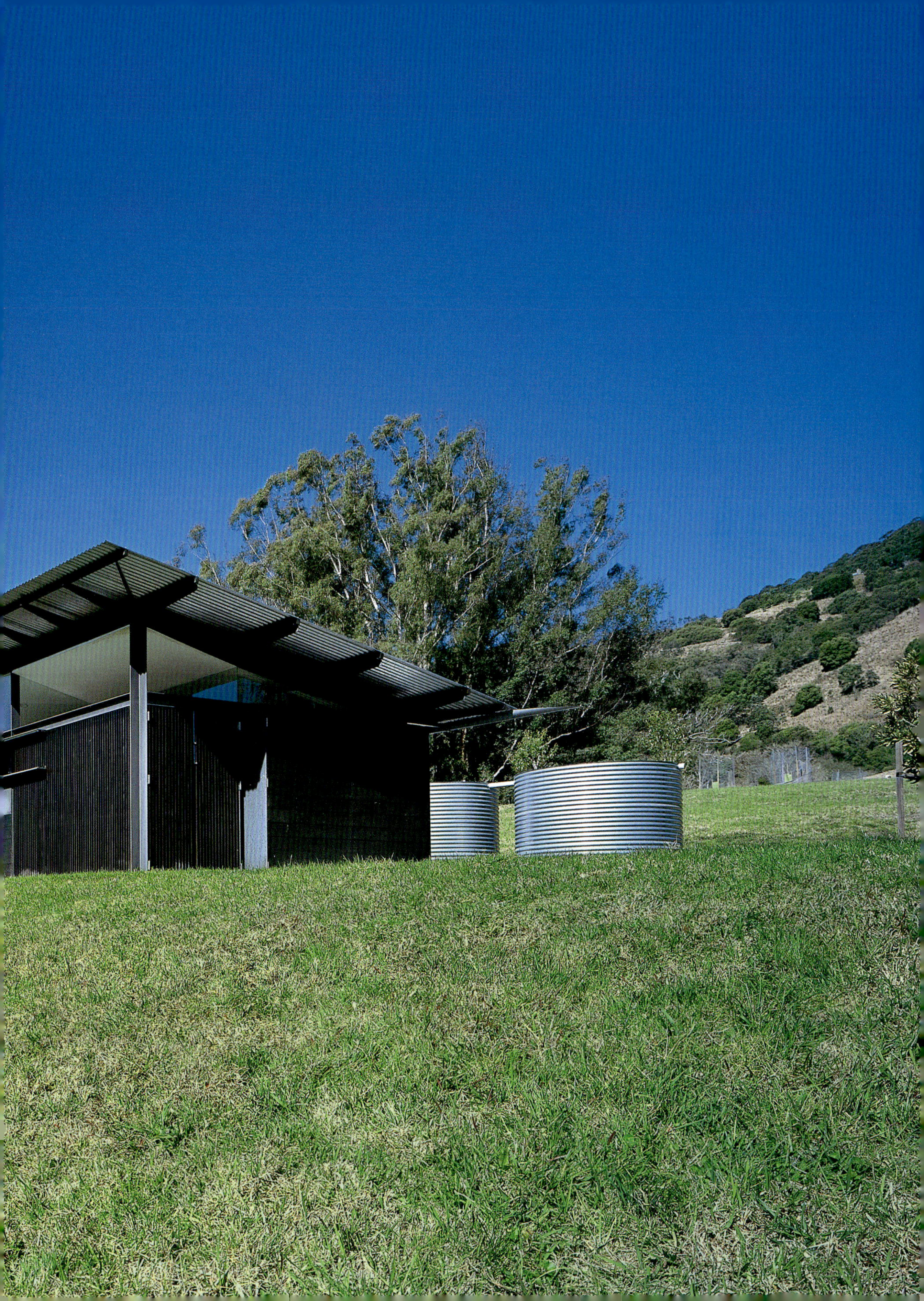

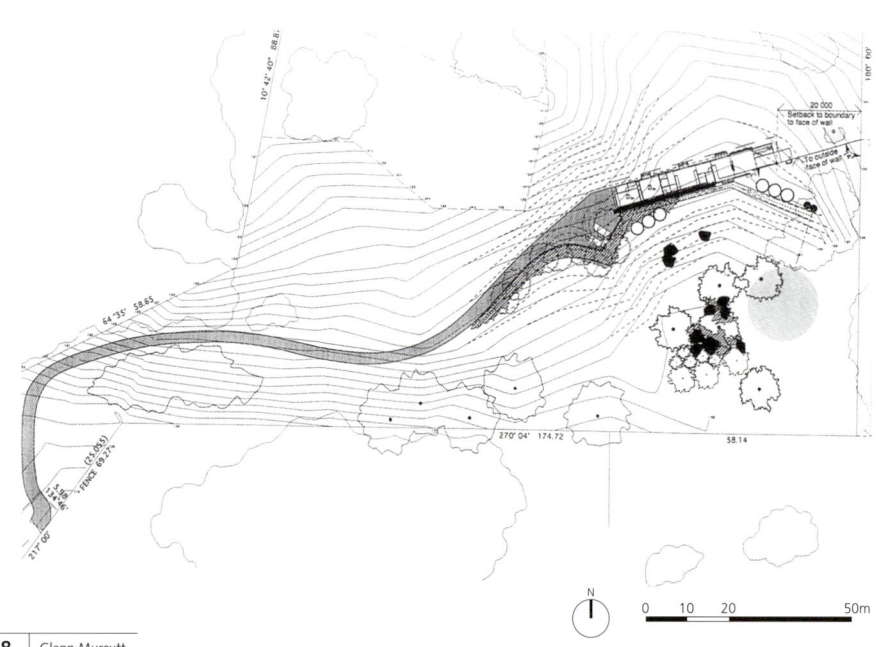

278 | Glenn Murcutt

屋根の深い庇は、上部の窓を夏の高度の高い直射日光から守り、冬には暖かさを採り入れる。下部の窓はスクリーンやルーバーにより保護するとともに室内の明るさを調節する。

The deep roof-projection shields the upper glazing from the high summer sun while admitting it into the house during winter. The projecting bay-windows are protected by adjustable screens and louvers, allowing each user to individually modify the lighting of their room.

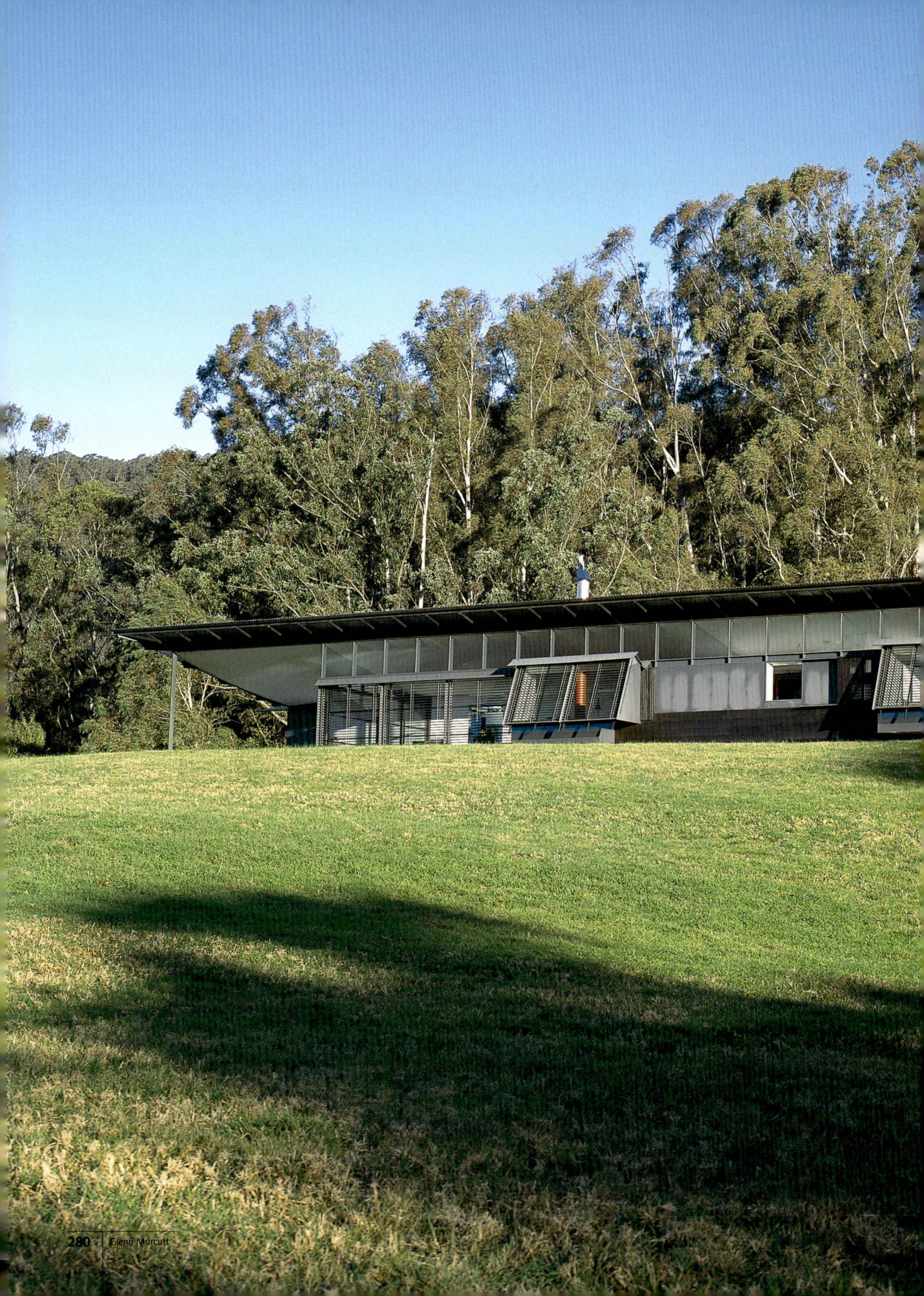

出窓は、左のダイニングルームと右の2つの寝室を明らかにしている。

The bay windows identify the dining room, to the left, and the two bedrooms to the right.

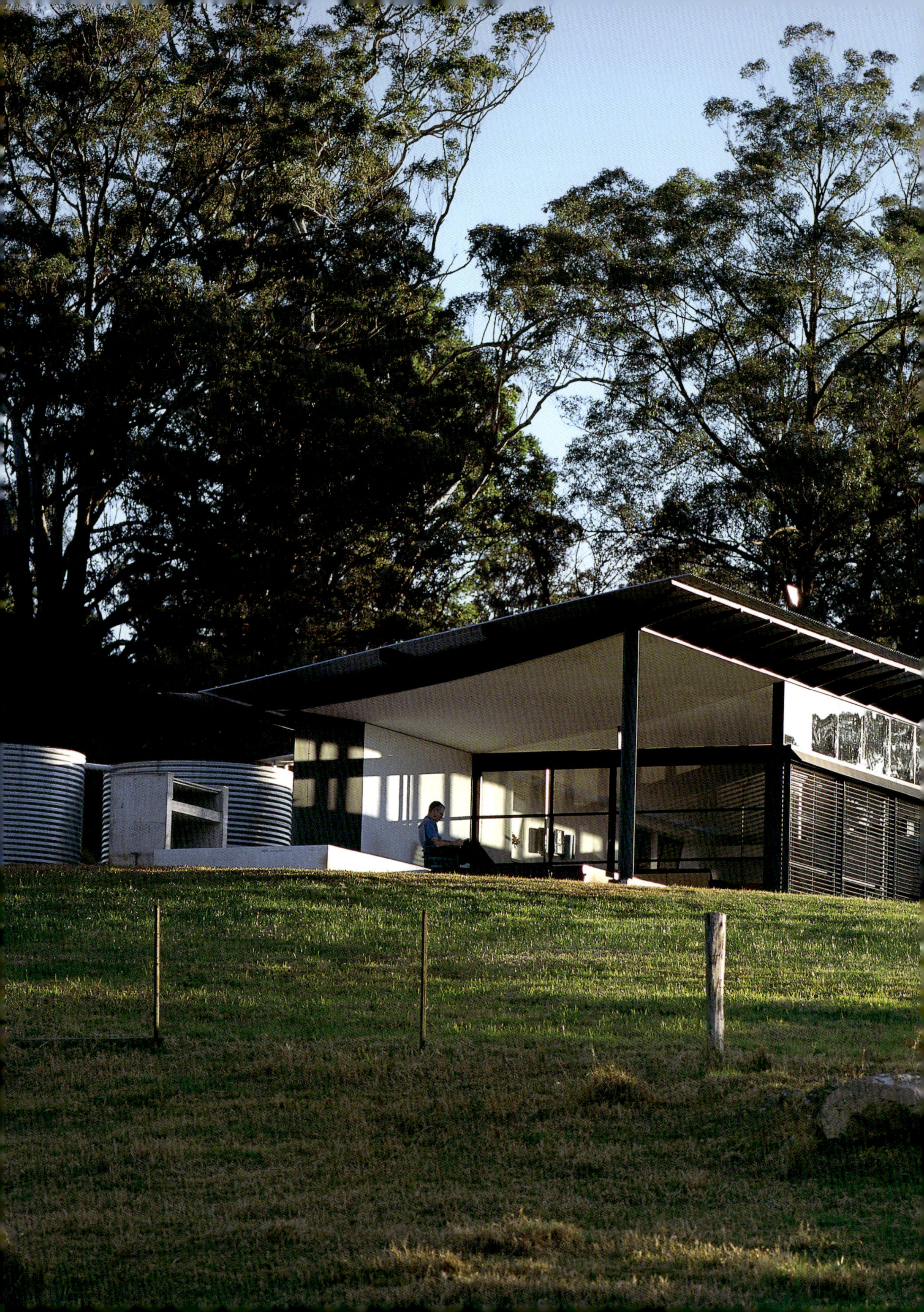

ベランダは東にあり、夏の暑い午後の日射しから陰になるように考えられている。

A veranda is located to the eastern side of the house, shaded from the heat of the summer afternoon sun.

住宅は4つの異なる立面をもつ。南と西面は、農家的な実際的なものであり、車庫、ガスタンク貯蔵庫、洗濯室、大きな雨水タンクである。北と東面は、より開かれ、周辺の美しい景色を示唆している。

The house presents four very different façades. To its south and west it has the working character of a farmhouse, with garage, gas-tank storage, laundry and large water-storage tanks, while its northern and eastern faces address the verdant surrounding views.

ダイニングルームは、家の中で唯一、北と南の両方への眺望がある場所として強調される。

The dining room is given emphasis as the only room which has both northerly and southerly aspect.

上部の窓は、深い庇で夏の直射光から守られて、北の丘陵への眺望を枠組みする。

The deeply-projecting roof shields the upper-level windows from direct summer sun, allowing these windows to frame the view of the northern hills throughout the year.

上：暖色の赤で塗られた鉄製の暖炉は、マーカット作品であることを表す「シグニチャー」である。
下：どのように夏の日射しを住宅に入れないか、また周辺の丘への視線をどう確保するかという、マーカットによる建物の形状のスケッチ。

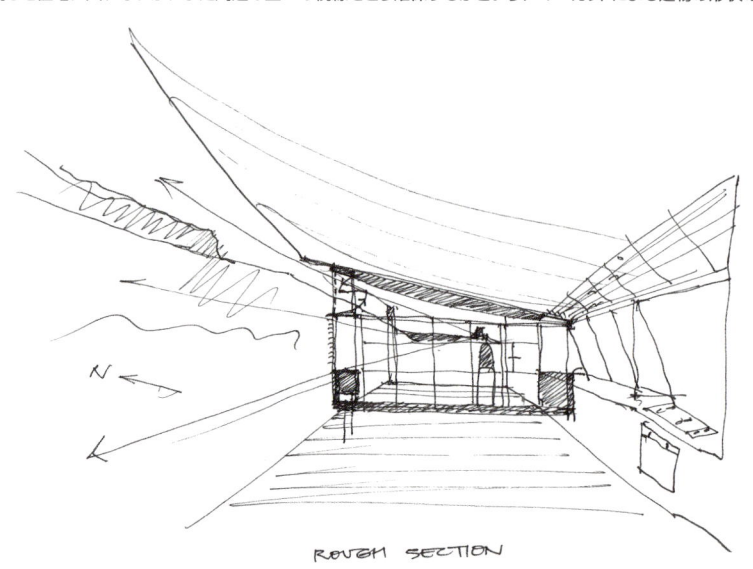

ROUGH SECTION

Above: The steel firechest, painted warm red, is a 'signature' Murcutt component which he has used in several houses.
Below: Some of Murcutt's numerous studies showing how the building frames view of the surrounding hills.

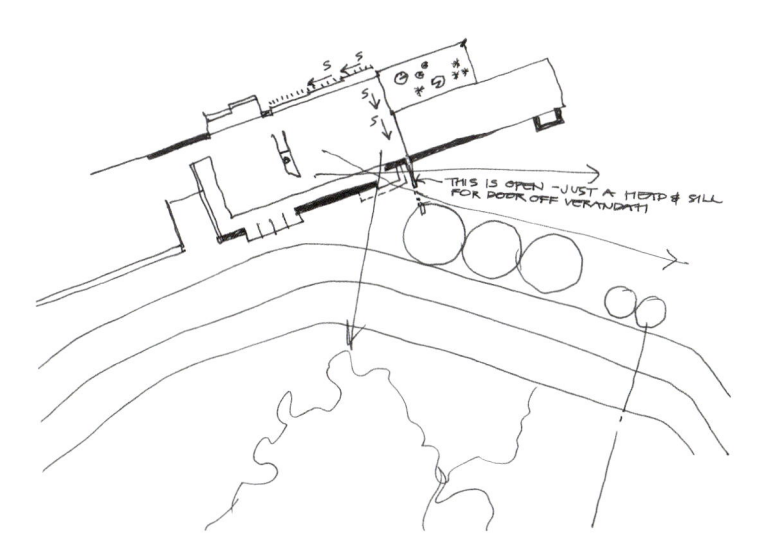

Glenn Murcutt | 295

2つの寝室の出窓は長椅子となっている。
Bay windrows in the two bedrooms accommodate day-beds.

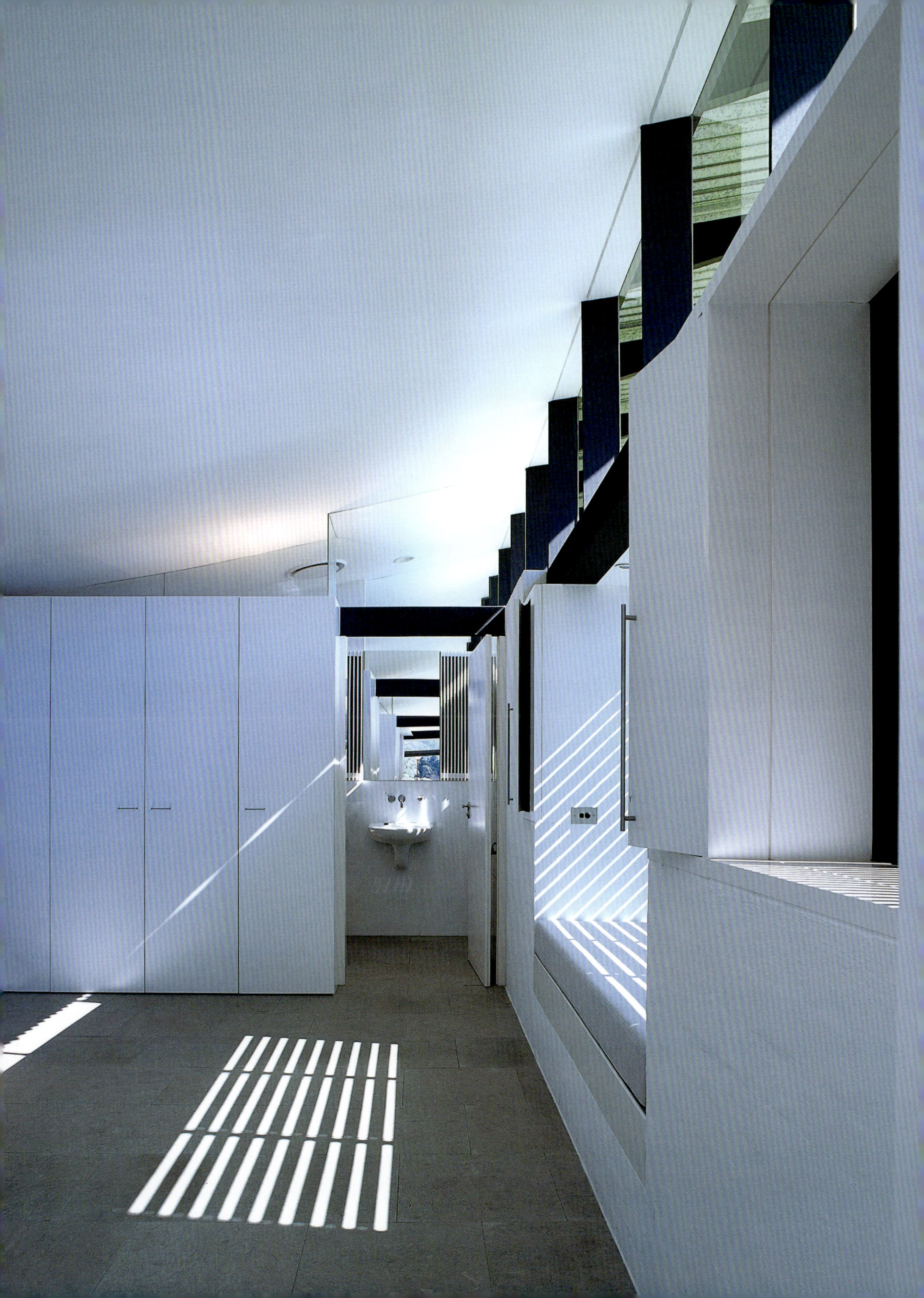

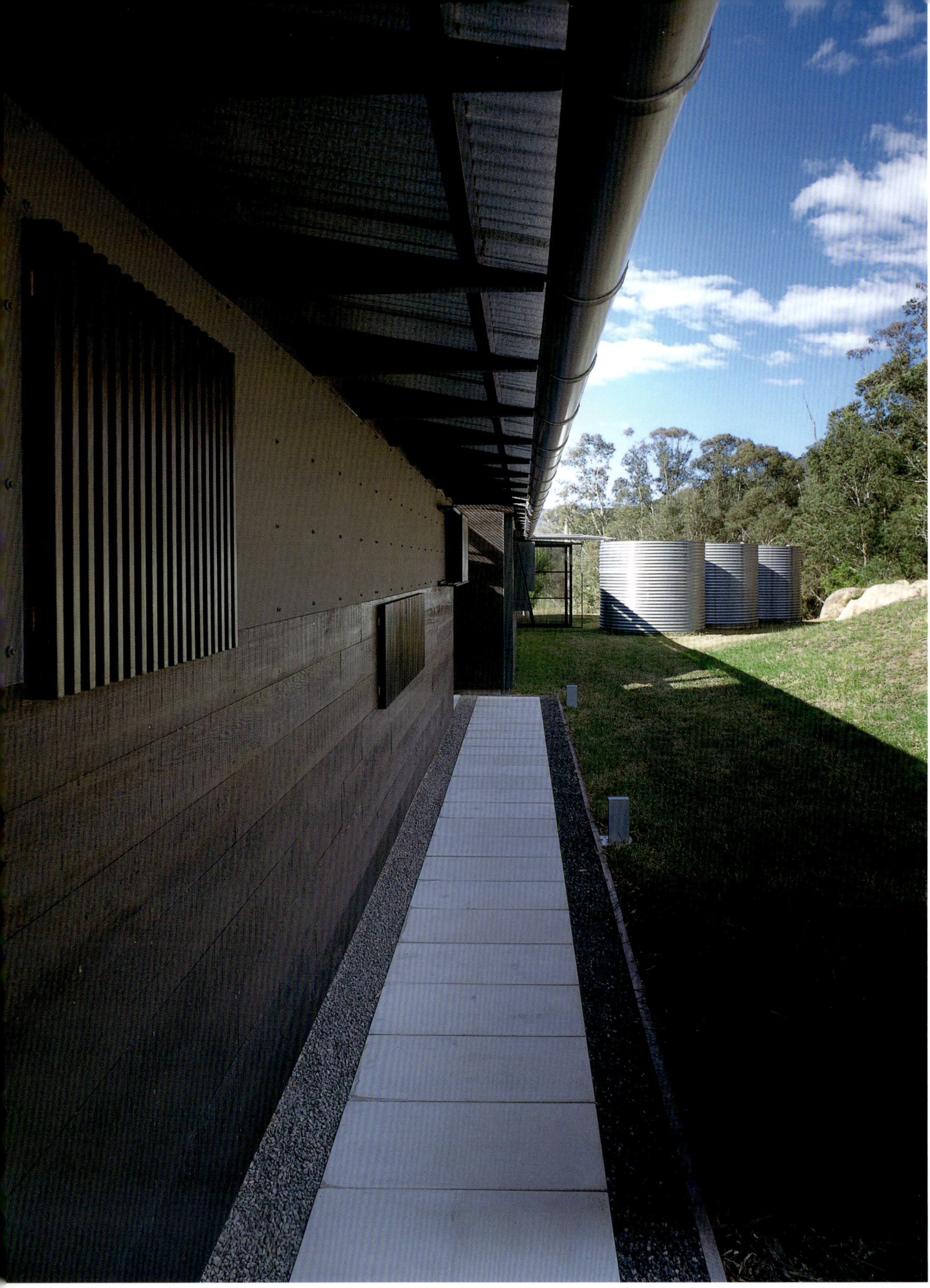

住宅は優美でありながら、最も実際的な素材でつくられた。工業色の灰色で塗られた鉄板、漆黒に染められた幅広の板、波板鉄板、波板ポリカーボネートの天窓である。

This refined architecture is achieved using the most elementary materials—steel sheet painted industrial grey, wood board stained ebony, corrugated steel and ribbed acrylic glazing.

東面のガラス戸は建物の南側背後へ完全に引き込まれ、リビングとテラスは一体となる。南側の壁は屋外へと延び、ベランダを冷たい南西の風から守る。

The glazed eastern wall of the house slides out entirely, to the southern side of the house, to unite the sitting room with veranda. The southern wall is extended to protect the veranda from cold south-west winds.

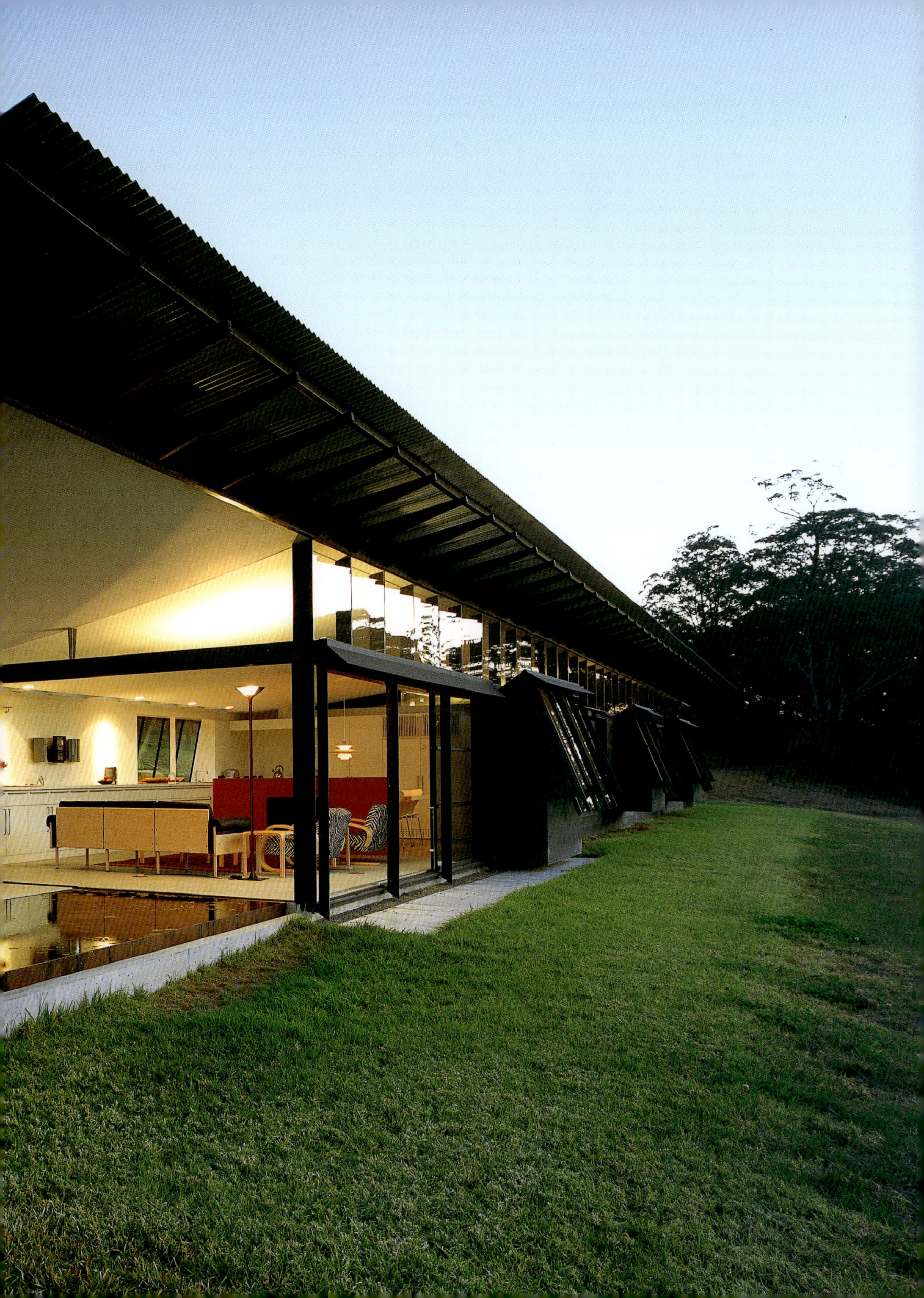

浅い池は、テラスの天井に水紋を反射するとともに、夏の室内気温を下げる。池の縁のディテールにより、水面を居間の床と同じレベルに保っている。

The shallow pond plays reflected patterns of sunlight onto the canopy ceiling, and tempers the heat of the summer air. Meticulous detailing of the pond edge maintains the plane of water at precisely the same level as the living room floor.

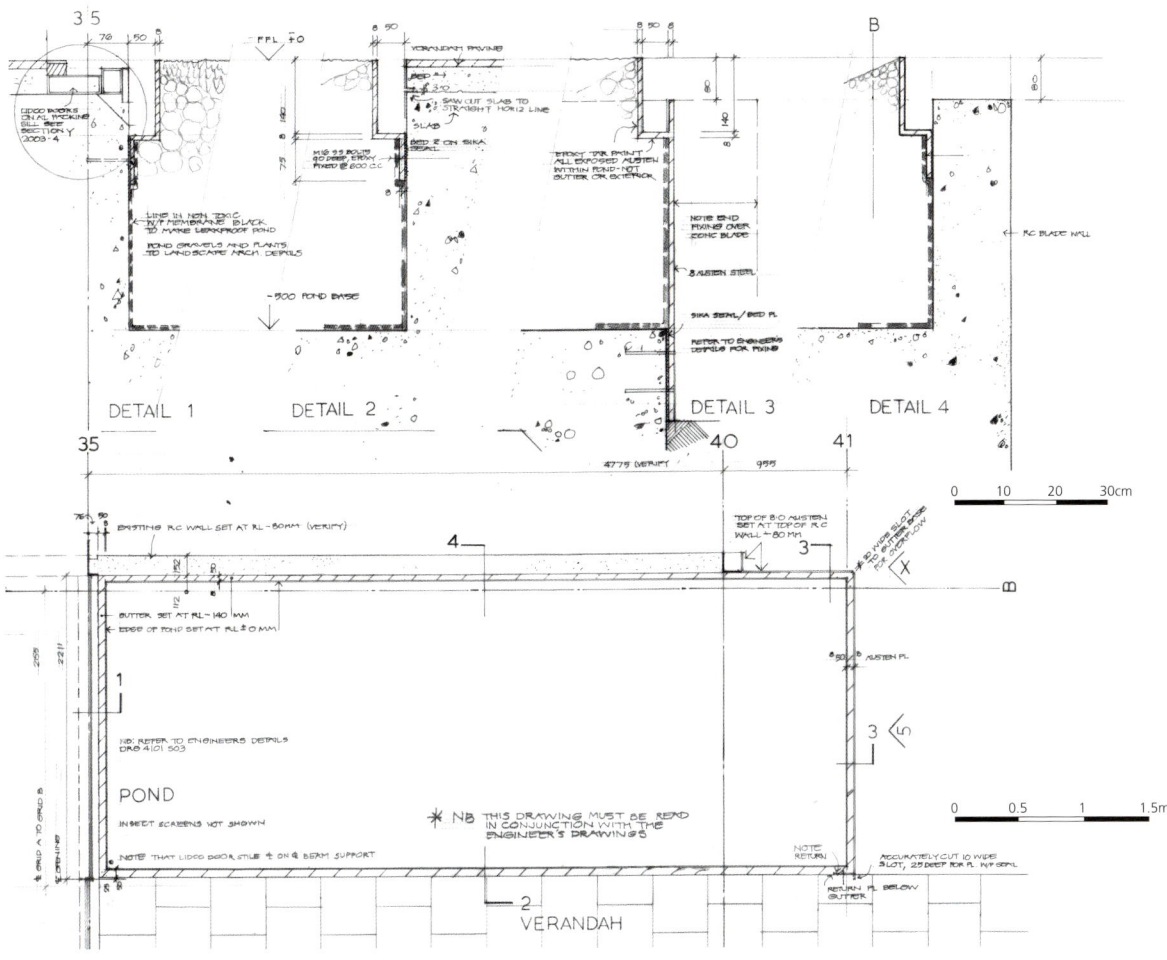

Details of the pond

Walsh House

ウォルシュ邸

この住宅は、シドニーから南へ200kmの距離にあるカンガルーバレーにあり、フレッチャー＝ペイジ邸に近く、形態もいくつかの共通点をもつ。2邸とも、平面が細長い片流れ屋根のパビリオンで、似た幅と高さ、長さをもつ。しかし、内部の使われ方、周辺ランドスケープへの関わり方はまったく異なるものである。

ウォルシュ邸は開けた草原に建ち、北の鬱蒼とした尾根に正面を向けている。長手の軸は、まっすぐに東の遠方に見える大きな隆起した岩を指している。マーカットの多くの住宅と同じように、深い庇が上部の北向きの窓を直射日光から守り、ブラインドの必要をなくし、1年中、尾根への眺望を得るようにしている。しかし、例えばシンプソン＝リー邸とは異なり、ウォルシュ邸の室内は流れるような1つの空間ではない。ここでは違う性質の部屋が連結されており、外部から見るとそれは、出窓の構成によって明瞭に区別されている。出窓のガラス面は、各部屋の明るさを調節する可動のブラインドによって保護される。それぞれの出窓は、例えば長椅子、書斎机、小さな温室などに使えるように考えられた。

住宅は4つの異なる立面をもつ。冬の冷たい南西の風が吹きつける南面と西立面は、農家的な実際的なものであり、直裁的かつ簡素な素材でつくられ、窓は少ない。北と東面は、より洗練された素材とディテールで構成され、周辺の美しい景色へとより開かれている。

ダイニングルームは南北両側への眺めがある唯一の部屋である。南の大きな窓からは岩を凌いで生える古木が見え、南東へは小さなコーナー・ウィンドウから雨水タンクの先へと斜めに視線を導いて、ランドスケープが傾斜していることを明らかにしている。北面には大きな2枚の引戸があり、東面のガラス戸は南側の建物の後ろへ完全に収納できる。これにより、リビングとテラスが一体化されて、浅く穏やかな水面をもつ池の上を眺望が渡る。池は、夏の暑い空気温度を下げるとともに、日光を水面に反射させてテラスの天井に水紋を投射している。

The house is located in Kangaroo Valley, close to the Fletcher-Page House, with which Walsh House has some formal similarities. Both are linear, mono-pitch pavilions, of comparable dimensions. However, in their ways of use, and in the ways that they engage with the landscape, the two houses are extremely different.

Walsh house stands on open grassland, with its principal façade addressing a forested ridge to its north, and with its long axis directed precisely towards a large knoll of rock in the distance, to its east. As at a number of other houses by Murcutt, the roof projects deeply to shield the upper, north-facing windows from direct summer sun, allowing these windows to be unscreened, and to frame the view of the ridge clearly throughout the year. However, unlike Simpson-Lee House, for example, Walsh House is not conceived as a single, fluid, interior space but as a series of connected rooms, each clearly identified from the outside by an individual glazed bay, protected by adjustable louvers, which allows the user to individually adjust the daylighting of their room. Each bay is intended for variable use, as for example a day-bed, writing desk, or small greenhouse.

The house presents four very different faces. Its southern and western elevations, facing the cold south-western winds of winter, have the character of a working farmhouse, crafted in rustic materials, with few windows. The northern and eastern façades are of far more refined materials and detailing, and are more open to the luxuriant surrounding view.

The dining room/kitchen is the only room in the house with both a northerly and southerly aspect. The large southern window frames a view of the ancient tree which surmounts the adjacent hillock, and a small corner window frames a selected, diagonal south-easterly view, past the water tanks, which reveals the sloping form of the land. The two ultimate windows of the north façade can be slid back, and the glazed eastern end-wall can be slid completely away to the south side of the house. This both unites the sitting room with the veranda and sets up a north-easterly diagonal view across a shallow, tranquil pond which plays reflected patterns of sunlight onto the canopy ceiling, and tempers the heat of the summer air.

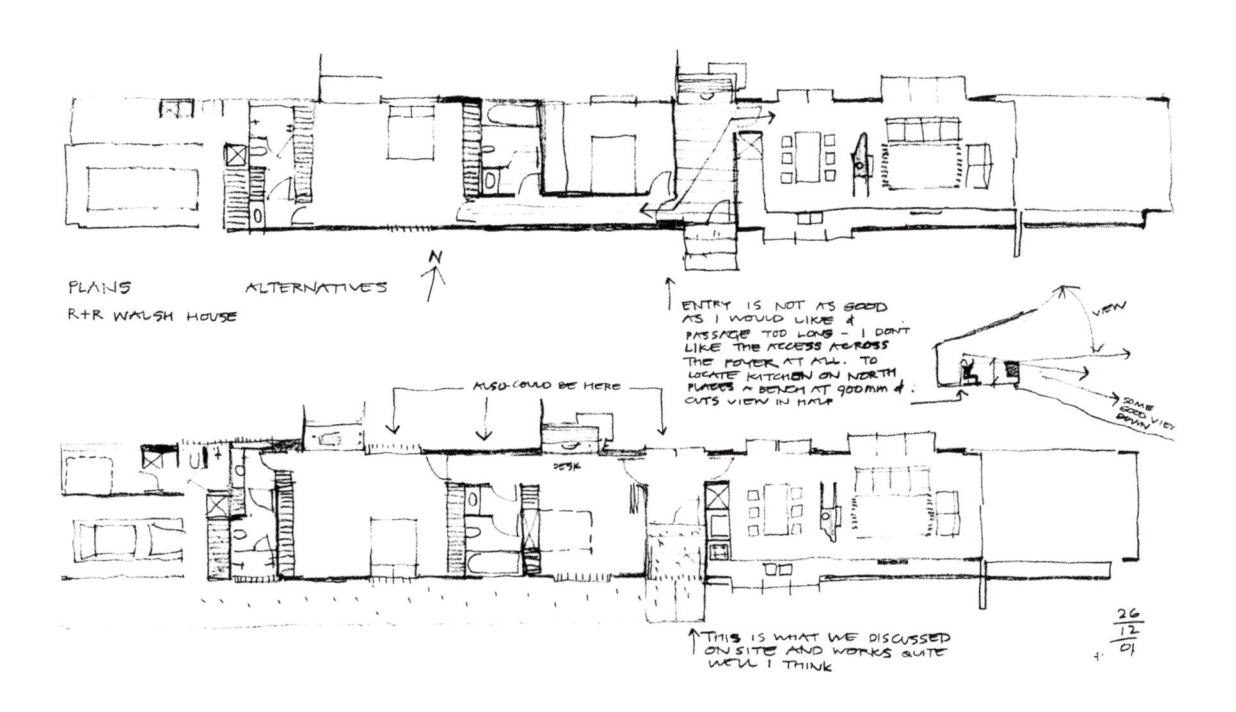

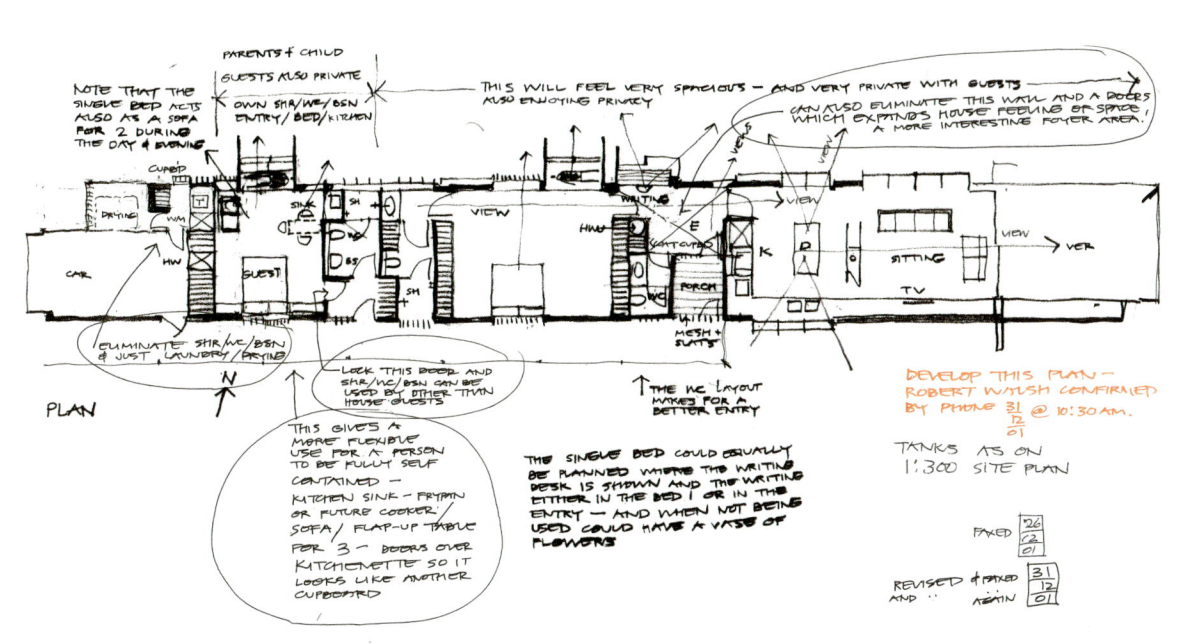

施主へのアイデア説明に使われたマーカットによる平面スタディ。一番下のスケッチが最終形に近い。

Three sketch plans made by Murcutt at different stages to explain his developing ideas to the client. The lowest plan shows roughly the final version.

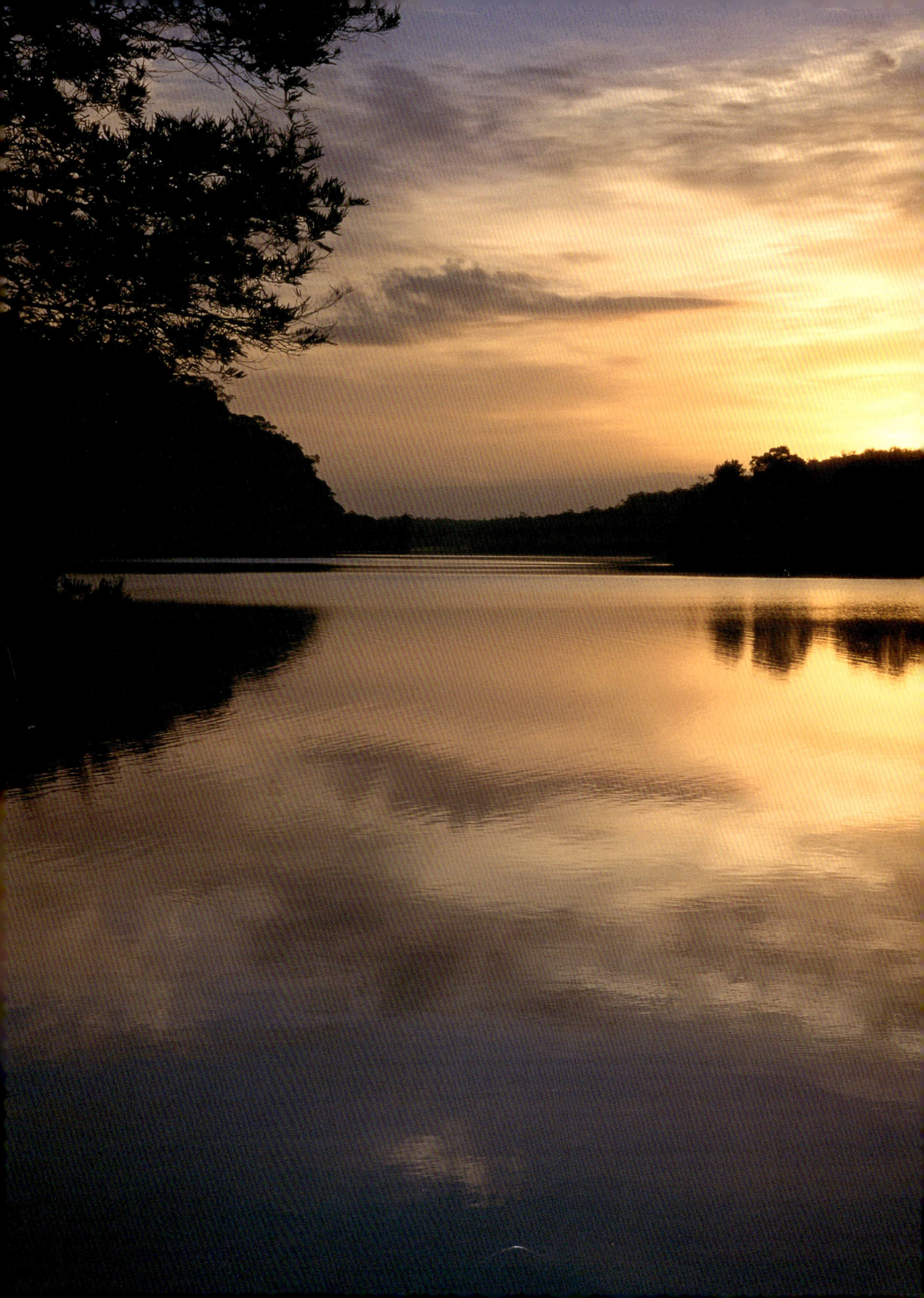

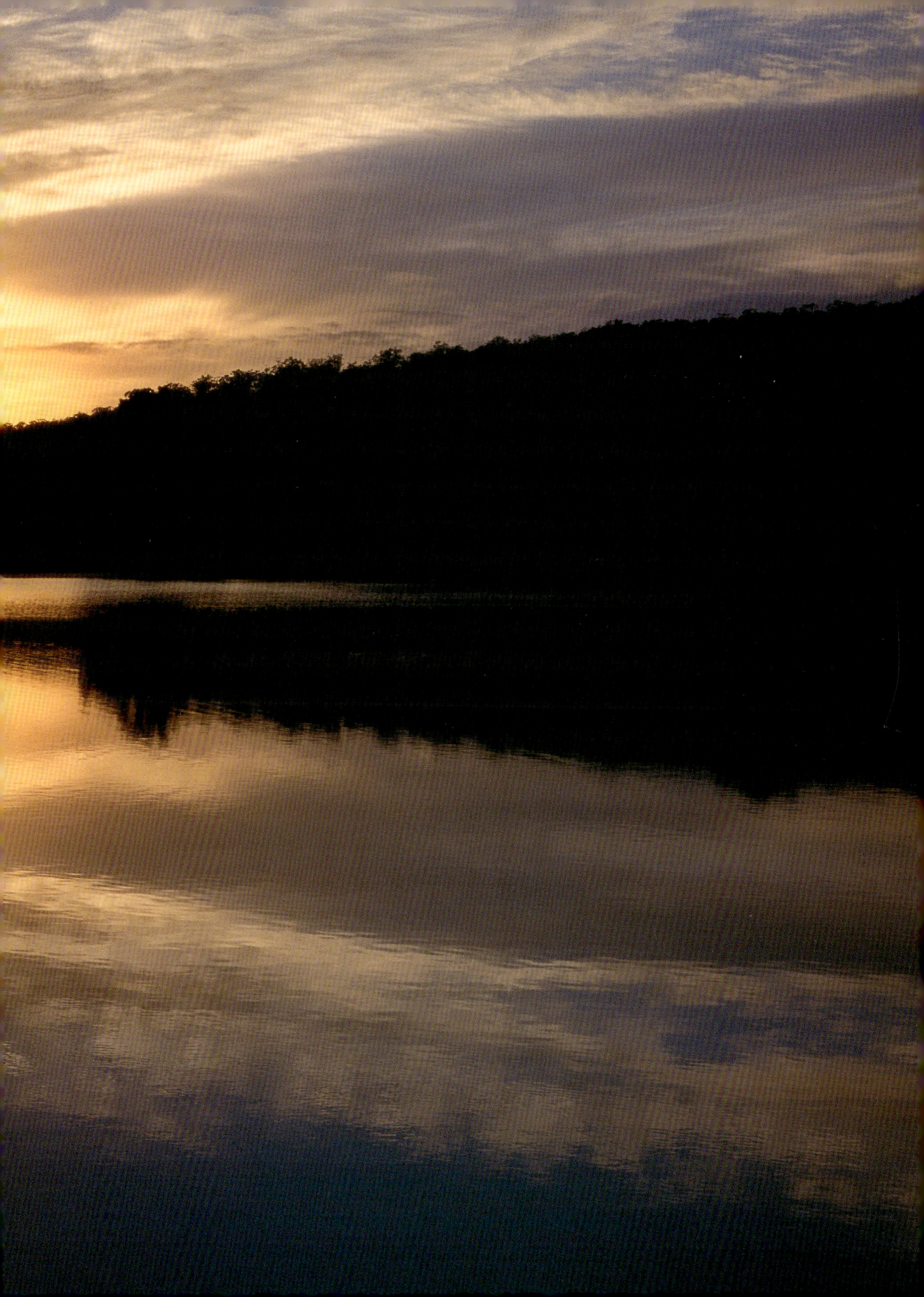

対話と発見

トム・ヘネガン

「建築の本質的な主題は、人間であり、その歴史と文化である。空間、光、素材をどうつなげて建てるか。土地への責任。よいデザインとは、これらを理解してその答えを見つけるまで模索を続けることである。建築とは、見出す過程そのものである」[1]

グレン・マーカット

マーカット＝ルーウィン邸の背面にある、洗練された佇まいのガラス・スクリーンは、マーカットの建築を原始的なものへの郷愁と誤ってとらえている人々を驚かすかもしれない。そのスクリーンは、単純なかたちをもつにもかかわらず、その日の天気と時間によって室内の状況を「調節」するようにあつらえられた創意に満ちた仕組みである。これは、マーカットが自身の建築を語る時によく使う言葉で言えば、「空間装置（コントラプション）」*である。エリザベス・ファラリーが指摘したように、「建築は、マーカットにとっては、興味深い多次元の問題なのだ。そこでは空間的な仕掛けが解決方法なのである」[2]。

ここで「問題」とは建築をどう自然の中へ建てるかという入り組んだ問いである。しかし彼には「自然界」は不安定で無秩序な場所ではない。「私たちの（オーストラリアの）ランドスケープには……」とマーカットは説明する。「厳密な秩序がある。ひどく雑然と見えても、土の酸性やアルカリ性レベル、地下水位の深さ、海抜高さ、海への近さなどが規定する厳密な秩序をもっている」[3]。マーカットにとってランドスケープは、周辺の環境が関連して成り立つ文脈（コンテクスト）であるだけでなく、それ自体を「読む」ことのできる「文章（テキスト）」でもあるのだ。平原に立つ樹木の種類の違いは、土の深さやその種類の違い、地面には現れていない積層した岩の在り処、地面の形状によって雨が降ると川の流れとなる場所、そして自然から守られている土地を明らかにする。このようなすべての情報が、デザイン過程の中で消化されて建物となる。建物では、周囲の自然環境の一番よいところが生かされて、それが住み手の日常となるのである。

マーカットの、ランドスケープを「読む」行為は、分類学の手法に似ている。それは相互関係により物事を理解する科学であり、その差異が意味をもちうる学問である。そして彼の一連の建築を分類学的にとらえることは適切であろう。それは彼の建物と周辺自然との間にある「秩序」、そしてマーカッ

---

*訳者註：「空間装置（コントラプション）」とは、本稿では、風力や自然光などの自然エネルギーを利用して空間環境を調節する、建築的な仕掛けや仕組みを指す。

[1] See invitation to exhibition *Thinking Drawing/Working Drawing*, Gallery Ma, Tokyo 2008.
[2] Elizabeth Farrelly, *Three Houses—Glenn Murcutt*, Phaidon Press Limited, 1993.
[3] Glenn Murcutt, interview with author, Sydney, 2007.

トの建物が互いに関連してもつ「秩序」である。

　自然の中では、「物事はぶつからず、姿を変えるのだ。要素は序列に従い、あるべきところに収まるように構成されている」[4]とマーカットは言う。明らかな工法で、建築要素が明確に分けられている彼の建築にもこの説明は当てはまる。しかしその建築は、ランドスケープに応答しながらも景色と一体化はしていない。それは精密な、幾何形態をもつパビリオン建築で、低い「ピロティ」として地面からもち上げられていることが多い。「調和とは、異種性の認識である。異なる音が和音となって心地よく響く……。（自然と建築が）それぞれの完全無欠さを保っているならば、対峙するものを描写することができる。一方がもう一方の〈秩序〉を規定するのである」[5]。

　この相互関係により、マーカット設計のどの住宅図面を見ても、方角、年間の気温、風の向き、敷地における浸水や山火事の危険性、辺りにある特徴的な自然のおおまかな位置が基礎情報としてわかり、そして、彼の環境にあわせて建物の色彩を決める習慣から、その敷地が鬱蒼とした林にあるかまで、その場合は外壁の種類や色までも言い当てることができるかもしれない。「建物は環境に根本的に関連しているのがいいと思う——もしくは受動的であってほしい。それゆえに木材で外壁を仕上げる時は、そこに生えているユーカリの落とす影の濃さによって、灰色か黒に塗装する。ニューサウスウェールズ州の南海岸では、ランドスケープは灰色か黒だが、北海岸では、より灰色に近い。だから、マリー・ショート邸は黒ではなく灰色なのだ」[6]。

●

しかしながら、より注意深く彼の住宅を見ると、彼の美的な決定は倫理的な決定に比べると数少ないことがわかる。なぜならその建物の立脚点は、使われ方であり、立ち姿ではないからである。マーカットにとって、環境への負荷を最小限にとどめる建築を設計することは、創造的な仕事である。生産時の環境負荷が少ない素材を使って、解体や再利用がたやすい工法によって建てられている。

　今になってやっと、現実的で火急な建築の問題となった環境への配慮は、仕事を始めてから現在に至るまでのマーカットの基盤となっている。その環境に対する強い決心は、彼の幼少に起因する。オーストラリア人の両親の短い滞在期間中に英国で生まれた後、「冒険家」である父親のアーサーが、

---

[4] Haig Beck and Jackie Cooper, *Glenn Murcutt, A Singular Practice*, The Images Publishing Group, 2002.
[5] Elizabeth Farrelly, *Three Houses—Glenn Murcutt*.
[6] Glenn Murcutt, interview with author, Sydney, 2007.

船大工や発明家、大工や金の探鉱という型にはまらない仕事をしたニューギニアの森の中で5年間過ごした。彼の父親はまた、アメリカの自然主義者で哲学者のヘンリー・デイビッド・ソロー（1817-1862年）の熱心な読者であった。ソローは自伝『ウォールデン—森の生活』で、自然の簡潔さにならい、自立して暮らすことを説いたが、白人入植村から何マイルも離れたところに住んだマーカット一家はその2つの教訓の実践者であった。彼らの父親が建てた住宅は、浸水や爬虫類、攻撃的な原住民を避けるために地面から高くもち上げられ、波板鉄板で屋根を葺かれていた。謙虚さと独立という家訓は、マーカットのその後の人生と仕事におけるガイドラインとなった。フィリップ・ドリューが記したように、「問題や難関に対して誰にも頼らず自分自身で考え抜くことは、アーサー・マーカットがニューギニアで学んだ一番重要なことで、その教えは幼少のグレン・マーカットへも叩き込まれた」[7]。そしてソローの最も根本的な言葉、それはマーカットの父親もよく口にした教訓だが、「ほとんどの人間はその一生をありふれた仕事をして過ごすのだから、重要なのは、その仕事を並外れてうまくやることだ」[8]。

　一家は1946年にシドニーへ辿り着き、アーサー・マーカットはさらにデザイナー兼大工という新しい分野の仕事を始めた。そして、大工仕事とレンガ積み工として熟練し始めた2人の青春期の息子の助けを借りて何軒かの住宅を建てた。型にはまらない新しいものに夢中になるたちの父親は、当時の名高い国際的な建築雑誌を一心に取り寄せていた。「父は、私の現代建築に対する原思想を吹き込んだのだ。フィリップ・ジョンソン邸、イームズ邸、そして誰にもましてフランク・ロイド・ライト。14歳か15歳の頃には、ライトの仕事をすべて知っていたほどだ」[9]。しかし一番の影響を与えたのは、1951年の『アーキテクチュアル・フォーラム』誌であり、マーカットのすべての建築の出発点となるミースのファンズワース邸であった。彼の父親は建築家として訓練を受けることはついぞなかったが、「父はいくつかのとてもよい住宅を建てた。そして確実に言えることは、美しくものを組み立てるやり方を知っていて、それを徐々に私に教えることができたということだ」[10]。

●

知性を用い、経済的で——そして最も重要な——「正直な」架構方法で「美しい」建築をつくるのは、もちろん現代建築家（モダニスト）たちの主題であり、マーカットの建築をその流れに沿ったものと見ることも可能で

---

[7] Philip Drew, in *The Tin Man*, Television Documentary, Catherine Hunter Producer, Chanel Nine Telecast, 2000.
[8] Glenn Murcutt, *Architecture Australia*, May/June 2002.
[9] Elizabeth Farrelly, *Three Houses—Glenn Murcutt*.
[10] Glenn Murcutt, in *The Tin Man*.

ある。しかし彼の仕事をモダニズムから一線を画しているのは、それがモダニズムの伝承された決まりごとから自由である点である。その野心や優先順位のつけ方からおそろしく無関係なのだ。「ミースは、無意識のうちにいまだ私の判断基準だ」[11]という言葉のように、ミースの形態の残照があるとしても、マーカットにとって1931年に建てられたパリのメゾン・ドゥ・ヴェール（ガラスの家：ダルザス邸）訪問は衝撃的であった。「そこにはロマンティックなモダニズムがあった。決まりにとらわれない……。あの住宅で私は〈発見すること〉について解き放たれた。現代建築でありながら、1つの解答へ収束せず、主義ももたない」[12]。その住宅こそ、建築家ベルナルド・ヴィボエと、家具とインテリアのデザイナーであるピエール・シャロー、そして金属職人のルイス・ダルベが協同した作品だった。ガラス戸やパンチングメタルの引戸、折りたたみ戸、回転スクリーンが室内空間を変化させ、また軸回転する衣装棚などのさまざまな仕掛けや、キッチンからダイニングへ頭の上を走る食膳、図書室の可動はしごや、回転して移動できる衛生器具など、現代生活が仮定上必要とするものがメカニックな発明品によって応えられた独創的な住宅である。それは、最高の「空間装置（コントラプション）」であった。

●

建築は空間的な装置であるという考え方——マーカットにとっては因習にとらわれないまったくの目的をもった仕掛けなのだが——は、彼の建築の基礎をなす。その理由は、ヨットを繰る船乗りの行動がヨットの中心的存在であり、そしてヨットが船乗りの自然を楽しむ際の中心的存在であるのと同じく、施主が住まいの中心的存在であることを強調するからである。実際、マーカットは「舟」を「家」の比喩として用いる。「私の建築はヨットを繰るように使うのだ。舟を進ませるにはうまく操縦しなければいけない。いろいろな仕掛けを動かさなければいけない。私の建築も同じである。これは重要なことだ。建物は静止した物体ではないことを理解するのはとても大切なことだ」[13]と言っている。議論はさらに、幼少を過ごしたシドニーの家の7台のピアノや、いろいろな工程段階の競争艇（スキフ）があったことが変じて、住まい方を、音楽を奏でる行為になぞらえる。マーカットは彼の建築を「楽器」もしくは「自然を感知する道具」と呼んで、その表面にある窓などを「ピアノを弾くのを習うように」[14]使い方を習得する装置だと説明する。

---

[11] Glenn Murcutt, in *Architecture Australia*, May/June 2002.
[12] Elizabeth Farrelly, *Three Houses—Glenn Murcutt*.
[13] Glenn Murcutt, in *The Tin Man*.
[14] Glenn Murcutt, interview with author, Sydney, 2007.

空間的な仕掛けが室内にあったメゾン・ドゥ・ヴェールとは対照的に、その建物において仕掛けは表面——そこをマーカットは「変化がおこるエキサイティングなゾーン」というが——にあり、スクリーン、ブラインド、引戸、軸回転扉などが設置される。実際、マーカットの建築を性格づけているものは手動による調節可能な表皮である。その建築は、ほぼ共通して3層の建具をもち、「ルーバーを外側に、鎧戸、網戸付きのガラス戸がある。これらの3種類の建具は住み手に自由度を与える。暑い日にはすべてを開け放して換気する。防犯には鎧戸を閉める。虫がいれば網戸を閉める。寒い夜にはガラス戸を閉める。もしくは日中暖をとりたければ、鎧戸を引き込み、ガラス戸にする。常に建物を変化させるのだ。建物の中にいるだけでなく、建物と暮らすのだ」[15]。

●

マーカットの住宅は敷地に対して東西に長く配置される。これは日射しを効果的に採り入れて換気条件をよくするためである。立面は、住み手による能動的な機構調節装置として使われ、屋根は夏の高い太陽光を防ぎ、冬の暖かい日射しを採り入れる受動的な存在である。さらに屋根は、その翼形状によって夏の涼風を加速するように働き、上水道から離れた敷地において水を確保するために雨水を収集する。共通項であるこれらの前提はしかし、各プロジェクトの詳細において常に新たに考え直される。言い換えれば、マーカットは、自然の中の住まいという普遍的な問いに対して研究を重ねているのだと言える。

この見方は、マーカットの建築の型が、回顧的なオーストラリアの羊毛刈り小屋の系列であるという言論や、彼がミニマリスト・モダニズムやブッシュ・バナキュラーという幻想によって現代「オーストラリア建築」なる分野をつくったという論への問いとなるだろう。ケネス・フランプトンは「地域（工法）の参照という起点……。（実現されたのは）実際的な、高度に美的な奥地方式」[16]と形容したが、「奥地様式」ではなく「奥地方式」としたところに意味がある。フランプトンによれば、マーカット建築の素晴らしさは環境負荷を最小にする建て方に由来する美しさである。マリー・ショート邸の二重屋根は近くにあるいくつもの農家の二重屋根に認められるが、その他の特徴については、建物の各要素が複雑で洗練された機構調節装置をつくりだすように考えられた試行の産物だと言える。施主の小屋

---

[15] Glenn Murcutt, interview with author, Sydney, 2007.
[16] Kenneth Frampton, in letter of support for award of Honorary Doctorate to Glenn Murcutt by the University of Sydney, 2003.

にあった木材のみを利用して、将来の移築に対応するように組まれたマリー・ショート邸は、マーカット自身の言葉によれば「たぶん、その組み方にまでサスティナビリティというデザインの核をもった最初の建物の1つだろう」[17]。

ほぼ40年にわたり、これまでマーカットは500以上の建物をすべてオーストラリア国内に建ててきた。ほとんどすべての住宅が、彼自身によって設計され、図面が引かれ、現場監理がされた。マーカットは所員を雇わない。たまに大きな仕事で、例えばボイド・アートセンターでは彼の妻であるウェンディ・ルーウィンと協同したが、通常は各プロジェクトのすべての面において責任を1人で負う。それにより、デザインのコンセプトの一貫性を保ち、図面に引かれたものと制作物の完全な一致が図られるのである。この理由によりマーカットはオーストラリア国外の仕事を断る。それは成果物に対する同等の監理が不可能だからである。そしてほとんど確実に施主の意向によって彼の目指すものが妥協させられるであろう大きなプロジェクトや商業施設を設計しようという気はないようである。

　マーカットの引く施工図面は、それに基づいて建てられる建築のもつ精密さと力強さそのものである。その図面はマーカットの頭の中にはっきりと見える現実を表すものであり、大工への指示というよりは「実測図面」に近いものである。平面図と断面図によってアイデアを案出するのと同時に、マーカットはどうやったらそれを建てることができるかという詳細スケッチを検討する。そのために「設計図面」と「実施図面」の違いがほとんどない。例えば、フレッチャー＝ペイジ邸の施工図面には、素材や工法について触れられると同時に、建物配置の理由づけまで示されている。住宅からの一番よい景観である崖へ向かう視線がその平面図に描かれている。

　マーカットの図面は、局地的な敷地条件、気候や地理性——そして大抵はそこの文化まで——を記した地図ともとれる。毎回、彼は基本の問いから始める。「建築をつくることは、素晴らしい発見の過程なのだ」と彼は言う。「それは質問の答えは知らないが、そこに辿り着くであろう道筋を知っている科学者のようなものだ……。発見という道程の喜び、それがまさしく私がやっていることだ」[18]。

---

[17] Glenn Murcutt, interview with author, Sydney, 2007.
[18] Glenn Murcutt, in *Architecture Australia*, May/June 2002.

Dialogue and Discovery   Tom Heneghan

"The central design issues of architecture are humans and their history and culture; space; light; how things are put together; and responsibility to the land. Good design involves an understanding of these issues and pursuing the questions they raise until you make appropriate discoveries. Architecture is a path of discovery." [1]

Glenn Murcutt

The sophistication of the glazed screen to the rear of the Murcutt-Lewin House may surprise those who incorrectly sense in Murcutt's work a romantic nostalgia for primitive things. The screen, although simple, is a compendium of ingenious, custom-made mechanisms that permit the complex relationship between the inner and outer worlds to be continuously 'tuned', as wished, in response to the climate and to the time of day. It is a 'contraption'—a word Murcutt uses frequently to describe his buildings. As Elizabeth Farrelly has pointed out, "Architecture, for Murcutt, is an intriguing multi-dimensional problem; the contraption is the solution." [2]

This 'intriguing problem' concerns the issues involved in responding to the natural world through architecture. For him, the 'natural world' is not a place of capricious randomness. "In our native [Australian] landscape," he explains, "there's a very strict order. It looks incredibly informal, but it's a very strict order, related to the acidity level, or the alkalinity level, related to the level of the water-table, related to the altitude, to proximity to the sea." [3] For Murcutt, a landscape context is a 'text' that may be 'read' if one knows how to do so. The change in species of plants across a field reveals the differences in the types and depths of soil; the location of hidden rock layers; the location where heavy rain is channelled by the form of the land; the location where the wind blows fiercely and where the land is sheltered. All such information becomes fused, in his design process, into buildings that draw the most beneficial qualities of the natural context into the daily experience of the occupants.

Murcutt's 'reading' of the land is analogous to taxonomy—the science of understanding things in terms of their relationship with each other, and the lessons that can be drawn from their difference. And, it is apposite to consider his body of work in those terms, also—the 'order' of his buildings relative to that of their surrounding nature; and the 'order' of those buildings relative to each other.

In nature, he says, "Things don't smash together, they transmute. There is a hierarchy of parts,

---

[1] See invitation to exhibition *Thinking Drawing/Working Drawing*, Gallery Ma, Tokyo 2008.
[2] Elizabeth Farrelly, *Three Houses—Glenn Murcutt*, Phaidon Press Limited, 1993.
[3] Glenn Murcutt, interview with author, Sydney, 2007.

and a rational language in how the parts fit together"[4]—a description that equally applies to his architecture, in which the parts and methods of making are clearly articulated. But, while Murcutt's architecture corresponds to its landscape, it does not merge with it. His buildings are precise, geometric pavilions, often elevated above the ground on short *piloti*. "Harmony," he explains, "is about disparateness, about disparate sounds that when put together make a pleasing whole…If [nature and architecture] both hold their integrity, each will tell about the other. One clarifies the 'order' of the other."[5]

Due to this reciprocity, from a study of the working drawings of any Murcutt house, one could at least approximate its orientation, the seasonal temperatures, the wind directions, whether the site is susceptible to flooding or fire, the probable location of nearby natural features, and—since Murcutt colours his buildings in response to their context—one might even deduce whether this is a location of heavy planting and, if so, its probable type: "I like buildings that are tonally related to the environment—or recessive. So, in timber buildings I'll often stain the outside grey or black, depending on the depth of shade at the site and the type of eucalypts that are growing there. Along the south coast of New South Wales much of the landscape is grey or black. Along the north coast there are more greys. That's why the Marie Short House is grey and not black."[6]

A close study of a house would, however, tell one less about the architect's aesthetic preferences than about his ethics, since the polemic of his buildings lies in their way of their operation rather than in their appearance. For Murcutt, the design of buildings with minimal impact on the environment is the real work of a creative mind. His materials are chosen for their low embodied-energy, and are jointed for easy dis-assembly and re-use elsewhere.

Concern for the environment—which has now become such an urgent and contemporary issue in architecture—has underlain all Murcutt's work. His resolve in this area originates in his upbringing. Although born in England during a short visit there by his Australian parents, he spent his first five years living in the forests of New Guinea, where his 'adventurer' father, Arthur, followed a variety of unconventional careers—boat-builder, inventor, carpenter, gold-prospector— and was a profound devotee of the writings of the American naturalist and philosopher Henry

---

[4] Haig Beck and Jackie Cooper, *Glenn Murcutt, A Singular Practice*, The Images Publishing Group, 2002.
[5] Elizabeth Farrelly, *Three Houses—Glenn Murcutt*.
[6] Glenn Murcutt, interview with author, Sydney, 2007.

David Thoreau (1817-1862) whose memoir, 'Walden,' advocated a life of natural simplicity and self-reliance. The Murcutt family's life, many miles from the nearest white settlement, was both of those. Their house, built by his father, was perched high above the ground on stilts to keep out water and reptiles—and some dangerous local tribesmen—and roofed in corrugated iron sheet. The humility and independence of this existence established the guidelines by which Murcutt would route his subsequent life and career. As Philip Drew notes, "The message of being able to think through and respond to challenges and problems—by yourself, not relying on others—is the single most important lesson that Arthur Murcutt learned in New Guinea, and drummed into Glenn Murcutt as a young child."[7] And, Thoreau's most fundamental dictum, frequently recited by the father, is now Murcutt's explanation of his approach to architecture: "Since most of us spend our lives doing ordinary tasks, the most important thing is to carry them out extraordinarily well."[8]

In Sydney, to which the family returned at the start of war, Arthur Murcutt embarked on another new career—this time as a designer and builder of houses, often constructed with the help of his two teenage sons—both becoming adept at carpentry and bricklaying. Fascinated by the unconventional and the experimental, the father subscribed to all the leading international architectural journals of the time. "My father imbued my psyche with modern architecture. The Philip Johnson House, the Eames' House and Frank Lloyd Wright more than anybody. I knew all of Frank Lloyd Wright's work by the time I was 14 or 15."[9] The most influential, though, was a 1951 edition of *Architectural Forum* illustrating Mies van der Rohe's Farnsworth House—the building which has become a touchstone for all of Murcutt's architectural works. While his father had no formal training as an architect, "He designed some very good buildings, and I can say that he was able to instil in me the idea of putting things together in a way that was beautiful."[10]

The achievement of 'beauty' through intelligent, efficient and, above all, 'truthful' assembly was, of course, one of the leitmotifs of modernist architecture, and it is possible to see Murcutt's works as part of that tradition. But, what separates his works from those of Modernism is his architecture's freedom from received doctrine. His works are formidably independent in their ambitions and priorities. While remaining formally in thrall to Mies—"Mies, almost unconsciously, is still

---

[7] Philip Drew, in *The Tin Man*, Television Documentary, Catherine Hunter Producer, Chanel Nine Telecast, 2000.
[8] Glenn Murcutt, *Architecture Australia*, May/June 2002.
[9] Elizabeth Farrelly, *Three Houses—Glenn Murcutt*.
[10] Glenn Murcutt, in *The Tin Man*.

my conscience"[11]—he cites a visit to Paris' 'Maison de Verre,' built 1931, as showing him that "There was a poetry to modernism, an absolute freedom…it unlocked for me the whole notion of discovery, because it was a modern building, but it was open-ended, it had no dogma."[12] That house, a collaborative work by the architect Bernard Bijvoet, the furniture and interior designer Pierre Chareau and the metal-craftsman Louis Dalbet, could be transformed internally by sliding, folding or rotating screens in glass or perforated metal, and by a variety of devices including pivoting closets, an overhead food-trolley running from the kitchen to the dining room and rotating sanitary equipment. It was an entirely original work in which the imagined necessities of a modern lifestyle were met by a series of mechanical inventions. It was the 'contraption' *par excellence*.

This notion of architecture as a 'contraption'—by which Murcutt means an unconventional but entirely purposeful appliance—is the fundamental concept of his work since it emphasises the client's central, active role in the inhabitation of their building—in the same way that the actions of a yacht sailor are central to the performance of the yacht, and that the yacht is central to the sailor's experience of the natural environment. Indeed, Murcutt regularly uses 'boat' as metaphor for 'house': "You operate my buildings like you sail a boat. To make a boat go well, you have to work with it. You have to work with the elements. To make my buildings go, you have to work with them —to make them go well. That's a very important issue. It's important to understand that a building is not a static element."[13] He extends the argument by equating the 'act' of inhabitation with the making of music—a mixture of metaphors perhaps originating in his childhood home in Sydney where there were seven pianos, and in which racing skiffs were frequently to be found in different stages of construction. Murcutt describes his buildings as 'instruments', or as "devices with which to sense nature", and his external skins as 'mechanisms' which one must "learn to 'play' as one does a piano."[14]

In contrast to the Maison de Verre, where the mechanisms were predominantly internal components, it is at the edges of Murcutt's architecture—which he describes as the "zone of change and excitement"—that the screens, the louvers, and the sliding and pivoting planes are found. Indeed, the defining characteristic of Murcutt's architecture is the manual adjustability of

---

[11] Glenn Murcutt, in *Architecture Australia*, May/June 2002.
[12] Elizabeth Farrelly, *Three Houses—Glenn Murcutt*.
[13] Glenn Murcutt, in *The Tin Man*.
[14] Glenn Murcutt, interview with author, Sydney, 2007.

his perimeter skins. Typically, his façades are triple-layered, "There are louvers on the outside, and slatted screens, and glass windows with insect screens. These tri-partite elements give you flexibility. If the weather is hot and you want full ventilation you have everything open. For security you can just have the slats across. If there are insects you can just have the insect screens. If it's a cold night, you slide the insect screen in and the glass in. Or, during the day, if you want to get warm, you slide the slats and the insect screen back and let the glass take in the heat of the sun. So the whole time you're modifying the building. You're living with the building; you're not just living in it."[15]

He lays his long, thin houses east-west across their sites—maximising solar access and opportunities for cross-ventilation—with the walls configured for active climate modification by the clients, and with the roofs operating passively—as shade elements which exclude the high summer sun but admit the winter sun into the interior; as aerofoils, which speed sluggish summer breezes; and as rain collectors, since his houses are generally distant from town water supply. While these strategies are fairly consistent across all his works, their detailed resolution is constantly re-invented. Indeed, his body of work can be understood as a program of continuous research into appropriate architectural solutions to the universal questions of dwelling in nature.

This contradicts propositions that Murcutt's architecture is a retrospective linear descendant of the rustic Australian woolshed, or that he has created a contemporary 'Australian architecture' by the fusion of bush vernacular and minimalist modernism. Kenneth Frampton writes of Murcutt's "Invention of a regionally referential…but nevertheless practical and highly aesthetic 'outback' mode."[16] His use of the term 'outback mode' rather than 'outback style' is telling. The significance of Murcutt's architecture, he argues, is in the way that its aesthetic originates in the *methods* by which the buildings' impact on the ecosystem is minimised. The double-roofed Marie Short House does acknowledge the numerous double-roofed farm buildings that are found in its vicinity, but in every other respect is an experimental work in which every element is part of a complex and sophisticated climate-modifying 'mechanism.' Designed to be built entirely from lengths of wood that were laying in the client's shed, and jointed for easy dismantling in anticipation of the client's

---

[15] Glenn Murcutt, interview with author, Sydney, 2007.
[16] Kenneth Frampton, in letter of support for award of Honorary Doctorate to Glenn Murcutt by the University of Sydney, 2003.

plan to move the building to a different site in the future, it is, argues Murcutt, "Probably one of the first buildings, anywhere, in which sustainability was at the core of every aspect of the design, including its assembly."[17]

During his nearly 40 years of practice Murcutt has built more than 500 buildings, all in Australia, almost all houses, and almost all designed, drawn and supervised on site by him—alone. He employs no staff. While he occasionally collaborates on larger projects, such as the Boyd Art Centre, with his wife Wendy Lewin, he customarily takes sole responsibility for every aspect of a project so that there is absolute consistency of concept throughout the design, and absolute compliance between what he has drawn and what is fabricated. For that reason, he declines offers of work outside his homeland—since equivalent control over the product would be impossible—and he has no interest in designing large-scale or commercial buildings where his vision would almost certainly be compromised by competing factional client bodies.

Murcutt's extraordinary working drawings parallel the precision and intensity of the architecture that is their result. They describe what exists in Murcut's mind as a manifest reality, and have more the character of 'measured drawings' than of instructions to a builder. As he evolves his ideas in plan and section, Murcutt immediately sketches possible construction details to see how the ideas might be made real. There is, consequently, little difference between a 'design drawing' and a 'construction drawing'. The working drawings of Fletcher-Page House, for example, describe not only the materials and the manner by which it is to be assembled, but also the reasons for its orientation—the principle view-lines to the nearby cliff are marked on the plans.

Murcutt's drawings can be read as climatic, geological—and often cultural—maps of their sites, each of which has very different conditions and microclimate. He responds, each time, by thinking out the issues from first principles. "Architecture is a marvellous expression of the process of discovery," he explains, "It's like being a scientist who doesn't know the answer, but knows the path to it…That is what I'm in it for, the joy of the path, the discovery."[18]

[17] Glenn Murcutt, interview with author, Sydney, 2007.
[18] Glenn Murcutt, in *Architecture Australia*, May/June 2002.

グレン・マーカット

略歴

1936	・イギリス、ロンドン生まれ。両親はオーストラリア人
1950-1955	・マンリー高校（シドニー）
1956-1961	・シドニー・テクニカル・カレッジ（現ニューサウスウェールズ大学）にて建築学の学位取得
1962-1964	・イギリス、ヨーロッパ、北欧に研究旅行
1964-1969	・アンカー、モートロック、マリー & ウーレイ建築事務所勤務（シドニー）
1969	・事務所開設
1973	・メキシコ、アメリカ、イギリス、ヨーロッパに研究旅行
1984-1985	・ヨーロッパ、北アフリカに研究旅行
1986-1987	・メキシコ、アメリカに研究旅行

教育活動

1970-1979	・シドニー大学 デザイン講師
1985	・ニューサウスウェールズ大学 客員教授
1989-1997	・メルボルン大学建築学修士課程 客員クリティック
1990	・ペンシルヴァニア大学芸術大学院 客員クリティック
1990-1992	・シドニー工科大学 客員教授
1991-1995	・ペンシルヴァニア大学芸術大学院 招聘教授
1991	・アリゾナ大学 客員名誉建築家
1992	・パプアニューギニア工科大学 マスタークラス
1994	・ヘルシンキ工科大学 客員教授
1995	・シドニー工科大学 客員教授
1996	・ハワイ大学 客員教授
1997	・テキサス大学オースティン校 オニール・フォード教授
	・パプアニューギニア工科大学 マスタークラス
1998	・ヴァージニア大学 トーマス・ジェファーソン教授
1999	・アーフス建築学校（デンマーク）客員教授
	・モンタナ州立大学 マスタークラス
	・キャンベラ芸術学校 客員研究員
2000	・カルフォルニア大学ロサンゼルス校 客員教授
2001	・イェール大学 ウィリアム・ヘンリー・ビショップ客員教授
	・ニューキャッスル大学（オーストラリア）グレン・マーカット・マスタークラス

2002	・ワシントン大学 ルース+ノーマン・ムーア客員教授
	・ニューキャッスル大学（オーストラリア）グレン・マーカット国際マスタークラス
	・カンザス大学 J・L・コンスタント講師
	・パプアニューギニア工科大学 マスタークラス
	・イェール大学 ウィリアム・ヘンリー・ビショップ客員教授
	・コーネル大学 マスタークラス
2003	・ミシガン大学 エリエル・サーリネン客員教授
	・ダブリン工科大学 客員教授
	・モンテレー工科大学（メキシコ）ルイス・バラガン客員教授
	・ニューキャッスル大学（オーストラリア）グレン・マーカット国際マスタークラス
2004	・イリノイ工科大学 モーゲンシュタイン客員教授
	・ワシントン大学 カリストン客員教授
	・シドニー大学〈リバースデール〉グレン・マーカット国際マスタークラス
	・バッファロー大学ニューヨーク クラークソン客員教授
2005	・ワシントン大学 カリストン客員教授
	・ノースカロライナ大学 クリティカル・マス講座
	・シドニー大学〈リバースデール〉グレン・マーカット国際マスタークラス
	・イェール大学 ウィリアム・ヘンリー・ビショップ客員教授
2006	・リュブリャナ大学建築学校（スロヴェニア）客員教授
	・〈リバースデール〉グレン・マーカット国際マスタークラス
2006-2008	・ニューサウスウェールズ大学 招聘教授
	・ニューサウスウェールズ大学 第3学年デザイン教授
	・ワシントン大学 カリストン客員教授
	・ダブリン工科大学建築学校 CRH 教授
2007	・パレルモ大学（アルゼンチン）名誉教授

出版物

1985	・『鉄の葉っぱ——グレン・マーカット：オーストラリア建築形態のパイオニア』 フィリップ・ドリュー著
1993	・『3つの家——ディテールの建築』E・M・ファレリー著
1995	・『グレン・マーカット——ワークス＆プロジェクツ』フランシャス・フロモノ著
1999	・『大地にやさしく触れる——グレン・マーカットの言葉』フィリップ・ドリュー著
	・『グレン・マーカット』フローラ・ジャルデッロ・ポスティグリョーネ著
2002	・『グレン・マーカット——類例のない建築的実践』 ハイグ・ベック＆ジャッキー・クーパー著
2003	・『グレン・マーカット——ビルディングス+プロジェクツ 1962-2003』 フランシャス・フロモノ著
2006	・『グレン・マーカット・アーキテクト』ケネス・フランプトン著

受賞と栄誉

RAIA 州支部建築賞

1973	・王立オーストラリア建築家協会（RAIA）／グレイ＆マロニー修復／リノベーション賞
1973-2005	・2作品に RAIA ニューサウスウェールズ支部スルマン公共建築賞
	・6作品に RAIA ニューサウスウェールズ支部ウィルキンソン住宅賞
	・RAIA 北部準州支部トレーシー公共建築賞
	・RAIA 北部準州支部バーネット住宅賞
2004	・RAIA ニューサウスウェールズ支部25年賞（マリー・ショート／グレン・マーカット邸）

RAIA 建築賞

1973-2000	・「木造建築」賞
	・「鉄骨造建築」10年賞
	・ゼルマン・コーワン賞（ボワリ・カカドゥ・インフォメーションセンター：トロッポ・アーキテクツと協同）
	・ゼルマン・コーワン賞（アーサー＆イヴォンヌ・ボイド・アートセンター：ウェンディ・ルーウィン、レッグ・ラーク・アーキテクツと協同）
	・ゼルマン・コーワン公共建築選奨（ケンプシーの博物館）
	・ロビン・ボイド住宅賞（マグニー邸、ビンジーポイント）
	・ロビン・ボイド住宅選奨（マグニー邸、パディントン）
	・アボリジニの住宅に対する審査員特別賞（マリカ＝アルダートン邸）
	・RAIA25年賞（マリー・ショート／グレン・マーカット邸）

国内の受賞と栄誉

1992	・RAIA ゴールドメダル
1993	・RAIA 終身メンバー
1995	・ニューサウスウェールズ大学 名誉科学博士号
1996	・オーストラリア勲章
2003	・シドニー工科大学 名誉博士号
2004	・シドニー大学 名誉科学博士号

国外の受賞と栄誉

1982	・ビエンナーレ展（パリ、フランス）
1985	・イギリス連邦建築家連合（CAA）「場所と文化」建築賞
1991	・ビエンナーレ展（ヴェネチア、イタリア）
1992	・アルヴァ・アアルト・メダル
1996	・ビエンナーレ展（ヴェネチア、イタリア）
1997	・アメリカ建築家協会（AIA）名誉会員
	・王立英国建築家協会（RIBA）国際名誉会員
1998	・ノイトラ財団およびカルフォルニア・ポリテクニックよりリチャード・ノイトラ建築・教育賞
1999	・王立オランダ建築家アカデミーより「グリーン・ピン」国際建築・エコロジー賞
2001	・ケネス・F・ブラウン・アジア太平洋文化・建築デザイン賞（アーサー＆イヴォンヌ・ボイド・アートセンター：ウェンディ・ルーウィン、レッグ・ラーク・アーキテクツと協同）
	・トマス・ジェファーソン建築メダル
	・王立カナダ建築協会 名誉会員
2002	・王立オランダ芸術アカデミー国際賞
	・フィンランド建築家協会 名誉会員
	・プリツカー賞
2003	・ケネス・F・ブラウン・アジア太平洋文化・建築デザイン賞（マリカ＝アルダートン邸）
2004	・王立スコットランド建築家協会 名誉会員
2005	・台北建築家協会 名誉メンバー
	・シンガポール建築家協会 名誉会員
2008	・アメリカ芸術院 名誉会員

Glenn Murcutt

Biography

1936	· Born in London, UK. Parents Australian
1950-1955	· Manly Boys High School, Sydney
1956-1961	· Diploma of Architecture, Sydney Technical College (UNSW)
1962-1964	· Study travel United Kingdom, Europe and Nordic regions
1964-1969	· Joined Ancher Mortlock Murray & Woolley Architects, Sydney
1969	· Entered private practice
1973	· Study travel Mexico, USA, UK and Europe
1984-1985	· Study travel Europe and North Africa
1986-1987	· Study travel Mexico and USA

Teaching

1970-1979	· Design tutor, University of Sydney, Sydney
1985	· Visiting professor, University of New South Wales, Sydney
1989-1997	· Visiting critic, Master of Architecture, University of Melbourne, Melbourne
1990	· Visiting critic, Graduate School of Fine Arts, University of Pennsylvania, USA
1990-1992	· Visiting professor, University of Technology, Sydney
1991-1995	· Adjunct professor, Graduate School of Fine Arts, University of Pennsylvania, USA
1991	· Visiting Distinguished Architect, University of Arizona, Tucson, Arizona, USA
1992	· Master Class, PNG University of Technology, Lae, Papua New Guinea
1994	· Visiting professor, University of Technology, Helsinki, Finland
1995	· Visiting professor, University of Technology, Sydney
1996	· Visiting professor, University of Hawaii, Honolulu, USA
1997	· O'Neill Ford Chair, University of Texas at Austin, Texas, USA
	· Master Class, PNG University of Technology, Lae, Papua New Guinea
1998	· Thomas Jefferson Professor, University of Virginia, USA
1999	· Visiting professor, School of Architecture, Aarhus, Denmark
	· Master Class, Montana State University, Bozeman, USA
	· Visiting Fellow, Canberra School of Art, Canberra
2000	· Visiting professor, UCLArts, Los Angeles, USA
2001	· William Henry Bishop visiting professor, Yale University, USA
	· Glenn Murcutt Master Class, University of Newcastle, Australia

2002	• Ruth + Norman Moore visiting professor, University of Washington, St. Louis, USA
	• International Glenn Murcutt Master Class, University of Newcastle, Australia
	• Distinguished J.L. Constant Lecturer, University of Kansas, USA
	• Master Class, PNG University of Technology, Lae, Papua New Guinea
	• William Henry Bishop visiting professor, Yale University, USA
	• Master Class, Cornell University, Ithaca, USA
2003	• Eliel Saarinen visiting professor, University of Michigan, Ann Arbor, USA
	• Visiting professor, Dublin Institute of Technology, Ireland
	• Luis Barragan Visiting Chair, TEC de Monterrey NL Mexico and TEC de Monterrey, Mexico City, Mexico
	• International Glenn Murcutt Master Class, University of Newcastle, Australia
2004	• Morgenstein visiting professorial chair, Illinois Institute of Technology, Chicago, USA
	• Calliston visiting professorial chair, University of Washington, Seattle, USA
	• International Glenn Murcutt Master Class, 'Riversdale'/University of Sydney, Sydney
	• Clarkson visiting professorial chair, University of Buffalo, New York, USA
2005	• Calliston visiting professorial chair, University of Washington, Seattle, USA
	• CriticalMass, University of North Carolina Charlotte, USA
	• International Glenn Murcutt Master Class, 'Riversdale'/University of Sydney, Sydney
	• William Henry Bishop visiting professor, Yale University, USA
2006	• Visiting professor, School of Architecture University of Ljubljana, Slovenia
	• Glenn Murcutt International Master Class, 'Riversdale' West Cambewarra
2006-2008	• Adjunct professor, University of New South Wales, Sydney
	• Year 3 design professor, University of New South Wales, Sydney
	• Calliston visiting professorial chair, University of Washington, Seattle, USA
	• CRH professor, School of Architecture, Dublin Institute of Technology, Ireland
2007	• Honoris Causa Professor, Universidad de Palermo, Buenos Aires, Argentina

Publications

1985	• *Leaves of Iron—Grenn Murcutt: Pioneer of an Australian Architectural Form* by Philip Drew
1993	• *Three Houses—Architecture in Detail* by E. M. Farrelly
1995	• *Glenn Murcutt—Works and Projects* by Françoise Fromonot
1999	• *Touch This Earth Lightly—Glenn Murcutt in His Own Words* by Philip Drew
	• *Glenn Murcutt* by Flora Giardiello Postiglione
2002	• *Glenn Murcutt—A Singular Architectural Practice* by Haig Beck and Jackie Cooper
2003	• *Glenn Murcutt—Buildings + Projects 1962-2003* by Françoise Fromonot
2006	• *Glenn Murcutt Architect* by Kenneth Frampton

Awards and Honours

RAIA State Chapter Named Architecture Awards

1973	• Royal Australian Institute of Architects (RAIA) /Gray and Mulroney Restoration/Renovation Award
1973-2005	• Two Sulman Awards for Public Buildings, NSW
	• Six Wilkinson Awards for Housing, NSW
	• Tracy Award for Public Buildings, Northern Territory
	• Burnett Award for Housing, Northern Territory
2004	• RAIA NSW Chapter 25 Year Award for the Marie Short/Glenn Murcutt House, Kempsey, NSW

RAIA National Named Architecture Awards and National Awards

1973-2000
- 'Timber in Architecture' Award
- 'Steel in Architecture,' Award of the Decade
- Sir Zelman Cowan Award for the Bowali Kakadu Visitors Information Centre, in collaboration with Troppo Architects
- Sir Zelman Cowan Award for the Arthur and Yvonne Boyd Art Centre, in collaboration with Wendy Lewin and Reg Lark architects
- Sir Zelman Cowan Commendation for Public Buildings—Museum Kempsey, NSW
- Robin Boyd Awards for Housing—Magney House, Bingie Point
- Robin Boyd Commendation for Housing—Magney House, Paddington, Sydney
- National Jury Special Award for Aboriginal Housing—Marika-Alderton House, Northern Territory
- RAIA National 25 Year Award for the Marie Short/Glenn Murcutt House, Kempsey, NSW

National Awards and Honors

1992
- Royal Australian Institute of Architects Gold Medal

1993
- Life Fellow, Royal Australian Institute of Architects

1995
- Honorary Doctorate of Science, University of New South Wales, Sydney

1996
- Order of Australia (AO)

2003
- Honorary Doctorate of Letters, University of Technology, Sydney

2004
- Honorary Doctorate of Science, University of Sydney, Sydney

International Awards and Honors

1982
- Biennale Exhibition, Paris, France

1985
- Commonwealth Association of Architects (CAA) Award for Architecture of its 'Place and Culture'

1991
- Biennale Exhibition, Venice, Italy

1992
- Alvar Aalto Medal, Helsinki, Finland

1996
- Biennale Exhibition, Venice, Italy

1997
- Honorary Fellow of the American Institute of Architects
- International Fellow of the Royal Institute of British Architects

1998
- Richard Neutra Award for Architecture and Teaching from the Neutra Foundation and CalPoly, Pomona, USA

1999
- The 'Green Pin' International Award for Architecture and Ecology from the Royal Danish Academy of Architects

2001
- The Kenneth F. Brown Asia Pacific Culture and Architecture Design Award for the Arthur and Yvonne Boyd Art Centre, Riversdale—in collaboration with Wendy Lewin and Reg Lark architects
- Thomas Jefferson Medal for Architecture, USA
- Honorary Fellow of the Royal Architectural Institute of Canada

2002
- The Royal Danish Academy of Fine Arts International Award for 'Making a Difference' to the thinking and practice of architecture
- Honorary Fellow ot the Finnish Association of Architects, SAFA
- The Pritzker Architecture Prize

2003
- The Kenneth F. Brown Asia Pacific Culture and Architecture Award Honorary Mention for an Aboriginal House, Arnhem Land, Northern Territory

2004
- Honorary Fellow, Royal Incorporation of Architects in Scotland

2005
- Honorary Member, Taipei Architects Association, Taiwan
- Honorary Fellow, Singapore Institute of Architects, Singapore

2008
- Elected, Honorary Member, American Academy of Arts and Letters, USA

クレジット
Credits

写真　Photography
アンソニー・ブローウェル　Anthony Browell
下記以外の全ての写真　Except:
マックス・デュパン　Max Dupain
pp.38-43, pp.102-103, p.112, pp.116-117
グレン・マーカット　Glenn Murcutt
pp.148-154, pp.156-161
レイナー・ブランク　Reiner Blunck
pp.168-169

図版　Drawings
グレン・マーカット　Glenn Murcutt

特別協力への謝辞
Acknowledgement for special contributions
ウェンディ・ルーウィン　Wendy Lewin
ニューサウスウェールズ州 州立図書館
State Library NSW

作品解説＆キャプション
Project descriptions and captions
トム・ヘネガン　Tom Heneghan
Douglas Murcutt House, Fletcher-Page House,
House in the Southern Highlands,
Murcutt-Lewin House & Studio, Walsh House
マリアム・グーシェ＆キャサリン・ラッセン
Maryam Gusheh & Catherine Lassen
Marie Short/Glenn Murcutt House, Fredericks/White House,
Magney House (Bingie Point), Magney House (Paddington),
Simpson-Lee House, Marika-Alderton House,
Murcutt Guest Studio, Arthur and Yvonne Boyd Art Centre

和訳　Japanese Translations
勢山詔子　Shoko Seyama

アシスタント　Assistants
サーシャ・クロッカー　Sascha Crocker
カーラ・ドハティー　Cara Doherty

お願い　Request to readers:
本書に掲載された住宅は、個人住宅であり非公開です。
マーカット氏は個人事務所として設計活動をされており、
所員やインターンを受け入れておりません。お断りの手紙
を書く時間もなく非礼を詫びることもできませんので、
どうか履歴書などを送らないで下さい。
読者の皆様のご理解をお願い申し上げます。

The houses illustrated in this book are private
residences and are not open to visitors.
Mr. Murcutt reminds readers that he operates his
office as a sole-practitioner and does not employ
staff or interns. He requests you not to send job
applications or CV's as he does not wish to be rude,
but he has no time to reply.
The publisher asks readers to understand and
support Mr. Murcutt's position.

著者プロフィール
Authors' Profiles

マリアム・グーシェ　Maryam Gusheh
ニューサウスウェールズ大学 建築環境学部講師
Lecturer, University of NSW, Faculty of The Built Environment
ニューサウスウェールズ大学卒業。2001年に大学に籍をおくまで建築家として働く。異文化間の建築活動に注目した研究や論文を執筆。ルイス・カーン設計のバングラデシュ国会議事堂についての博士論文がある。
Maryam Gusheh graduated from the University of New South Wales. She worked as a practicing architect prior to joining UNSW in 2001. Her research and publications have focused on cross-cultural architectural practices. Her doctoral dissertation undertakes a close reading of the Parliament Building in Bangladesh, designed by the American Architect Louis Kahn.

トム・ヘネガン　Tom Heneghan
建築家／シドニー大学 建築・デザイン・都市計画学部 建築学部長
Architect / Chair of Architecture, Faculty of Architecture, Design and Planning, University of Sydney
AAスクール卒業後、1990年に東京にアーキテクチャー・ファクトリーを設立するまで同校で教鞭をとった。1994年熊本県草地畜産研究所で日本建築学会賞。2002年福島県あだたらの森キャンプ場で公共建築賞環境賞受賞。
Tom Heneghan graduated from the Architectural Association, London, where he taught until establishing his office 'The Architecture Factory' in Tokyo in 1990. In 1994, he won the Award of the Academy of the Architectural Institute of Japan. In 2002 he was awarded the Japanese Government public building award for ecological building.

キャサリン・ラッセン　Catherine Lassen
建築家／ニューサウスウェールズ大学 建築環境学部講師
Architect / Lecturer, University of NSW, Faculty of The Built Environment
1995年ハーバード大学建築学科修了。2000年シドニーへ移住するまで、レム・クールハース主宰のOMAロッテルダム事務所とボストン事務所に勤務。2002年事務所設立。2007年シドニー大学における改築プロジェクトでRAIAの建築遺産賞であるグリーンウェイ賞受賞。
Catherine Lassen received her Master of Architecture from Harvard University in 1995. She worked for Rem Koolhaas at OMA in Rotterdam and in Boston Massachusetts before moving to Sydney in 2000. Her office was established in 2002. She was awarded the RAIA Greenway Award for Heritage Architecture for a project she completed at the University of Sydney.

勢山詔子　Shoko Seyama
建築家（一級建築士／王立オーストラリア建築家協会公認建築士）
Architect (Japan/RAIA)
東京芸術大学建築科卒業後、1995年にアーキテクチャー・ファクトリーに参加。2002年にシドニー移住。主なプロジェクトに、北京常青区タウンハウス（ヘネガンと共にプロジェクトアーキテクト）。2006年より180戸の住宅建設が始まっている。
Shoko Seyama graduated from Tokyo National University of Fine Arts, and joined the Architecture Factory in 1995. She moved to Sydney in 2002. Her projects include the Beijing Townhouse project, involving the construction of 180 houses, which she co-designed with Tom Heneghan.

The Architecture of
GLENN MURCUTT
グレン・マーカットの建築

2008年6月15日　初版第1刷発行
2021年7月20日　初版第4刷発行
●
監修協力 ——— グレン・マーカット
著者 ——— マリアム・グーシェ
　　　　　　トム・ヘネガン
　　　　　　キャサリン・ラッセン
　　　　　　勢山詔子
写真 ——— アンソニー・ブローウェル
発行者 ——— 伊藤剛士
デザイン ——— 太田徹也
●
プリンティング ディレクション ——— 高柳昇
印刷・製本 ——— 株式会社東京印書館
●
発行所 ——— TOTO出版（TOTO株式会社）

〒107-0062 東京都港区南青山1-24-3
TOTO乃木坂ビル 2F
[営業] TEL: 03-3402-7138　FAX: 03-3402-7187
[編集] TEL: 03-3497-1010
URL: https://jp.toto.com/publishing

落丁本・乱丁本はお取り替えいたします。
本書の全部又は一部に対するコピー・スキャン・デジタル化等の無断複製行為は、著作権法上での例外を除き禁じます。本書を代行業者等の第三者に依頼してスキャンやデジタル化することは、たとえ個人や家庭内での利用であっても著作権法上認められておりません。
定価はカバーに表示してあります。

© 2008　Glenn Murcutt

Printed in Japan　ISBN978-4-88706-293-1